POWER AND POLITICS IN THE UNITED STATES

Power and Politics in the United States

A Political Economy Approach

G. DAVID GARSON   *North Carolina State University*

D. C. Heath and Company
Lexington, Massachusetts/Toronto

To Cindy, with love

Preface

This book is a primer. It is meant to accompany a text on American government or political science, or to be a text in courses on elitism and pluralism, power-structure research, business and government relations, or political sociology. It presents political economy as a framework for analyzing American politics. In so doing the advantages and limits of elite theory and pluralism are contrasted. As a primer it is meant to be only an introduction to political economy. The principles introduced are not original or sophisticated, but the political-economic framework used nonetheless provides a clear alternative to the two most common paradigms now in use: elite theory and pluralist theory. These principles, more accurately labeled "starting points" for political economic analysis, are presented in the final chapter.

It is my hope that this work will be a significant contribution to moving political science beyond the sterile elitism-pluralism debate. While the political-economic model will not provide a general theory of political science, it does engender many insights into American politics, avoiding the simplifications of elite and pluralist theory. I hope it will promote a fruitful and even lively discussion. The limits of political economy disqualify it from any pretension to general political-sociological theory, but as a paradigm it provides a most useful next step for the introduction of political science analyses of American politics.

I owe a debt of gratitude to all those who have helped in

this enterprise, even where they did not agree with my views. Special appreciation is owed to William Wolff, Jeffrey Berry, and Ann Drallios for their contributions. Of course, I alone take responsibility for any errors which may remain.

Contents

Part I   Theoretical Bases

1   An Introduction to Power and Politics in the
    United States   3
2   The Distribution of Power in the United States:
    Alternative Views   31

Part II   Power in the United States

3   Methods of Studying Power   61
4   The Structural Approach: Power in the Military   79
5   The Decisional Approach: The Vietnam War   119
6   The Reputational and Positional Approaches   155
7   The Distributional Approach: Economic Stratification
    and American Politics   175

Part III   Class Analysis and Business Power

8   Is Class Consciousness Important in American Politics?   203
9   An Historical Case: The Politics of Oil   231

Part IV   A Political-Economic Model

10 America's Political Economy: Revolution to the
    Civil War   269

11   America's Political Economy: Reconstruction to
the Present   297
12   Political Economy as an Alternative to Pluralist or
Elite Theory   327

Index   347

Part I

Theoretical Bases

1. An Introduction to Power and Politics in the United States

Power is the central concept of political science, yet it is among the most difficult to explain or measure. In the Articles of Impeachment drawn up against former President Nixon by the House Judiciary Committee in 1974, for example, burglary at the Watergate headquarters of the Democratic National Committee was attributed to "agents of the Committee to Re-Elect the President, on behalf of Richard M. Nixon, and solely in his interest in preserving political power. . . ." [1] But what does "preserving political power" mean?

To some, preserving political power means the same thing as defending incumbency in office: power is the set of rights that attach to governmental position. To others, preserving political power means maintaining personal influence: power is the set of resources (not just official position, but also money, information, control over jobs) which may be used by the power-holder. To yet others, preserving political power has less to do with either position or resources than it has to do with the deference of others: power is in the mind of the one who is influenced.

Suppose we find that a certain city employee, whom we shall call Bill Jones, is spending his spare time campaigning for the mayor, Mayor Alice Smith, and we want to know if this shows that the mayor has power over Bill Jones. We might start by asking if Mayor Smith said or did something that got Bill Jones to do what the mayor wanted—to campaign for her— when Jones would have preferred to be doing something else. If the answer is "Yes," we are likely to conclude *power* was used. This logic is simple and most people think this way. Therefore in the last half of this chapter we will spend some time considering why the question of power is not that simple. For now, however, we may briefly say that what has just been talked about is the *overt* use of power, and what makes power not simple is that it is sometimes *implicit*.

Some political scientists and most members of the public discuss politics only in terms of overt power. Political scientists, though, are likely to make a number of fine distinctions about power that most people would call just jargon. While admitting some truth to this charge, it is also true that we can learn a little about power by making these distinctions, all having to do with overt power.

If what got Bill Jones to campaign for Mayor Smith was the mayor's official position, then political scientists say this power relationship was one based on *authority*. If what got Jones to respond was based on Mayor Smith's resources apart from her official position, then the type of power relation was one of *influence*. Finally, occasionally it happens that the response is based on the power-holder's (the mayor's) personality characteristics over and beyond position or resources. In such cases the type of power relation is one of *affinity*. Authority and influence, of course, are far more pervasive in American politics than is affinity.

These three types of power relationships—authority, influence, and affinity—correspond to three basic types of *compliance* outlined by Amitai Etzioni in his famous essay on how organizations get members to comply with organizational needs.[2] Compliance based on *coercion* tends to lead to *alienative involvement* as in prisons and some high schools. Members resent complying but are forced to do so. Compliance based on *remuneration* involves *calculative involvement* as in most businesses. Employees comply because they are paid to. Finally, *norms* may be the basis of compliance. Normative compliance is associated with *moral involvement,* as in many voluntary associations. Here members comply because of their commitment to the goals and ideals of their group.

Power relations and compliance relations are actually two sides of the same coin. The exercise of power is actually a transaction. To exercise command (power) requires understanding obedience (compliance); obedience is not a simple mechanical response. Thus President Harry Truman complained: "One word from me, and everyone does as he pleases!" Of Dwight Eisenhower, Truman remarked, "He'll sit here and he'll say, 'Do this! Do that!' And nothing will happen. Poor Ike—it won't be a bit like the Army. He'll find it very frustrating." [3] Some types of power-compliance relationships are much more important to political science than others. Those involving affinity, for example, are relatively atypical. The power of authority often involves coercive compliance, but it may involve remunerative or normative compliance as well. Influence often involves remunerative compliance but it, too, has variants. Moreover, the exercise of power is usually complex. More than one type of power and of compliance is often involved. Prisons, for example, at first impression seem to be run by authority and coercion, but sociologists studying penal systems have found an underlying intricate system of tangible rewards and privileges (remuneration) which support the authority of the guards.

Examples of Overt Power-Compliance Relationships

Authority is the most obvious form of power, and coercion is the bluntest form of compliance. A power-compliance relation of this type (see type 1a in Table 1–1) is often dramatically visible, as in the violent police repression of demonstrators at the 1968 Democratic National Convention in Chicago. Of this "orgy of violence," *Time* magazine wrote, "Thanks to Mayor Daley, not only Chicago but the rest of the United States as well was pictured as a police state." [4] Less visible examples occur in the forced evictions of renters and homeowners in the urban renewal programs of the 1950s and 1960s. Coercion, by

Table 1–1   *Types of Power-Compliance Relationships*

	Authority	Influence	Affinity
Coercion	1a	2a	3a
Remuneration	1b	2b	3b
Norms	1c	2c	3c

arousing often bitter resentment, may be viewed by officials as counterproductive. It is not as well recognized, however, that authority-coercion relationships can exist in the private sector as well. The American Medical Association, for example, is but one of many interest groups that has succeeded in gaining the mantle of state power. The AMA, acting through state medical boards, for example, uses its position to coerce chiropractors to cease performing certain medical tasks. An even more common illustration is the frequent use of court injunctions by business to prevent labor strikes and boycotts.

Because of the drawbacks of coercion, officials often rely on authority-remuneration relationships. Patronage in the dispensation of government jobs is the time-honored use of power which fits into this category (type 1b in Table 1–1). Until recently the Army Corps of Engineers was notorious for building up its power vis-à-vis U.S. presidents in this way, developing a friendly constituency in Congress and among private interests based on its role in pork-barrel public construction projects.[5]

Much of what authorities accomplish depends upon the moral commitment of citizens. If officials could operate only through coercive penalties and self-interested remuneration, they would be able to do very little. Instead, society must be largely self-regulating, based on some minimal shared belief in the values enunciated by authorities. If such a normative belief system is operating, sanctions and rewards serve merely to reinforce the basic social cement of normative compliance. Patriotism, civic duty, nationalism—all are of critical importance, for they bear on the *implicit* exercise of power, which will be discussed in the last half of this chapter.

Influence is as important in politics as authority is. A business lobby may exert influence through control of resources such as campaign funds, information, or jobs. Influence-remuneration relationships (type 2b in Table 1–1) are occasionally direct, as in bribery, but are usually indirect, as in contributions to campaigns. During the preliminary impeachment proceedings against Nixon, for example, it was charged that this type of power was operative in the $2 million pledge of the dairy industry to Nixon's campaign, following which his administration suddenly reversed its milk-price-support policies in a direction favorable to dairy interests. In a more subtle way this type of power relation aided the oil industry which, because of its control over information about oil reserves, was able to influence decision-making during the 1973–1974 "oil-shortage" crisis.[6]

In other cases the will of the lobby coincides with the will of the legislator, and the two cooperate out of mutual normative commitment. The lobby provides suggestions, technical information, staff work, even drafts of legislation which aid the legislator to do what he or she intended to do anyway (but might not have had the resources to accomplish). For example, Congressman David Henderson (D , N.C.) described the aid of the conservative National Right to Work Committee in a successful effort to bar union-shop provisions among postal employees during the 1971 postal reorganization: "The Right to Work Committee and its staff served as coordinator not only for my office and other involved legislators, but also for other organizations participating in the fight. . . . [They] coordinated their own efforts fully with us. . . ."[7] Henderson, a representative from a traditionally anti-union state, was opposed to compulsory union membership on principle and did not have to be remunerated to act on this belief. He did, however, need help in getting his amendment to the postal reorganization act passed. This the National Right to Work Committee provided. It is customary for lobbies to work most with legislators already friendly to their interests rather than with those who must be converted.

Power relationships involving affinity are far less important in American politics, though they do occur. A recent example occurred during the 1972 fight over no-fault auto insurance. Shortly before the final vote, one senator told the *Washington*

Post that he had received phone calls from twenty of his lawyer friends urging he table the legislation.[8] Similarly the American Medical Association has long used the personal relations of legislators and their doctors as an avenue for exerting power over legislation.[9] Such examples are exceptions, however.

Most political scientists today place much less emphasis on the direct power of lobbies, quite in contrast to the "group-theory" approach to political science in vogue during the 1950s and early 1960s. (This will be discussed in Chapter 2.) Work by political scientists like Milbrath and Bauer, Pool and Dexter have, since 1963, emphasized the obstacles faced by, and the limited success of interest groups in, the American political process.[10] Most interest groups do *not* enjoy the quasi-official status which, as mentioned earlier, many states accord to the American Medical Association. Only a handful enjoy the tremendous resources of such a lobby. And even an interest as well-entrenched and with as much money as the AMA commands is often forced to flow with the times, in this case acceding to the increasing demand for government playing a major role in health care. Some have interpreted this as a further indication of the tremendous fragmentation and pluralism of the American political system. Others have seen in the relative weakness of the lobbies the danger of unchecked bureaucratic tyranny. Still others have concluded that although *direct* lobbying is not of paramount importance, business interests still dominate politics through other, *implicit* uses of power.

The Implicit Aspects of Power

Thus far we have outlined power relationships of the usual sort: Mayor Smith exercises power on the basis of authority, influence, or personal affinity, and her employee, Bill Jones, complies, motivated by coercion, remuneration, or normative agreement. We suggested that overt power relationships of these types could be investigated by examining instances where the powerholder got the person influenced to do something which he or she would not otherwise have done. But in this instance, what if Bill Jones were disposed to do what the mayor wanted in the first place? Would this mean no power relationship was present?

Not at all. We have already touched on this aspect of power when we discussed compliance based on *norms*. Normative compliance is based on shared value orientations common to both the powerholder and the person influenced. In such situations it is difficult to observe power-compliance transactions because cooperation with the will of the power-holder is yielded freely. True, we may define *overt* power to require the person influenced (Bill Jones) to yield *when he would rather do otherwise*. By observing this person changing from doing what he wanted to what was asked, we may "observe" a power relationship at work. But in practice there is no clear line between overt power (in which the one influenced does what he or she would not otherwise do) and implicit power (in which the will of the power-holder is fulfilled because the one influenced has been indoctrinated, trained, or socialized to desire or accept the same goals as the power-holder). What people "want to do" is commonly ambiguous, multipurposed, and unstable. By invoking appropriate value symbols, cultural cues, and definitions of the situation, the power-holder may tap a reservoir of compliance. The person influenced may easily feel he or she is "spontaneously" acting in accord with the power-holder through free will.

Power is present even when there is no overt exercise of power. Many, ranging from conservative southerners to the late black leader Malcolm X, have called attention, for example, to the presence in the ante-bellum South of many slaves who supported the slave system. A British traveler in the Old South wrote, "There is an hereditary regard and often attachment on both sides, more like that formerly existing between lords and their retainers in the old feudal times of Europe." [11] But though slaves at times might support slavery and wish to do as their masters wanted, who would deny that a power relationship exists between master and slave?

Could we not argue that the apex of power has been reached when the overt exercise of power is no longer needed because the socialization into obedience is complete? This kind of power is reminiscent of divine authority: "I will put my laws into their mind and write them in their hearts, and I will be to them a God and they shall be to me a people." [12]

As a second example, Stanley Elkins has compared the adjustment made by some American slaves—childlike conformity to authority—with the identification of certain Jewish prisoners with their German captors during World War II.[13] Bruno Bettelheim has studied this process in greater detail: "Old prisoners tended to identify with the SS not only in their goals and values, but even in appearance. . . . The lengths prisoners would go to was sometimes hard to believe, particularly since they were sometimes punished for trying to look like the SS. . . . Since old prisoners had accepted or been forced to accept a child-like dependency on the SS many of them seemed to want to feel that at least some of the people they were accepting as all-powerful father images were just and kind." [14]

But are these examples of slavery and the concentration camp relevant to studying power and politics in America? In the following sections we outline three bodies of literature that argue implicitly that there *is* a connection—that the psychological stress that affected the slave on the plantation or the prisoner in the concentration camp also affects the citizen in American politics, albeit in different ways. These three areas revolve around the concepts of *nondecisions, symbolic action,* and *political hegemony.*

Decisions and Nondecisions

Unlike overt power exercised in, say, a political decision, implicit power cannot be observed directly. By definition, implicit power is not the subject of a confrontation between power-holder and the person influenced. Since political science is often construed as the study of group conflicts, political scientists have been disposed to concentrate on the overt kinds of power-compliance relationships evidenced in conflicts. Implicit power has been largely ignored even though what is *not* decided because of the absence of conflict may say far more about the nature of power in a society than what *is* decided as a result of some overt conflict process.

A nondecision is a potential outcome of a possible decision, one which was not made because it seemed to be outside the realm of desirability or feasibility. Some nondecisions are simply a rational ignoring of the inappropriate: not to direct national resources into the continued construction of clipper ships after the invention of the steamship, for example. But other nondecisions might seem far less rational to an observer from another culture: the tendency of Americans to dismiss the possibility of nationalization of industry (because it is thought to be inherently socialistic and inefficient), for example. Observed from another culture, such a tendency to dismiss nationalization out of hand—really not to consider it seriously at all—might seem wholly prejudiced and irrational. Nondecisions of this sort, we could argue, reveal the nature of the American political system far more than any amount of case studies of the regulation of business.

The problem is, how do you go about studying a nondecision, much less the net effect on a society of many nondecisions? The answer is, regrettably, "With a great deal of difficulty." We must make inferences on the basis of indirect evidence and from history. Different bases for inference are the subject of later chapters in this book.

How the Concept of Nondecisions Became Important in Political Science

The 1950s and early 1960s were marked in political science by a running debate between the "pluralists" and the "elitists" over the nature of power in America.[15] In simplest terms, the pluralists argued that political decisions were the outcome of a plurality of many competing interest groups, political leaders, and other influences. The elitists, on the contrary, argued that major decisions were made by a few unrepresentative men in an undemocratic manner. The basis for the pluralistic approach was synthesized in David Truman's classic work, *The Governmental Process* (1951). The elitists cited empirical studies by Floyd Hunter (*Community Power Structure*, 1953) and C. Wright Mills (*The Power Elite*, 1956).

Both the pluralists and the elitists (whose views are to be

discussed more fully in Chapter 2) looked at decisions to validate their views. Truman believed, for example, that decisions in
the area of regulation of business showed a pluralist democratic
pattern, while Hunter said city government decisions in Atlanta
showed elite dominance. Mills concurred with Hunter, pointing
to the dominance by elite groups of national foreign policy and
other "big decisions." But Hunter tended to rely on decision-
makers' *reputations* for power as a measure, while Mills emphasized the social-class *backgrounds* of leaders.[16] Both ways of
measuring power relationships were felt by the pluralists to be
inferior to the direct approach. If decisions, or at least "big decisions," can be accepted as the key to understanding how democratic or undemocratic this country is, why not study these decisions themselves? [17]

For example, one leading pluralist, Robert Dahl, held that
power could be pinpointed at the "point in the process of forming opinions at which the one group will be seen to initiate and
veto, while the rest merely respond. And we can only discover
these points *by an examination of a series of concrete cases
where key decisions are made*." [18] Another leading pluralist, Nelson Polsby, wrote that by emphasizing decision-making behavior, pluralists "concentrate on power exercise itself." [19] The
direct decision-making approach appeared at first to most political scientists to be the best way of assessing power. The study
of decisions apparently vindicated the pluralist view of power.
Whether one looked at welfare, tax policy, or education, one
found many competing forces at work, with no one group (not
business, for example) dominant in all issue areas or even always successful in any one area.

This view prevailed in political science as long as everyone
accepted the underlying assumption that *overt* power (as in
explicit decisions) was the only important kind to study. So the
methodological point—that the direct-decision case-study approach was a better way of measuring overt power than was
reputation for power or inference from social background—was
purely secondary to acceptance of this basic assumption. By the
1960s, however, the study of people's socialization to acceptance
of political values and attitudes had become important in politi-

cal science. And on this basis it became easy to believe that *implicit* power relations might be much more important than the pluralists (or elitists) believed. Consequently it seemed that the results of the many studies of political decisions might not give a very true picture of how power was distributed in America. More than any other, the work of Peter Bachrach served to underscore this realization by political scientists. Though the basic ideas had been put forward much earlier, Bachrach's concept of *nondecision-making* forced political scientists to confront the possibility that their work might have been, in the main, short-sighted and misleading.

Bachrach's Concept of Nondecision-Making

Peter Bachrach and others who began emphasizing nondecisions in the early 1960s based their work on the earlier work of E. E. Schattschneider and his idea of "mobilization of bias." [20] Schattschneider put forward the simple view that as conflict at the center of power radiates out, each side calls on its potential allies. There is a mobilization of the "predominant values, beliefs, rituals, and institutional procedures ('rules of the game') that operate systematically and consistently to the benefit of certain groups at the expense of others." [21]

This mobilization of bias can take extreme forms, as in the Ku Klux Klan (KKK) in the South during Reconstruction or in the Palmer Raids against radical immigrants after World War I. In these cases dominant values are asserted with terroristic ferocity. More often, however, dominant values are subtly put forward through the schools, the churches, the media, and other institutions.

As a result of the mobilization of bias, some demands may come to be viewed as illegitimate or outside the realm of discussion. In this way a nondecision occurs: certain demands are not processed through normal political channels. Instead they are screened out of the political process in four ways:

1. *Force* may be used to suppress dissident ideas, as in the KKK and Palmer Raid examples.

2. *Influence* and rewards may be used to co-opt (token participation on advisory committees, for example), or sanctions may be used to intimidate (dismissal from employment, for example).
3. *Authority* may be used to establish political rules which frustrate dissident forces (as when officials define landlord-tenant relations as private in order to rebuff tenant demands on government).
4. *Norms* may be used to deny legitimacy to ideas (as through statements by religious or other respected leaders, branding ideas as socialistic, unpatriotic, and immoral).

Bachrach believed that nondecisions *could* be examined empirically,[22] and on this point many exponents of the decision-making approach to power attacked his work. Raymond Wolfinger, for example, said Bachrach's approach would require knowledge of politicians' motivations, their anticipations of alternative courses of action (including those not taken or even seriously considered), and understanding how cultural values and social institutions like schools affected specific people and specific decisions.[23] These requirements seemed to make the nondecision-making approach impossible; better to stick with tried-and-true case studies of decisions.

A Famous Example: Urban Renewal Politics in New Haven

The nondecision-making issue can be made more concrete by looking at one of the best-known case studies of decisions, which was undertaken by a leading pluralist scholar, Robert Dahl, in his study of urban renewal decision-making in New Haven, Connecticut. It was this study that Bachrach used as his case in point in criticizing the decisional approach to power.

Dahl's *Who Governs?* had become commonly regarded as the first major study empirically rebutting Mills's elitist approach, using the decision-making approach to do it. Dahl concluded that his study showed the city to be characterized by a broadly democratic, pluralistic decision-making process. Business, in particular, played a subordinate political role in New Haven politics—quite in contrast to the elite role assigned to business by Mills. "Perhaps the most significant element in the history of city planning," Dahl wrote, "is that very little happened until redevelopment became attached to the political fortunes of an ambitious politician." [24] Business was viewed as but one force among many in which Mayor Lee played the crucial, orchestrating role.

Dahl's statement seemed to say more than it did. When urban renewal is actually implemented—that is, when "something happens"—the program then "becomes attached" to the "political fortunes" of the mayor, as does any major program. But why did Mayor Lee make urban renewal a major issue in the first place, rather than some other issue?

Dahl's own analysis revealed a long history of business pressure in New Haven for urban renewal. In fact, business was the dominant pressure group. As early as 1907 the city's Civic Improvements Committee was dominated by business people, and this group led to the establishment of the New Haven Planning Commission in 1913.[25] Dahl characterized this period as one of rule by the entrepreneurs, anticipating a business influence decline in later years. This did not occur.

In the late 1920s and 1930s the call for renewal action centered on James Hook, a leading New Haven business figure. In 1941, the New Haven Planning Commission was finally allocated enough funds to hire professional help. Its work was led by Angus Fraser, a prominent businessman.[26] World War II delayed planning, but in 1953, four years after urban renewal had been adopted by Congress as a national policy, the New Haven Chamber of Commerce adopted a ten-point program reflecting the work of the Fraser group.

The national program made it financially possible for New Haven politicians to meet the long-standing demands of the business community for urban redevelopment. Lee, the future mayor and a Democrat, became convinced that his party might capture control of the city if they "seized upon urban renewal as a program." [27] Democrats on the board of alderman got the process started by establishing a redevelopment agency. Celentano, the Republican mayor, perceived the political dangers of this Democratic power play,[28] but acquiesced because many members of the business community had long insisted that improvements were essential.[29]

Lee defeated Celentano in 1953 on a platform emphasizing the need for urban renewal. After the election Lee appointed a prominent bank president to head the citizen's redevelopment committee, a committee composed primarily of utility heads, manufacturers, bankers, and business people. Another banker was made head of the redevelopment agency.

How, one may ask, could Dahl have presented this as case evidence for the subsidiary role of business as merely one force among many? Dahl cited the fact that initiation of renewal policy emanated from the mayor's planning staff, while the citizen's committee merely rubber-stamped the plans. Thus, as quoted earlier, one group could be seen to initiate (Lee and his administrative staff), while the rest merely responded (the business community). But does this really show the more important power of politicians as compared to those in business?

Perhaps not, if nondecision-making is taken into account. Lee took the initiative in campaigning on urban renewal in 1953, but his motive was to attract business support away from the Republican party by catering to a long-standing business desire. All urban renewal decisions of major importance were arrived at after considerable consultation with the business community, and the mayor refrained from advancing policies he felt they might oppose.[30] Moreover, the federal laws required Lee's staff to select renewal sites that would be profitable for private developers, so other sites were not considered.

Power—which at first seems a simple concept—becomes, in concrete cases, much less clear. The mayor and his staff *did* initiate most proposals, and most of them were carried out. Moreover, the mere fact that the business community wanted urban renewal was not sufficient for it to happen. Renewal was carried out only when the Democrats came into office. On this basis one may conclude that the power of professional politicians and their staff administrators was paramount.

By extension, just as most political decisions are made by those elected and appointed, so most economic decisions are made by people in business, and in education it is educational professionals who tend to make decisions. Thus the decisional approach leads to the pluralist conclusion that in each area of decision, those most involved (by reason of their occupation) are likely to dominate. The logic of pluralism is completed by noting that the division of labor assures that different people will have different occupations, and so power will be spread among many people in many decision-making areas.

But the same case may be looked at through the lens of nondecision-making. No one had to pressure Mayor Lee into selecting sites profitable to the business community, because Lee had no other choice. The decision, or rather nondecision, was predetermined by the economic criteria of the federal law. Nor did Mayor Lee have to be pressured into advocating urban redevelopment in the first place. The political advantages of business support did not appear to be "giving in to business"; rather, it seemed to Lee to be a natural move in his own interest. Yet urban renewal *was* something business wanted, got, and benefited from disproportionately. Redevelopment in other cultures might involve far more low-income housing or community-owned housing construction enterprises, but these were not issues in New Haven because they seemed economically and politically unfeasible. In this view, business *was* the paramount political force in this case.

Wolfinger is correct that the direct study of a nondecision is impossible, but it is wrong to conclude that the direct study of a decision case will provide the "right" answer. No methodological approach can easily solve our problem, but in later chapters we will set forth several alternative approaches and seek to understand what each has to offer as we seek to discover the nature of power in America.

Politics as Symbolic Action

A second area of political science that suggests that overt exercise of power can pale in comparison with implicit control is associated with the concept of *symbolic action*. Politics as symbolic action means that many governmental acts are undertaken for their symbolic rather than their ostensible real purpose. For example, a new agency may be created not because leaders have any serious expectation it will solve a given social problem, but because its very creation shows leaders are doing something about it and recognize those who have demanded action. Appointing a blue-ribbon study commission amid great publicity (but later quietly ignoring its report) is another common example. The regulatory commissions, such as the Federal Communications Commission and the Food and Drug Administration, have been charged as being examples of symbolic action: their creation reassures the public that business abuses are under government control, while in fact their net effect on the industry is collusive rather than regulatory. Whenever acts of government are used to reassure citizens of one thing when the substance of what is done is something else, symbolic action is present. Second, symbolic action is also present whenever leaders directly seek to manipulate national symbols. This happens in various public-relations images projected by the president: giving his televised reports with flags in the background, being present at major sporting events, or being shown conversing with national religious figures.

Politics as symbolic action is a means by which leaders may take advantage of the *implicit* power they hold by virtue of the response to symbols socialized into citizens by the schools, churches, media, political campaigns, and so on. Because of implicit power, often associated with people's response to symbols of patriotism, religion, Americanism, the American way of life, individualism, prosperity, efficiency-in-government, and the like, it is often possible to induce citizens to support (or at least accept passively) what they otherwise would not. That is, the implicit power evoked through symbolic action may often make serious political conflict and the *overt* exercise of power unnecessary.

How the Concept of Symbolic Action Became Important in Political Science

The earliest work in political science to call attention to politics as symbolic action was that by Harold Lasswell. In *World Politics and Personal Insecurity* (1935), Lasswell interpreted politics in terms of elite symbols of identification, demand, and expectation.[31] Government leaders seek to use these elite symbols in their efforts to counter new dissident groups who, in turn, seek to put forward new social myths. These myths are new visions of social order, appealing to the personal insecurities of individuals in societies undergoing crisis. In the 1930s, when Lasswell wrote, the allusion was to Nazi manipulation of nationalistic and racial symbols in their struggle against dissident groups that were raising new visions of socialism and communism. But Lasswell interpreted American politics, as well, in terms of manipulation of the public through symbolic action, with the central strategy being to stimulate "effective class-consciousness among the middle-income groups." [32]

After World War II the importance of symbolic action in politics was studied in well-known works by Erik Erikson. Erikson specifically related politics as symbolic action to childhood perceptions of the world and, implicitly, with the burgeoning postwar political-science literature on socialization to political attitudes. In adolescence, Erikson wrote, political symbolism has its greatest effect. Thus, "the polarity Big-Small is the first in the inventory of existential oppositions such as Male and Female, Ruler and Ruled, Owner and Owned, Light Skin and Dark, over which emancipatory struggles are now raging both politically and psychologically." [33] Symbols were seen as crucial to the adolescent's internal identification with one side or another in such political struggles.

In *Young Man Luther* (1958), Erikson sought to illustrate the interplay between social and political symbols on the one hand and adolescent identity crisis on the other. Erikson attempted to show how Martin Luther's own fears, his feelings of being oppressed by an avenging God, were shared by many others in his society, and how Luther's Protestantism found a sympathetic response among others as an alternative symbolic system which allayed their fears.[34] Like Lasswell, Erikson said that in normal times the prevailing, institutionalized imagery (the avenging God imagery of Luther's day, the German super-race imagery of Nazi Germany, the patriotic American-Way-of-Life imagery of present-day United States) is dominant. But he went beyond this to emphasize how national symbols become corrupted over time. They gain and lose in their solidity and legitimacy; they fluctuate and may collapse. Disasters, wars, and changes in technology or leadership may "cause a shrinkage in the world image, a kind of chill attacking the sense of identity of large masses." [35]

When this happens political leaders can no longer rely on their *implicit* power based on a well-socialized citizenry. Politics tends to collapse into *overt* forms. Normative compliance begins to diminish. There is more reliance on what Marxists call the "cash nexus" between the power-holder and the one influenced. Finally, if the social crisis deepens, even remunerative compliance is insufficient to maintain the state, and leaders resort to coercion and force. Marxists argue that in America today, as capitalism falters the old symbols of rugged individualism and free enterprise ring hollow; social malaise deepens, and as people turn from corporate ideology to private goals, the scene is set for privatization of political life and for corruption. Like Erikson, the Marxists believe that the dominant system is maintained in prosperous times by a supportive world view, obscuring the latent panic which waits for the catastrophe that comes when the prevailing order ceases to advance, making possible the emergence of alternative social orders and social symbols.

Even though the whole concept of politics as symbolic action may be fitted into a Marxist view, in American political science the idea of symbolic action has been developed in a somewhat different direction. Its main developer has been a student of Harold Lasswell, Murray Edelman.

Edelman's Concept of Politics as Symbolic Action

Edelman was struck by the fact that the hopes people attach to government are in many ways irrational. He observed that groups are often satisfied with mere symbolic reassurance that their goals are being achieved (such as by the creation of new agencies, by sympathetic speeches and proclamations, by new laws, and so on), even though the actual and tangible benefits received from government amount to little. Edelman concluded that political processes were "easy objects upon which to displace private emotions, especially strong anxieties and hopes." [36] That is, the use of political symbols is successful in tapping vast implicit power for leaders because people often have a strong emotional need to believe in them.

The pluralist model of politics predicted that groups would mobilize politically around certain shared interests and would compete with other groups for the attention and favor of government, being satisfied to the extent their demands were met. Edelman suggested a different model was truer to reality: interest groups will continue in their discontent regardless of the extent to which their demands are met. In fact, satisfying demands predictably leads the group to advance demands for even more benefits! [37] For example, the poverty programs of the 1960s served to politicize those affected and to arouse more intense political pressures.

Stability is a prime virtue for political leaders. And political quiescence is more likely to be achieved, Edelman stated, by (1) frequent ritualistic assertion of progress toward achievement of group goals, and (2) dedicating the state to the goals of the group by creating new constitutional amendments, laws, or agencies (even though the effect of these is minimal, except symbolically).[38] Edelman's basic premise is that citizens are re-active. That is, most people take little interest in the details of legislation or administration until events seem either threatening or promising.[39] And even then citizens respond to cues found in political speeches and actions.

On this basis Edelman wrote that "it is therefore political actions that chiefly shape men's political wants and 'knowledge,' not the other way around . . . ." [40] While political elites do react to pressures from below, they are not passive: they help to determine what people know about politics and help to define what is good, legitimate, and possible. New political outlooks can be created relatively quickly, as in the cold-war transformation of Russia from a patriotic ally of the United States to a menacing threat.[41] Though such changes are never instantaneous or unanimous, they are possible because people find comfort and a reduction in tension in believing national symbols.[42]

On many controversial issues, Edelman wrote, "the impact of government actions upon mass beliefs and perceptions is, in fact, the major or the only consequence of political activity." [43] Government efforts to elicit supportive attitudes is evidenced in voting and election campaigns (which function to cue a belief in popular participation, the dramaturgy of consultation with various groups and minorities, a cue that the regime tolerates dissent), in drives against particular groups (as in repression of radicals in the McCarthy era), or in public prouncements of political leaders, reassuring the public about their ability to cope with social problems.[44]

In summary, emphasis on politics as symbolic action leads to an expectation of considerable leeway for political leaders to define public issues, assign legitimacy to various purposes or groups, and to suggest new political perspectives. Earlier we stated that implicit power has to do with situations in which the one influenced is predisposed to act in accordance with the desires of the holder of power. Edelman's work leaves us with the suggestion that people may want what their leaders *say* is legitimate and possible. In this view, popular claims and demands may be satisfied on a symbolic level. This symbolic function of government may provide even greater discretionary power for political elites.

Edelman's work also suggests that a public mood of satisfaction and support for government may be a sign, not that government is responsive to public opinion, but rather that it exerts great control over it. It suggests that the paramount form of power is *implicit* power: power based on the internal identification of the citizen with political symbols legitimated by governing elites.

Political Hegemony

The third area of political science which shows implicit power to be more important than the overt forms of power is associated with the concept of "political hegemony." This area is emphasized by Marxist scholars. Political hegemony was what Marx and Engels were talking about when they wrote in 1846 that "in every epoch the ideas of the ruling class are the ruling ideas, that is, the class that is the ruling *material* power of society is at the same time its ruling *intellectual* power." Each ruling class "has to give its ideas the form of universality and represent them as the only rational, universally valid ones." [45] Though it may appear that certain ideas have an independent force-of-reason which does not depend on ruling-class support, this appearance is an illusion. When the ruling class is displaced, the old ideas subside, revealing that their true force was rooted in the previous class distribution of power.

Political hegemony refers to the preponderant intellectual influence of self-serving ideologies of the ruling class. It is the Marxist way of looking at what Bachrach called mobilization of bias around nondecisions or what Edelman called symbolic action by governing elites; its function is to make possible the exercise of implicit power over those who accept ruling ideologies and are therefore predisposed to act for elites and against their own interests.

When the ruling class is on the ascendant, the system of ideas which supports it gains hegemony over older ideas. For example, as the bourgeois state displaced feudalism, classic liberalism (with its defense of individual liberties against feudal restrictions and its glorification of bourgeois-dominated parliaments) became ascendant. When industrial capitalism displaced merchant capitalism, the ideology of Adam Smith displaced mercantilism. At a general level, such ruling ideologies rationalize the interests of the elite. But what about the role of the lowly citizen?

In normal times the state holds a religious-like attraction for the individual. In modern capitalist societies such as the United States this attraction takes the form of the ideology of satisfaction in the workplace (such as the Horatio Alger myth) and the ideology of citizenship in the state.[46] As a private individual under capitalism, the worker is "the plaything of alien powers," treating others and being treated as a mere means, thereby degrading him- or herself. Citizenship in the state is an attractive alternative fiction, carrying the pretense of equality and dignity. In citizenship, Marx wrote, the worker may pretend to be fulfilled as "an imaginary member of an imagined sovereignty."

The religious-like hold of the state over the citizen is a sham, Marxists believe, because the state responds to class functions rather than to electoral majorities. Similarly, in the workplace an ideology of satisfaction reigns not because work is satisfying but because one can view one's life in the least stressful way by accepting one's lot. This is called *pragmatic role accept-*

ance: accepting the inevitability of one's political and economic place under the social system. Such acceptance is far from being support, but it may seem *like* support for the government so long as leaders are able to perpetuate belief in ruling ideologies. Many scholars have been influenced by this Marxist interpretation of politics. Antonio Gramsci wrote, for example, about the role of intellectuals in organizing successful political hegemony and orchestrating the "spontaneous" consent of the masses to the general direction of ruling ideologies.[47] And Herbert Marcuse has written about the subtle process whereby political conformity is encouraged through the implicit definition of what is politically legitimate and possible and by the unspoken neglect of alternatives which would challenge the social arrangements of dominant groups in America.[48] As with other writers interested in the concept of political hegemony, the underlying theme concerns the amassing of implicit power by leaders who may enjoy the "support" of passive masses predisposed to accept their general goals.

Consensus or Conformity?

All the literature on nondecisions, symbolic action, and political hegemony suggests the paramount importance of implicit power compared to overt forms of power. Many political scientists have come to accept its implications, but many remain unpersuaded. One of the central questions at issue is whether the popular acceptance of and support for government given by the American people to their leaders should be interpreted as *spontaneous consensus* or as *socialized conformity*. The work we have been discussing points to conformity as a passively reactive if not slavish mentality, but many political scientists argue that in America economic success has bred political consent of a spontaneous and genuine nature.

One scholar who has investigated this issue is Michael Mann. In Mann's survey of dozens of recent public-opinion studies, the thesis of value consensus was not sustained. Mann concluded that "value consensus does not exist to any significant extent." [49] Most Americans, for example, hold such "unconsensual" beliefs as feeling that the laws favor the rich, that they have no influence on government, and that business has too much power. The lower in the social stratification system, the less consensus.

That is, Mann argued that *both* the Marxists *and* their pluralist critics were wrong: the working class is neither indoctrinated successfully by dominant values nor does it seem to give spontaneous consent. Rather, consensual attitudes exist side-by-side with dissensual political beliefs, forming a kind of "multiple consciousness." Workers may believe *both* that the rich get the profits *and* that they, as workers, are satisfied with their work. A citizen may believe *both* that he or she has no influence on government *and* that voting is important and America is democratic. In each of us, critical and supportive attitudes coexist.

Mann's survey leads us to believe that alongside consensual processes of voluntary deference, nationalism, and rational support for the government (the mobilization of bias, deference to political symbols, or indoctrination in hegemonic ideology—according to various viewpoints) there also exists a vast reservoir of dissensus. Mann wrote that "a significant measure of consensus and normative harmony may be necessary among ruling groups, but it is the *absence* of consensus among the lower classes which keeps them compliant." [50] In Mann's view the power to control has more to do with dividing than with gaining consensus.

Clearly this is not an either-or issue. America is not a closed political system destined either to perpetual value consensus or to inevitable pragmatic role acceptance and manipulative socialization to dominant ideologies. In any society, rulers may benefit at one and the same time from the ostensibly contradictory strategies of (1) encouraging religious, racial, ethnic, and other political differences among the masses of citizens; and (2) encouraging universal acceptance of symbols and ideologies that legitimate the goals of those who rule. Both overt and implicit power are intertwined in the art of governance. But in this chapter we have tried to suggest that even though consensual socialization will never eradicate conflicting ideas, governing has more to do with implicit power based on the predispositions of those who comply than it has to do with the overt forms of power-compliance transactions discussed at the outset.

Summary

The purpose of this introductory chapter has been to raise the concept of power as the central focus of political science. In doing so we have surveyed a wide range of conceptions of power. We started by observing that power is defined by a relationship in which the holder of power gets another to do (or not do) something the person being influenced would not otherwise do. This relationship, exhibited in the exercise of overt power, was said to be a transaction; compliance was its other aspect.

The first portion of this chapter discussed various types of power-compliance relationships. These types include most of what is ordinarily meant by power. In these types, power took the forms of authority, influence, and affinity; and compliance took the forms of coercion, remuneration, and normative commitment. While no pretense was implied that the nine types of power-compliance relationships treated in this section constituted a unique or comprehensive typology, the diverse and varied nature of overt forms of power was emphasized.

The second portion of this chapter treated the broader or implicit aspects of power in which there need not be any overt exercise of power or even any recognition of compliance. That is, the power-holder need not do or say anything, and the people influenced were not necessarily aware that the power relationship made any difference in their behavior.

After discussing slavery and the concentration camp as two dramatic examples of implicit power relationships, we examined three areas of political-science literature that point to the importance of the implicit aspects of power: Bachrach's concept of nondecisions, Edelman's concept of politics as symbolic action, and Marx's concept of political hegemony. While recognizing the problematic nature of studying implicit power, it was argued that an exclusive focus on overt power would be misleading at best.

Given this general background, we are prepared to begin our study of the distribution of power in America and the way in which it affects politics. The next chapter sets forth the contending political-science viewpoints on power distribution, and later chapters descend from the level of theory to the more challenging level of evidence. At the end of the book we will return to a central theme of this work: the utility of political economy as an approach to understanding politics.

Notes

1. *New York Times*, 20 July 1974, p. 17.
2. Amitai Etzioni, *A Comparative Analysis of Complex Organizations* (New York: Free Press, 1961), pp. 3–21.
3. Richard Neustadt, *Presidential Power* (New York: Signet, 1960), p. 22.
4. Excerpted in Theodore Becker and Vernon Murray, eds., *Government Lawlessness in America* (New York: Oxford University Press, 1971), p. 8.
5. See, for example, Grant McConnell, *Private Power and American Democracy* (New York: Knopf, 1967), p. 216.
6. For a study of the importance of information-control as a political resource, see H. Owen Burter, "Legislative Experts to Outsiders: The Two-Step Flow of Communication," *Journal of Politics* 6 (August 1974): 703–30.
7. Congressional Quarterly, *The Washington Lobby* (Washington: Congressional Quarterly, 1971), p. 7.
8. Mark Green, James Fallows, and David Zwick, *Who Runs Congress?* (New York: Bantam/Grossman, 1972), p. 49.
9. Richard Harris, *A Sacred Trust* (rev. ed.; Baltimore: Penguin, 1969), pp. 24–25, 46.
10. T. Bauer, L. A. Dexter, and I. Pool, *American Business and Public Policy* (New York: Atherton, 1963); Lester Milbrath, *The Washington Lobbyists* (Chicago: Rand McNally, 1963); L. A. Dexter, *The Sociology and Politics of Congress* (Chicago: Rand McNally, 1969); R. Peabody, J. Berry, W. Frasure, and J. Goldman, *To Enact a Law* (New York: Praeger, 1972), ch. 3; John Kingdon, *Congressmen's Voting Decisions* (New York: Harper, 1973).
11. Ulrich B. Phillips, *Life and Labor in the Old South* (Boston: Little, Brown, 1963; orig. 1929), p. 211.
12. *Hebrews* 8:10.
13. S. Elkins, "Slavery and Personality," in B. Kaplan, ed., *Studying Personality Cross-Culturally* (New York: Harper, 1961), p. 244, excerpted in Richard Lazarus, *Psychological Stress and the Coping Process* (New York: McGraw-Hill, 1966), p. 416.
14. B. Bettelheim, *The Informed Heart* (New York: Free Press, 1960), pp. 171–73, excerpted in Lazarus, *Psychological Stress . . .*, pp. 192–93.
15. For a fuller discussion, see G. David Garson, *Political Science Methods* (Boston: Holbrook, 1976), ch. 4.
16. For pluralist critiques, see Nelson Polsby, *Community Power and Political Theory* (New Haven: Yale University Press, 1963), pp. 45–56;

Raymond E. Wolfinger, "Nondecisions and the Study of Local Politics," *American Political Science Review* 65 (December 1971): 1063–79.

17. Arnold Rose, *The Power Structure* (New York: Oxford University Press, 1967), p. 494. See also Robert Dahl, "A Critique of the Ruling Elite Model," *American Political Science Review* 52 (June 1958): 463–69.

18. Dahl, "A Critique of the Ruling Elite Model," p. 469 (emphasis in original).

19. Polsby, *Community Power and Political Theory*, pp. 119 ff.

20. E. E. Schattschneider, *The Semi-Sovereign People* (New York: Holt, Rinehart and Winston, 1960), p. 71.

21. Peter Bachrach and Morton S. Baratz, *Power and Poverty: Theory and Practice* (New York: Oxford University Press, 1970), p. 43.

22. Ibid., pp. 47–51.

23. Wolfinger, "Nondecisions and the Study of Local Politics," p. 1079. See also a critique of Wolfinger by F. Frey (pp. 1081–1101 of the same issue), and a rejoinder by Wolfinger (pp. 1102–1104).

24. Robert A. Dahl, *Who Governs?* (New Haven: Yale University Press, 1961), p. 115.

25. Ibid., p. 116.

26. Ibid.

27. Ibid., p. 117.

28. Ibid.

29. Ibid.

30. Ibid., p. 137.

31. Harold Lasswell, *World Politics and Personal Insecurity* (New York: Free Press, 1965; orig. 1935), pp. 4–7.

32. Ibid., p. 177.

33. Erik H. Erikson, *Childhood and Society* (2nd ed.; New York: Norton, 1963; orig. 1950), p. 418.

34. Erik H. Erikson, *Young Man Luther* (New York: Norton, 1958), pp. 73–74.

35. Ibid., p. 75.

36. Murray Edelman, *The Symbolic Uses of Politics* (Urbana: University of Illinois Press, 1964), p. 39. On p. 5 Edelman cites H. Lasswell, *Psychology and Politics* (Chicago: University of Chicago Press, 1930), pp. 75–76, on this point.

37. Edelman, *The Symbolic Uses of Politics*, p. 154.

38. Ibid., p. 164.

39. Ibid., p. 172.

40. Ibid., pp. 173–74.

41. Ibid.

42. Ibid., p. 174.

43. Murray Edelman, *Politics and Symbolic Action* (Chicago: Markham, 1971), p. 174.

44. Ibid., pp. 36–41.

45. Karl Marx and Friedrich Engels, *The German Ideology*, excerpted in Loyd Easton and Kurt Guddat, eds., *Writings of the Young Marx on Philosophy and Society* (New York: Doubleday, 1967), pp. 438–39.

46. See G. David Garson, "Automobile Workers and the Radical Dream," *Politics and Society* (Winter 1973), 163–77, for further discussion.

47. Antonio Gramsci, *Selections from the Prison Notebooks of Antonio Gramsci*, edited and translated by Quintin Hoare and Geoffrey Nowell Smith (New York: International Publishers, 1971), esp. ch. 1.
48. Herbert Marcuse, *One-Dimensional Man* (Boston: Beacon Press, 1964), pp. 7–8.
49. Michael Mann, "The Social Cohesion of Liberal Democracy," *American Sociological Review* 35 (June 1970). 437.
50. Ibid.

2. The Distribution of Power in the United States: Alternative Views

Most of us are aware of major political affairs such as the Watergate scandals, the Middle East situation, or the 1976 presidential election. A smaller public is somewhat informed about changes in cabinet officers or alternative national health insurance bills. But the bulk of what government does and what politics is about is a mystery to most. Indeed, mysteries may arouse curiosity, but most of what government does is a matter of public indifference.

An example of legislation which forms the stuff of politics but which few understand was the one-bank holding company bill passed not long ago by the Senate. It forbade firms owning two or more banks to acquire unrelated subsidiaries. Such legislation seems to most of us to be obscure, even unimportant. Yet of it Senator William Proxmire (D, Wisc.) said that in his entire thirteen years in the Senate he had never witnessed a more intense lobbying campaign than on this bill.

How is it that such legislation, of which the public is largely unaware, can be a matter of such intense political activity? How can there be such a gap between the intensity of political issues at the highest level of influence compared to the level of the ordinary citizen? Is this inconsistent with democracy?

The lobbies to which Senator Proxmire referred were business interests. Although political scientists are prone to talk about interest groups and pressure groups as a general category, the greater number of such groups are business groups; most of the remainder are professional and labor groups. Why is this so? Why are consumer groups, sports groups, cultural groups, racial groups, women's groups, and other types of organizations not as equally organized as political lobbies? What does this say about the distribution of power in America? What theories have been advanced to account for these facts?

Elite Theory: The European Heritage

We Americans have been relatively disinclined to think of our politics as having much of anything to do with class conflict or political elites. We have been more willing to believe that classes and elites might be more important in Europe, from which most of our ancestors came and from which some fled. Conceptions of elite-dominated politics are strongly rooted in European political theory. These concepts usually explain elite power by reference to *implicit* aspects of power, discussed in Chapter 1.

Though almost unknown among the general public, the European heritage of elite theory has deeply influenced how American political scientists view politics. One might think this would mean the belief that some ruling elite dominates politics. But as European elite theory developed in the early twentieth century it became a particular sort of interpretation of how politics works in a democracy. For this reason it is sometimes called *democratic elitism,* and many American political scientists believe American politics can be described as democratic-elitist. But what is democratic elitism? The best way to answer this is to look at the development of European elite theory.

Elite theory arose in reaction against Marxian *class* theory. Marx believed that those who owned industries, banks, and other capitalist institutions comprised a ruling class. This class controlled the state. The state, in turn, had three roles:

1. It served the interests of the ruling class.

2. It arbitrated rivalries among segments of the ruling class when these threatened instability.
3. Through bureaucracy it also developed some interests in its own right.

In Chapter 1 we mentioned the Marxist belief that in normal times, the ideas of the ruling class were also the ruling ideas. The ruling class was able to propagate its own self-interested world view as a popular ideology. The implicit power that was based on this enabled this class to proceed with its basic purposes of nurturing and subsidizing capitalist expansion and of suppressing dissent. But in these purposes the rulers remained isolated from the masses, using their control of the state to dictate their interests.

Early elite theorists argued, in contrast, that the masses were closely related to the rulers.[1] Though the rulers might comprise an elite, this was simply the inevitable nature of *all* government. The governing elite might be overthrown, but a new elite would invariably replace it. Theorists like Mosca and Pareto argued that the communist, classless society predicted by the Marxists was simply a myth.[2] They conceded that elections under representative democracy did not prevent the formation of a ruling stratum. But they argued that elections *did* oblige ruling groups to adapt themselves, at least in appearance, to the desires of the masses.[3] "It has the effect," Mosca wrote early in this century, "of forcing the ruling class to play up to the great majority of the people who are less aware of the true interests of society."[4]

But if the ruling elite did not serve class interests, but instead was forced to cater to the masses, politics was not really elite-dominated. In fact, Mosca argued, elites function to *protect* democracy from the authoritarian tendencies of the "uncultured strata"—the masses prone to submit to demagogues.[5]

Similarly, Mosca conceded that Marx was correct that the ideas of the ruling elite exerted tremendous hegemony (implicit power) over the population. (He called these ruling ideas "political formulae.") But he denounced Marx for thinking that *ruling* ideas are self-serving *class* ideas. Rather, Mosca said, ruling ideas have an independent nature. Far from being cynically used tools to manipulate the masses, ruling ideas serve to constrain *every* member of society, even members of the elite. In Mosca's words, a ruling idea or ruling political formula "serves as a check on the power of the ruler and ennobles somewhat the subjection of the ruled." [6]

The Problem with Early Elite Theory

The ideas of Mosca and Pareto became popular among those who wanted a clear, non-Marxist way of looking at modern politics. Early elite theory had much appeal. It was not simplistically legalistic, pretending that real-life politics was as democratic as constitutions and laws said it was. It admitted the existence of ruling elites and the implicit power of ruling ideas, while at the same time not falling into the revolutionary implications of Marxist class theory.

But many non-Marxists still disliked the ideas of Mosca and Pareto because of their essentially undemocratic and aristocratic nature. True, Mosca favored "mixed government," but by this he meant a mixture of liberalism and autocracy. Democracy was not something genuine. It did not, in Mosca's thinking, serve to prevent elite rule. Rather, its value was as a means to legitimate the rule of a "better class" of people, men with greater merit, rooted in wealth, contacts, and training.[7] The elite did renew itself by absorbing the "better elements" rising from the masses, but these few soon became socially oriented to the viewpoints of the elite. Mosca's aristocratic beliefs led to the virtual discrediting of his ideas among democratic thinkers when, after the rise of Mussolini in his native Italy, he failed to criticize fascism.

Pareto, writing during the same period, similarly believed that members of the elite were marked by superior personal attributes. They held more than others certain "instincts" toward organization, coalition-building, and use of ideologies to gain power. Elites thus formed a natural political stratum that was based, if not on aristocratic birthright, at least on innate psychological drives.

As one commentator summarized Pareto's views:

The elite maintains itself in power by a constant process of lying and cheating to make the many believe what the few do not. The strength to keep up such a harrowing task is to be found in the elites themselves and in the drive they have for power. Once the elite no longer believes in its task it is inevitably superseded by another elite, as well organized but with stronger intellectual force and closer contact with the residues and derivations [instincts] that make possible control of the public mind.[8]

This idea of a self-confident, popular, elitist intellectual force seemed to many, including Pareto, to be the fascist philosophy then sweeping Italy and Europe. Pareto became an enthusiastic supporter of Mussolini, and acted as his delegate to the League of Nations. As with Mosca, elite theory for Pareto apparently seemed more a stepping-stone to an acceptance of fascism than a defense of representative democracy against Marxism.

In summary, elite theory seemed to have as its outcome neither the expectation of rule by the capitalists nor rule by the people's representatives. Instead it suggested rule by the party machine. This concept was forged indelibly in the intellectual currents of the times by Roberto Michels, a former socialist. In *Political Parties* (1915) Michels had studied the seemingly democratic socialist parties of Europe and had pessimistically concluded that *all* political organization leads to rule by a tight hierarchy. "He who says organization, says oligarchy," he wrote.[9]

Michels's "iron law of oligarchy" taught that any organization, however democratic in form, tended to become ruled by elites. This was due simply to the ability of leaders to control party funds, party newspapers, party patronage, and so on.[10] His conclusions were similar to those of Mosca and Pareto: the public mind was inevitably controlled by an elite. The end result was the same, even if elite theory suggested four different reasons:

1. The public mind is controlled because of the economic hegemony of the ruling class (Marx).
2. The public mind is controlled because of the aristocratic, superior qualities of elites (Mosca).

3. The public mind is controlled because of the instinctual drives of elites for power (Pareto).
4. The public mind is controlled because of the organizational advantages of elites (Michels).

Regardless, there was little prospect for democratic hopes.

How Modern Elite Theory Avoided Fascism

Among those who developed modern elite theory in a democratic direction was one of the intellectual leaders of the Spanish Republican government, José Ortega y Gasset, a bitter opponent of the fascist movement. In *The Revolt of the Masses* (1930) Ortega attributed fascism not so much to the economic, psychological, or organizational attributes of elites, as to what he called "mass man." Mass man was a new type of political being, Ortega wrote, created by industrialism. The "mass man," he said, "proclaims the right to be common and refuses to accept any order superior to himself." [11] Mass man was prone to demagogic appeals, such as communism and fascism. Mosca's observation (or faith), that elites protect democracy while the masses continually threaten it, became in Ortega's work the main theme.

The Marxists attributed fascist power to capitalist elites and to elite theorists like Mosca and Pareto themselves. Later elite theorists like Ortega sought to deny that fascism flowed from the ideas of Mosca and Pareto; instead, later elite theorists blamed the industrial masses to whom the Marxists looked for hope! There was some truth in each position.

In Ortega's theories, then, we find the image of the common man and woman as the threat to democracy. Ironically, an intellectually superior and politically more tolerant elite is cast as the defender of republicanism. Here is the basis for the slogan of the American right wing: the United States is "a republic, not a democracy." Politics in liberal democracies (like the United States) is rule *by* elites *for* the masses. But to rule the elites must wield some great, unifying ideological ideal more powerful than the myths of communism and fascism that demagogues might seek to use. Ortega believed that the ideal of European unity, of a new supranationalism, might become the guiding ideology of democratic elites on the Continent.[12]

In retrospect the ideal of European unity—the Common Market notwithstanding—hardly seems the basis for implicit power that Ortega hoped. Supranationalism is not a powerful political symbol enabling rulers to guide masses of followers away from alternative ideologies like communism. Communism remains a major basis of appeal and is growing in several countries. But Ortega's work was important because it defined the problem of democracy as the problem of making elites democratic in ideology, *not* the problem of increasing the participation of the masses in government.

It fell to Joseph Schumpeter to present in the early forties an American version of democratic elitism. Schumpeter, an outstanding economist, agreed with Ortega in rejecting participatory democracy as anything but a dangerous myth. If attempted, it would open the state to the rule of demagogues. Schumpeter believed that people held no serious opinions; even when they did, they mattered only when mobilized by a political leader. The role of citizens was simply the "acceptance of leadership." [13] The sole purpose of elections was to accomplish the circulation of elites. Between elections, Schumpeter believed, citizens should not even write letters to their congressmen, much less participate in major decisions. While he expected leaders would come from the upper echelons of society, the choice of which specific leaders would be victorious Schumpeter thought to be a random matter of the "pyrotechnics of party management" as quite similar parties strove to gain office. In this process, he wrote, "the electoral mass is incapable of action other than a stampede." [14] Overall, true democracy was strengthened by insulating the ruling elites from the majority of ordinary citizens.

In this view politics in America was dominated by elites, but the elites competed with each other in elections. Elections, though irrational, served to legitimate leadership and circulate elites. Democracy was a device—a means to an end—enabling elites to govern in a broadly accountable manner.

Summary

Democratic elitism means the rule of a political few over the irrational many. The few who compose the elite are open to new faces from the middle and even lower classes. Competitive elections are held under conditions of civil liberties. Elites are ultimately responsible to the masses. But democratic elitism is *not* marked by several features classically assumed to be a part of democracy: rational voters, widespread participation in government, popular discussion of political issues, and public opinion as the basis for decisions of representatives.

Using the theory of democratic elitism as a guideline, we would expect American politics to reflect decisions made by relatively few. Even the discussion process leading up to decisions would be elite-dominated. The mass of citizens would be ill-informed and would not participate much in politics. In short, the example of the one-bank holding company legislation discussed at the beginning of this chapter would seem fully typical and understandable.

Criticisms of Elite Theory

The European heritage of elite theory has not been accepted without dissent, of course. Among the criticisms are the following:

1. Society is too complex to be dichotomized into "an elite" and "a mass."
2. Political leadership is not a distinct class, nor is it evident that it is innately superior in abilities.
3. It is not evident that the "masses" are particularly dangerous (membership in extreme political parties, for example, is more likely to involve intellectuals than workers in America).
4. Public opinion is not purely passive to political leadership.
5. Elites may use their positions for far more self-interested purposes than elite theorists cited here imply.
6. It is not evident that basic problems faced by the nation could be solved by informed elites if unhindered by "ignorant masses."

On the other hand, the heritage of elite theory has left some points of common agreement as well:

1. A considerable degree of elitism marks "democratic" politics.
2. Direct, participatory democracy ("classical democracy," involving an informed citizenry rationally participating in major decisions directly or through fully accountable delegates) is not an accurate description of modern democracies.
3. Political domination by an occupational elite is consistent with most contemporary definitions of "democracy" if the elite can be motivated to be accountable to the public.
4. There are several forces tending toward the accountability of elites, of which elections are only one.

By the time Schumpeter published his major book, *Capitalism, Socialism, and Democracy* in 1942, many of these ideas had become common in American political science. But American political scientists as well had by then also developed many of their own ideas about how power is distributed in this country.

American Political Science and the Interest-Group Concept of Politics

The general way American political scientists have looked at the distribution of power in America was different from the European views just discussed. But in the end, many of them arrived at the concept of democratic elitism all the same. It was different only because American political scientists were less concerned with Marxist ideas of a ruling class, which seemed hopelessly incorrect in a new nation far more mobile and democratic (they thought) than the class-ridden countries of Europe. Instead of class politics, what worried American political scientists was the rise of powerful pressure groups in the late nineteenth and early twentieth centuries. Groups, not classes, seemed to be the stuff of politics. By World War II the group-theory approach to politics was dominant in American political science. It found a classic summary in David Truman's *The Governmental Process* (1951). Later critics charged that the group approach was not different at all, however. They said it was just an Americanized version of democratic elitism.[15]

What was the group approach, and was it really an alternative way of looking at power in a modern democracy such as the United States? One way of answering this is to start by saying what group theory was *not*.

Group theory was not the jurisprudential approach to politics. Jurisprudence—the study of law—was the center of nineteenth-century American political science. Later group theorists charged the jurists with approaching politics legalistically, pretending that the Constitution and laws actually *described* how politics worked. Everyone knew, the group theorists said, that this was not so. "Real" politics took place between the lines of the law, in informal caucuses, in the workings of private pressure groups, and in the interaction of political personalities. This, not the law, was what American political scientists should study to find out how politics really worked.

Actually, the group theorists' criticism of the jurists was unfair. The jurists in general understood their studies to be *prescriptive*, not descriptive. Not only did they understand and study the difference between the law and actual practice, but they understood most aspects of group theory long before it was labeled such. They studied, for example, John Calhoun's theory of the "community as made up of different and conflicting interests" in which government "takes the sense of each through its appropriate organ, and the united sense of all as the sense of the entire community." [16] In studying Calhoun's views, Locke's theory of the social contract, and Rousseau's theory of the general will, the jurists wrestled with beliefs in the state resting on constituent groups and individuals. Most jurists opposed a group concept of politics because it seemed to weaken the ability of the state to act in the interests of all, over and above narrow group interests of the day. In extreme form, the jurists felt, group theory led to a rationale for states' rights and the divisions which underlay the Civil War.

The New Interest in "Pressure Politics"

The late nineteenth century brought the rise of giant corporations and, later, great labor unions. In a few short years dozens of trusts were formed, seemingly monopolizing every economic aspect of American commerce. The trusts became the prime targets of the Populist and Progressive movements. The tremendous power of the new corporate giants appeared to undermine the very sovereignty of the state. It became more and more plausible to believe that the study of the law did *not* get at the essence of politics. Should not the energies of political scientists be channeled *directly* into examination of these new interest groups rather than being wasted in scholarly treatises on jurisprudence?

A wave of writing developed to cover pressure politics. Lincoln Steffens's *The Struggle for Self-Government* (1906) was typical of dozens of exposés of how the new politics really worked. Many of these muckraking works (as Teddy Roosevelt called them) were serialized in leading magazines of the day. Political scientists were caught up in this surge of interest in and apprehension about pressure politics. And other social scientists added to this tendency by researching the historic role of economic elites in earlier periods of American history, notably in the works of Charles Beard.[17]

The upshot of these changes was not Marxism but rather a period of Populism and Progressivism in American life in general and in political analysis in particular. Textbooks changed. Young's 1915 text, *The New American Government and Its Work*, started its discussion by looking at business influence in politics, not the legal framework universal among earlier texts. In 1916 Jesse Macy, in his presidential address to the American Political Science Association, called on his colleagues to adopt the new "scientific spirit in politics." [18] By this he meant political scientists should apply their studies to the urgent tasks of reform—of finding ways to control the new pressures on American politics.

The Rise and Fall of Classic Pluralism

Against this background, a new theory, *pluralism,* became popular in American political science. (Pluralism again became popular after World War II in a different version, so this earlier theory will be called classic pluralism.) Classic pluralism was a group theory of politics. It held that politics was molded by the group influences upon it, not by the abstract forces of law, precedent, and reason so emphasized by the jurists.

Classic pluralism was associated with various European

thinkers (such as Figgis, Maitland, Duguit, and von Gierke) quite at variance with the European elite theorists discussed earlier. Americans learned about pluralism primarily through the work of Harold Laski, a brilliant political essayist and spokesman of the British Left.

On the surface, pluralism was a devastating rebuttal of traditional juristic views. Drawing on specific historical examples, Laski showed that, in practice, the state had ceased to be "absolutely sovereign" as the jurists claimed. For example, the English government had been forced to recognize the essential autonomy of religious groups after a long struggle in the nineteenth century. Laski's version of pluralism seemed to show that the jurists' legal theories about sovereignty were empirically false. Moreover, pluralism presented a new theoretical framework that appeared to be useful in explaining the new pressure politics just discussed.[19]

The jurists, of course, felt misrepresented, and they counterattacked by charging that Laski's pluralism tended toward anarchy. It was, they said, an implicit defense of group autonomy from the state. It would play havoc with social coordination and government control.[20] But in the end Laski's ideas became popular anyway. For many, including Laski himself, they served the political purpose of providing justification for the autonomy of the emerging labor movement from the intervention of an unfriendly and conservative state.

As its political implications became clear, however, most American political scientists rejected pluralism. For some it was too radical. For others its defense of group autonomy seemed wrong: it was an undesirable obstacle in the way of necessary governmental coordination of the economy. Laski himself eventually abandoned pluralism in favor of a version of Marxism. This was precisely because he came to favor a high degree of social control over economic groups.[21]

Early Group Theory

When Laski abandoned classic pluralism, the first major effort at a group theory of politics* collapsed. Though classic pluralism

---

* The first, at least, since Calhoun.

was abandoned, the approach of jurisprudence never revived. World War I was followed by a period of pessimism. Even the reform interest in pressure-group politics declined. Many political scientists turned to "purifying" political science. They wanted to discard what they regarded as moralistic reform ideas and concentrate on better describing how politics worked. (Of course this was what the reformers and the classic pluralists had *thought* they were doing, but in retrospect the postwar political scientists tended to believe they had not succeeded.)

In the period between the wars many aspects of political science tended toward a new group theory of politics. This theory postulated that government actions reflected the competition of group interests rather than the inertia of legal precedents, the power of ideals, or the appeal of personalities. Even though pluralist group theory was rejected at this time, another version of group theory was emerging. This theory eventually became among political scientists the dominant way of looking at how politics works.

Part of it grew out of the new interest in psychology. Social-psychological studies emphasized the importance of group relations and focused attention on the importance of group identifications to the individual.[22] But these studies were pessimistic about democracy. They emphasized the irrational nature of people, their susceptibility to suggestion and propaganda, and the critical role of emotion in their political preferences.

Walter Lippman's *The Phantom Public* (1925) crystallized the mood of pessimism. It became questionable whether democratic theory could ever again speak of a rational electorate making informed choices in participative elections. The fascist movements added their voices to this, charging the Western democracies with hopeless naiveté about how politics really worked and consequently with hopeless inefficiency.

In this context, some political scientists—such as Francis Wilson and E. Pendleton Herring—argued for a new group-theory way of looking at politics. This approach was a defense of democracy, but it did not require an optimistic faith in the average citizen. In fact, Wilson argued, the individual vote or the individual response in an opinion poll might be very *poor* ways of assessing the American public. Rather, the *real* will of the democratic public was to be found in their organization in interest groups.[23]

Herring had this in mind when he wrote that "the public interest cannot be given concrete expression except through the compromise of special claims and demands finally effected. Special interests cannot then be banished from the picture, for they are the parts that make the whole." [24] Herring said democracy was not the sum of rational individuals' choices. Individuals, it could be admitted, were irrational, emotional, and often lacked clear opinions. But the groups with which they were associated were fully capable of extracting the underlying interests of their individual members and expressing these in a far more rational and effective way. Thus, democratic politics was better seen as a sum of *group* interests. The writings of Herring and Wilson set the basis for present-day group theories of politics.[25]

In sum, through the new group theory one could see American politics as basically democratic, and one could defend our representative democracy as a system that effected the public interest through accommodating *group* conflicts. There was no need, as in classical democratic theory, to assume rational, participative, informed individual *voters*. After World War II this became the common way of interpreting American politics in political science.

Modern Group Theory

Following World War II, David Truman's *The Governmental Process* (1951) popularized the group-theory interpretation of how politics really works. This interpretation very nearly specified that politics was the optimal result of the competition of many interest groups, none of which had the power to control the state. But it stopped short of this mechanical model, which would have seen government decisions as simple "resultant vectors" based on the physics of "group forces." Instead, Truman said decision-makers took not only *existing* interest groups into account, but also *potential groups*. Group theory also came close to implying that lobbies were the key to politics, but Truman avoided this by defining the groups in his group theory very broadly: not only lobbies, but economic classes, ethnic groups, families, and any category of people were included, even if not organized.

Truman's group theory attracted much support. It was a non-Marxist, nonelite way of looking at American politics. It seemed to be value-free—devoid of the early reform prescriptions. It saw politics as evolutionary, not revolutionary. Change occurred incrementally, a bit at a time. This was because interest-group conflict always required long negotiations and intricate compromises. In short, it seemed to describe accurately the politics of the 1950s. It explained why lobbies were so evident in Washington, and why the formalities of congressional sessions appeared to be far less important than the informal politics of bargaining over interests. It explained why change was so slow and why comprehensive reforms almost never happened (because necessary compromises prevent strong, sweeping actions). And it fit in with Herring's defense of representative democracy as a democracy of articulate *groups*, but not of rational *individuals*. Finally, the group approach was apparently converting political science into a real "science" because it rejected metaphysical concepts like "the public interest." The *public* interest was a myth, the group theorists said. There are only *group* interests.

Criticisms of the Group Approach

It was not long before Truman's group theory became not only the dominant way of interpreting American politics, but also became itself the favorite target of political-science critics. The critics found five main problems with the group approach. These reasons, discussed below, they said showed that the group approach was not really a good alternative to Marxism or the European elite theories (democratic elitism) discussed earlier in this chapter.

1. *The Group Approach Is Not Really a Theory at All.*   If the group theory of politics simply said government decisions were the result of interest-group forces, it would be easy to interpret. We could look at the organized groups at work on a government decision, estimate their relative strengths and the positions they

seek, and predict the outcome on this basis. Unfortunately, politics does not work like that. And group theory does not say it does. But what does it say?

Group theorists like Truman emphasized the role of *potential* as well as *actual* groups. Potential groups could include "any mutual interest" or people with "any shared attitude." [26] This could be extended to include the effect on politics of diffuse forces like traditions and ideals. That is, the concept of potential groups meant virtually *all* causes were group variables. Group theory degenerated into a truism that all sorts of collective attributes affect politics.[27]

To say everything causes what happens in politics is accurate, but it is not helpful. It is not theory because you cannot use it to predict political outcomes. This sort of group theory becomes merely a *vocabulary* for discussing politics. Truman himself eventually disclaimed followers who still believed his work was a real theory of politics. He said his purpose was not theory at all, but only to "examine interest groups and their role." [28] He was *not* saying the key to understanding politics is understanding the power of interest groups. That would leave out consideration of *implicit* power, discussed in Chapter 1 and emphasized by the elite theorists in their ideas about control of the public mind.

2. *Group Theory Ignores the Issues of Elite Theory.*   The second major criticism of the group-theory approach was that it sidestepped dealing directly with its major alternative, elite theory. For example, Truman's section titled "Difficulties in a Group Interpretation of Politics" was confined to justifying his focus on groups rather than individuals or society at large. To the critics this was irrelevant. Practically no one really thought politics could be understood in terms of the personalities of great men or in terms of some diffuse national spirit. The real problems with the group approach, they said, were those being raised by C. Wright Mills* and other elite theorists. These modern elite theorists, like the European writers discussed in the first portion of this chapter, believed that elitism was an em-

* Mills's views are discussed later in this chapter.

pirical fact. Where group theory suggested politics was the competition of many relatively small groups—no one of which could dominate—the elite theorists thought it could be shown empirically that giant economic interests *did* dominate politics. Politics was not the competition of relatively equal and countervailing groups. Some groups were much "more equal" than others.

3. *Group Theory Wrongly Assumes Equilibrium Theory.* Equilibrium theory holds that political forces tend toward the reestablishment of equilibrium. In discussing group politics, Truman observed that "the institutionalized groups that exemplify these behavior patterns and the patterns themselves represent almost by definition an equilibrium among the interactions of the participants." [29] Critics find equilibrium theory too conservative in its implications. It suggests that the political system must always return to a stable center. Equilibrium theory seemed to be in tension with Truman's own passing acknowledgment that important political changes are due to more-or-less intense social disturbances. Therefore, these changes cannot be understood in terms of normal interest-group patterns of an equilibrating sort.

4. *Group Theory Neglects the Importance of Collective Behavior.* More generally, critics of group theory believed that Truman focused on lobby-type groups at the expense of forms of collective behavior such as social movements. They objected to his treating the process by which unorganized interests coalesce in rebellion under the label of "morbific politics." Morbific, meaning disease-producing, was a throwback to earlier conservative imagery in social science. Social movements were not part of a "social pathology"; they, more than the humdrum routines of the lobbies, had more to do with understanding political change than Truman admitted.

5. *Group Theory Is Too Conservative.* Overall, the critics concluded that group theory was biased toward a conservative political imagery. For example, Truman said that "the great political task now as in the past is to perpetuate a viable system by maintaining the conditions under which such widespread

understanding and appreciation (i.e., consensual acceptance of democratic 'rules of the game') can exist." [30] Critics found in Truman's emphasis on "perpetuation," "maintenance," "consensus," and other terms a conservative assumption, an assumption that the real purpose of government was maintaining order (a conservative view), *not* primarily providing for the general welfare.

Modern Pluralism

During the 1950s and 1960s many political scientists, influenced by group theory, began referring to their ideas as pluralist. They were not advocates of group theory because of one or more of the five criticisms just outlined, but they *did* disagree with elite theorists. The pluralists believed that American politics could be empirically shown to be based on a wide variety of group influences, ideas, personalities, traditions, and interests. Politics, they said, is relatively free from the domination of any single group or class of interests. Also, the modern pluralists differed from Laski and the classic pluralists because they were not seeking to justify group autonomy from the state.

Robert Dahl was among those pluralists who sought to rebut elite theory. "There is a high probability," he wrote, "that an active and legitimate group can make itself heard effectively at some crucial stage of the process of decision." [31] The result is that "the making of government decisions is not a majestic march of great majorities united upon certain matters of basic policy. It is the steady appeasement of relatively small groups." [32] There is no ruling class or governing elite. If there is any danger of tyranny, it is a danger of tyranny of the majority. That is, there is far more danger that the many will unjustly coerce the few than there is that the few will exploit the many.

Five propositions summarize pluralist theory:[33]

1. Modern society increases social complexity. Complexity requires more government intervention in society. It also requires more cooperation among individuals, and this in turn requires the existence of many groups. Groups inevitably tend to seek government cooperation to obtain their goals.

(In contrast, elite theorists often argue that modernization leads to the merger of public and private interests primarily at an *elite* level.)

2. Public policy is a function of: (a) the decision-maker's institutional interests and role perceptions; and (b) the effect of traditions and potential groups.

(In contrast, elite theorists see public policy as a function of elite bargaining.)

3. Group success is based on many factors, such as number of adherents, intensity of their commitment, mastery of political techniques (such as lobbying and public relations), and level of resources (legitimacy, wealth, time, and control over information). Ordinarily wealth is not necessary for a group to acquire at least some of these prerequisites for success.

(Elite theorists argue that group success is based primarily on the correspondence between group goals and elite purposes.)

4. Political stability depends on the counterbalancing of opposing groups, the overlapping of their memberships, consensual acceptance of rules of the game, the incentive the system gives to accommodation and compromise, and the pluralist fragmentation of power.

(Elite theorists say political stability rests on elite manipulation of symbols, control over institutions of socialization, such as schools and media, and control over agencies of force and repression; groups do not countervail because business dominates; dissensus is as common as consensus and consensual beliefs are often shallowly held and manipulated from above.)

5. There is no real public interest. The social interest can be assessed only through "summing" the often-conflicting interests of organized and potential groups. In practice, the perpetuation of the system becomes the dominant value of politics.

(Elite theorists believe system perpetuation is a conservative value, and one cannot take "potential groups" into account without having some concept of a *public* interest apart from what lobbies are demanding.)

In addition, some pluralists go beyond claiming their views simply describe politics. Some see pluralism as a prescription. These pluralists say the group process more nearly approaches a social optimum than any other political patterns. Specifically, they say, the attempt to override group pressures through central social planning will lead to more problems than benefits. Rational social planning is a dangerous socialist myth. In the words of Charles Lindblom, "muddling through" is better.[34] Elite theorists respond by saying that muddling through by reliance on group conflicts increases inequities and social problems because it allows them to mount to crisis proportions. Thus, the elite theorists say, acceptance of pluralist group process is the basis for eventual instability.[35]

Criticisms of Pluralism

Also during the 1950s and 1960s, when pluralism was becoming popular in political science, the contrary ideas of elite theory were also receiving much new attention. This was especially due to the work of C. Wright Mills (author of *The Power Elite*, 1956) and G. William Domhoff (author of *Who Rules America?*, 1967). Each wrote several books and many articles, all sharply critical of pluralism. They generally opposed the pluralists on the following grounds:[36]

1. Pluralists lack an adequate conception of the economic elite—they wrongly play down the political implications of America's relatively high degree of economic stratification.
2. Pluralists wrongly emphasize interest groups as the primary channels of business influence. (Elite theorists prefer to focus on peak business associations like the Business Council, presidentially appointed task forces and commissions composed of business people, advisory committees to administrative agencies, the business background of many governmental appointees, influence via campaign funding, and, especially, implicit power through control over information and hegemony over institutions of socialization.)
3. Pluralists, while admitting the elite character of foreign-policy-making, see popular influence in this area as undesirable. (Elite theorists tend to view the making of American foreign policy as a history of imperialism and mistaken interests, as in Vietnam, and popular controls over elite decision-makers are viewed as essential.)
4. Pluralists wrongly take New Deal and other progressive legislation as evidence that business loses as well as wins—it does not consistently dominate. (Elite theorists say such legislation is co-optive

in intent and merely symbolic in content, not really serving to redistribute wealth or power.)

5. Pluralists wrongly believe the government ultimately controls the economy. (Elite theorists see these "controls" as insignificant in content, unenforced in practice, and overseen by officials identified with the economic elite.)

6. Pluralists wrongly focus on Congress and the passage of legislation. (Elite theorists feel Congress is at a mere middle level of power.)

The Elitist-Pluralist Debate

Elite theory and pluralism are two poles in American political science. Together they raise questions mentioned at the beginning of this chapter. Is most of what government does democratic or not? Does the role of economic interest show America is elitist? Or are groups the mechanism through which real democracy is expressed?

These questions have raised a prolonged debate in political science and in sociology. Arnold Rose, a pluralist, and C. Wright Mills, an elite theorist, represent two of the best-known participants in this debate. Both died recently, but their viewpoints are still much argued, and others have taken up where they left off. By examining their ideas we can get a better idea of what these two alternative ways of looking at power are.

The Pluralist Viewpoint of Arnold Rose. Rose's *The Power Structure* (1967) argued that economic elites in recent years have never significantly controlled politics in America. People in business were pictured as concerned mainly with business, not politics. Moreover, they found their businesses subject to many governmental regulations. In Rose's view, even when business groups do intervene in politics, they do not act as a cohesive force. There are many divisions among business people. In certain instances, as in the case of some of the regulatory commissions, business people apparently dominate, but this is only because there is no real opposition. When counterpressures do become organized, Rose said, business is far less successful. In fact, it has been unable to prevent a torrent of restrictions on business since the New Deal, and the trend is for more of the same. Also, since business has less power at the federal than the state or local level—and since the federal level was increasingly important vis-à-vis the states and localities—we may expect even less business influence in the future. This is particularly true given the increasing importance of black people and other nonbusiness groups in American politics. Of course, given the resources, political skills, and control over economic information in the business community, business will never be an inconsequential factor in American politics. But it is far from being an economic elite.

The Elite-Theory Viewpoint of C. Wright Mills. Mills's *The Power Elite* (1956) sought to explain why most people feel almost powerless in relation to great political changes in America. He contrasted this with the key decision-making role of leaders at the top of the corporate, governmental, and military strata. Mills admitted that these key elites are not unified or sometimes even conscious they are elites. But overall their power is tremendous and they are aware of this. On crucial underlying issues like protection of the capitalist corporate system, they agreed. This agreement was rooted in similar class backgrounds, similar training, and socialization to elite ideas. Operating though a sub-elite of lawyers and managers, the power elite of business, government, and the military cooperated toward their common ends. Lower power levels like Congress are pressured into conformity through liaison men and direct communications from top bankers and lawyers, not through the interest groups emphasized by group theorists. With the decline of meaningful interparty differences, the "triple elite" of business, government, and the military has become more powerful than ever. Though not fully unified or omnipotent, this group of a few thousand key decision-makers rules America, in part through their direct authority and influence and in part through their implicit power rooted in Americans' acceptance of the current system of power.

A Summary of Contrasts. No brief summary can do full justice to the many books and articles written by Rose, Mills, and others to explain their views on the debate over elitism and pluralism. But the points listed in Table 2–1 indicate the extreme poles of this debate.

Conclusion

The purpose of this chapter has been to set forth some of the primary ways of interpreting power in America. In the first portion we looked at European elite theory and how it led to the concept of democratic elitism. Democratic elitism was a system in which elites ruled and in which the elements of classic democracy were absent. There was no rational, informed electorate actively participating in government decisions, instructing legislative representatives, and formulating public policy. But elites did change as new faces were brought in, and elections did force them to stay within very broad limits. Democratic elitism was rule *by* elites *for* the masses.

Later we discussed how group theory and pluralism became the main American political-science approaches to politics. These approaches portrayed American power as very fragmented. Politics was the conflict of many relatively small groups. All of them competed for the attention and favor of government. Though some government agencies had their own interests and acted like the private pressure groups, overall the government was seen as relatively neutral. It responded to the pressures upon it, but it was not just a matter of the strongest interests always winning. This was because, the pluralists argued, decision-makers take "potential" groups into account as well as actual ones. In any event, the pluralist fragmentation of power assured a politics of compromise. No one group could become a governing elite.

Democratic elitism and pluralism seemed to be two opposing ways of looking at politics. But contemporary elite theorists have argued they are basically similar. This is because, they argue, pluralist theory lacks the same classical democratic features that democratic elitism lacks. That is, under pluralism there is still no assumption of a rational, participative citizenry actively determining political policy. Rather, the interests of the citizenry are represented through hierarchically organized pres-

Table 2–1   *Pluralism vs. Elitism: Summary of Contrasts*

The Pluralist View

1. Politics is the competition of many relatively small groups.
2. Government oversees this competition in a basically neutral manner.
3. Business is only one of many competing interests.
4. Labor is on the same order of power as business, obtaining much of what they seek.
5. Progressive legislation shows popular forces can often override economic interests.
6. The New Deal and the Kennedy-Johnson years show government is often dominated by forces business dislikes.
7. This is because money cannot buy elections. (Otherwise the Republicans would always win!)
8. The poor and minorities can get their share of power if they overcome their apathy, and organize and participate in the electoral process.
9. Any legitimate group can get a share of benefits if it organizes.
10. Any needed changes can come through Congress and the electoral system.
11. Such changes have progressively improved the lot of the average citizen in America.
12. This is why America can be considered pluralist.

The Elite-Theory View

1. Politics is the cooperation of a relatively few elite groups.
2. These groups determine major government policies in their mutual class interests.
3. Business is the central and dominant interest in politics.
4. Labor unions are everywhere weak or co-opted, unable even to veto labor legislation they dislike.
5. Progressive legislation shows little because it has not changed the basic distribution of benefits in America.
6. Even under FDR, JFK, and LBJ, corporate power was further consolidated.
7. Except for the influence of money, the whole political spectrum would be much further to the left.
8. Elites create and depend on the subordination of the poor and of minorities. Their "apathy" results from manipulative socialization and from pragmatic role acceptance (that is, a realistic understanding of elite dominance.)
9. In normal, nonrevolutionary times, organized groups cannot get far unless their outlook is compatible with elite interests.
10. Basic social changes require social upheavals and mass movements directed against the elites.
11. Normal legislative changes have never really redistributed benefits in this country.
12. This is why America can be considered elitist.

sure groups. Elections only serve the same function as under democratic elitism: setting very broad limits. Really, elite theorists argue, there is no difference between democratic elitism and pluralism.

There is no difference between democratic elitism and pluralism because the interest groups which represent people are clustered into functional groups: military-related groups, business-related groups, education-related groups, and so on. And within each of these decision-making areas, a set of traditions develops which links the groups together. These traditions foster an in-group of elite influence-dealers, in and out of government. And since some functional groups—particularly that of business—are much more important than others, the whole system is one of democratic elitism. That is, there is a loose but highly evolved and specialized group of people (an elite) which is at the center of government. They rule for the people. The people's own participation in elections is primarily ritualistic, perhaps setting broad limits, but nonetheless several steps removed from the real policy-making process.

Of course, not all political scientists share the viewpoints discussed in this chapter. Marxists, for example, see American politics as dominated by a ruling class, not just a democratic elite. And many more moderate political scientists take a postpluralist path, deemphasizing the role of pressure groups altogether.[37] They still feel that American politics is pluralist, but decision-makers are seen as responding to a host of inputs, not just interest-group pressures. Because there are so many inputs and because legislators respond differently to them, the postpluralists maintain, it is impossible for any one group to become an elite.

How can we know which of these positions is most nearly correct? Or are there some other ways of looking at American politics that may be more helpful? These questions are taken up in the chapters that follow. Chapter 3 discusses various methods that have been proposed to gain answers, and later chapters examine what each of these approaches has to offer. Thus each chapter is a different approach to the question, "How is power distributed in America?" Some approaches are better for assessing *overt* power, while other methods seek to tap the effects of *implicit* power (recall Chapter 1). Chapters 10 and 11 provide an overview of American political history and ask how elitist or pluralist it has been. The final chapter concludes by suggesting a different interpretation of American politics that is neither elitist nor pluralist.

Notes

1. See James H. Meisel, *The Myth of the Ruling Class: Gaetano Mosca and the Elite* (Ann Arbor: University of Michigan Press, 1958). Mosca's first work appeared in 1896 as the last chapter of *Elementi Di Scienza Politica,* and went through many revisions until its last in 1933.
2. Ibid., p. 10.
3. Ibid., p. 383.
4. Ibid., p. 388.
5. Ibid.
6. Ibid., p. 384.
7. Ibid., pp. 388–90.
8. Renzo Sereno, *The Rulers: The Theory of the Ruling Class* (New York: Harper, 1968), p. 42.
9. Roberto Michels, *Political Parties* (New York: Free Press, 1958; orig. 1915), p. 418.
10. Gerant Parry, *Political Elites* (New York: Praeger, 1969), p. 43.
11. José Ortega y Gasset, *The Revolt of the Masses* (New York: Norton, 1957; orig. 1930), p. 133.
12. Ibid., p. 182.
13. Joseph A. Schumpeter, *Capitalism, Socialism, and Democracy* (New York: Harper, 1960; orig. 1942), p. 273.
14. Ibid., p. 283.
15. See G. David Garson, "On the Origins of Interest Group Theory: A Critique of a Process," *American Political Science Review* 68 (December 1974): 1505–19.
16. Elisha Mulford, *The Nation* (Boston: Houghton-Mifflin, 1881; orig. 1870), p. 212.
17. Charles Beard, *An Economic Interpretation of the Constitution of the United States* (New York: Macmillan, 1913); *Economic Origins of Jeffersonian Democracy* (New York: Macmillan, 1915); *The Economic Basis of Politics* (New York: Vintage, 1957; orig. 1922).
18. Jesse Macy, "The Scientific Spirit in Politics," *American Political Science Review* 11 (February 1917): 1–11.
19. Harold Laski, in Waldo Browne, ed., *Leviathan in Crisis* (New York: Viking, 1946), p. 120. See also Laski, *Studies in the Problem of Sovereignty* (New Haven: Yale University Press, 1917); *Authority in the Modern State* (New Haven: Yale University Press, 1919); and *The Foundations of Sovereignty* (New York: Harcourt, Brace, 1921).
20. For a critique of Laski, see Francis Coker, "The Technique of the Pluralist State," *American Political Science Review* 15 (May 1921):

186–213; W. Y. Elliot, "The Pragmatic Politics of Mr. H. J. Laski," *American Political Science Review* 18 (May 1924): 251–75.

21. Harold Laski, *A Grammar of Politics* (New Haven: Yale University Press, 1925), pp. 488–508.

22. Charles Merriam, "The Significance of Psychology for the Study of Politics," *American Political Science Review* 18 (August 1924): 469–88.

23. Francis Wilson, "Concepts of Public Opinion," *American Political Science Review* 27 (June 1933): 375–78.

24. E. Pendleton Herring, "Special Interests and the Interstate Commerce Commission," *American Political Science Review* 27 (December 1933): 916–17.

25. For criticism of this shift in democratic theory, see Peter Bachrach, *The Theory of Democratic Elitism: A Critique* (Boston: Little, Brown, 1967); and Carole Pateman, *Participation and Democratic Theory* (Cambridge, Eng.: Cambridge University Press, 1970).

26. David Truman, *The Governmental Process* (New York: Knopf, 1951), p. 511.

27. R. E. Dowling, "Pressure Group Theory: Its Methodological Range," *American Political Science Review* 54 (December 1960): 953.

28. David Truman, "On the Invention of 'Systems,'" *American Political Science Review* 54 (June 1960): 494–95.

29. Truman, *The Governmental Process*, pp. 47 ff. Truman acknowledges that "it would be idle to deny that a large proportion of organized interest groups have a class character" (p. 165), but most of his discussion appears inconsistent with class analysis. For further criticism, see S. Rothman, "Systematic Political Theory: Observations on the Group Approach," *American Political Science Review* 54 (February 1960): 15–33.

30. Truman, *The Governmental Process*, p. 524.

31. Robert A. Dahl, *A Preface to Democratic Theory* (Chicago: University of Chicago Press, 1956), p. 145.

32. Ibid., p. 146.

33. Based on Darryl Baskin, "American Pluralism: Theory, Practice, and Ideology," *Journal of Politics* 32 (February 1970): 71–95.

34. Charles Lindblom, "The Science of 'Muddling Through,'" *Public Administration Review* 19 (Spring 1959): 79–88; *The Intelligence of Democracy* (New York: Free Press, 1965); *The Policy-Making Process* (Englewood Cliffs, N.J.: Prentice-Hall, 1968).

35. A useful summary of the views sparked by C. W. Mills is contained in G. W. Domhoff and H. Ballard, eds., *C. Wright Mills and 'The Power Elite'* (Boston: Beacon Press, 1969). Useful anthologies include N. Crockett, ed., *The Power Elite in America* (Lexington, Mass.: Heath, 1970); and R. Gillam, ed., *Power in Postwar America* (Boston: Little, Brown, 1971). A bibliographic overview and interpretation is provided in A. H. Barton, "Empirical Research on National Power Structures," Bureau of Applied Social Research, Columbia University (1973).

36. Adapted from G. W. Domhoff, *The Higher Circles* (New York: Vintage, 1970), ch. 9. Domhoff was here criticizing A. Rose's work.

37. For a study of information control as a political resource, see H. Owen Burter, "Legislative Experts to Outsiders: The Two-Step Flow of Communication," *Journal of Politics* 6 (August 1974): 703–30.

Part II

Power in the
United States

3. Methods of Studying Power

Before we plunge into the study of power in America we must understand that there is a relation between our means and ends. How we go about studying power has a lot to do with what we will find. We must be careful not to take a research approach which will arbitrarily and misleadingly predetermine our conclusions. This problem was discussed briefly in Chapter 1. The decision-making approach, we said, tends to concentrate on *overt* power to the neglect of *implicit* power, for example. And in terms of the issues in Chapter 2, studying government decisions tends to favor *pluralist* rather than *elitist* interpretations of American power. This is because it focuses on political officials as the key decision-makers. Since they, not business people, make the actual decisions, there is a tendency for this approach to yield the finding that political officials are more influential in politics than any alleged business elite. Every approach is biased in one way or another.

Each main approach centers on a different type of evidence about how power really works. Early research emphasized the *formal prerogatives* of government office. These included constitutional powers, public laws, administrative rulings, and judicial precedents. Many contemporary political scientists use a *decision-making* approach, mentioned above. Other methods look to evidence on people's *reputations* for power, on the *social backgrounds* of leaders, and on the *distribution of benefits* in society. And, of course, the traditional *historical* approach is still important. Each of these has biases, but all contribute something to understanding power and politics in America. Later chapters in this book will look at each in greater detail. First, though, we will briefly discuss their advantages and disadvantages.

Evidence Based on the Formal Features of Government

No research approach concentrates purely on one type of evidence to the exclusion of all other facts. But the formalistic approach heavily emphasizes the formal powers, privileges, and responsibilities of the president, chief administrative officers, judges, senators, and congressmen. The strictly formalistic approach is no longer found in political science. That was associated with the nineteenth-century jurisprudential science mentioned in Chapter 2. In extreme form, it seemed to say: "If you want to know how power works, look at how the law says it works!"

While that seems too simple, every present-day textbook on American government still emphasizes basic information about the formal aspects of government. One learns, for example, about presidential powers vis-à-vis Congress. The expansion of the bureaucracy since the creation of the Office of Management and Budget in 1921 (formerly called the Bureau of the Budget) is discussed. Or one might learn about the expansion of the powers of the Supreme Court since John Marshall's early struggles in such cases as *Marbury* vs. *Madison* (1803), which established the principle of judicial review of the constitutionality of legislation. Finally, one might learn about the seniority system in the Congress. One could study, for example, what congressional rules and traditions allow the concentration of power in certain crucial committees. One could learn how the seniority rules in Congress have weakened a little in recent years, enabling new Democrats to oust certain conservative committee chairmen. Or one could learn how changes in Congress mean that the new Ways and Means Committee chairman, Al Ullman (D, Ore.), cannot be as powerful as his predecessor, Wilbur Mills (D, Ark.).

Clearly, much of what politics is about has to do with struggles over the formal aspects of government rules and organization. A case example would be Richard Bolling's 1974 attempt to reorganize the congressional committee system. Bolling's bill would have limited congressional leaders to holding only one major committee assignment at a time. It would thus disperse power among a larger number of representatives. It would have also split the Education and Labor Committee in two. Since this committee was a traditional liberal stronghold, this aspect of Bolling's reform dismayed organized labor. Any such proposal to change the formal structure of government meets powerful opposition from established leaders. In this case "many chairmen and other members whose power centers would be diminished" by the reform "helped draw up and promote a milder reorganization plan." [1] This milder bill gave the Speaker of the House more latitude in assigning bills to committees (this lowered committee chairpeople's power a bit), but it left basic committee jurisdictions unchanged. Nor did it prevent powerful people in Congress from holding more than one post. Had it passed, the Bolling reforms—directed at changing the little-known formal rules of Congress—would have been a major power change. The passage of the far milder bill (House Resolution 988) showed that the balance of power still lay with established leaders intent on protecting their influence. The formalistic approach to power, by focusing on such laws and rules and attempts to change them, directs our attention to an important aspect of politics.

Yet the formalistic approach has been strongly criticized. It calls attention to power in government, whereas the researcher may be interested in economic power in the private sector. The formal approach largely ignores the issue of nondecisions and implicit power discussed in Chapter 1. It emphasizes the rights and duties of officials and politicians while deemphasizing the influence on them of interest groups, public opinion, expert professionals, and other forces. Formalism, it is said, shows how power *should* work, not necessarily how it *does* work. There will always be some way to get around the formalities of politics, the critics suggest. The "real" underlying structure of power will have its way no matter how the superficial laws and rules change. Taken to an extreme, critics of the formal study of government operation believe that changing government structures is merely symbolic action. The forms of government are said to be far less important than the interests of decision-makers and those who back them.

Even though the formal approach is no longer popular or even present in political science, an imaginary formalist could make a number of responses to these criticisms. He or she would say that the formal approach includes four things: (1) study of constitutional and legal status of the government agency or other political unit being discussed; (2) description of its structure and organization; (3) its institutional history; and (4) its legislative record. While law and rules are abstractions incapable of being the causes of politics, they may be good *reflectors* of the underlying causes. A formalist might argue that it does not matter much what the relative political importance is of interest groups, powerful individuals, party officials, and so on. The formal aspects of government may be thought to reflect the *net effect* of all the informal and formal factors together. It may not really be necessary to look at the informal aspects of government.

Each of the four aspects of the formal approach is related to informal pressures on government, even if the formal approach does not study them directly. The legal status and powers of the Commerce and Labor departments, for example, can be taken as partial indicators of the relative political importance of business and labor in American politics. The legislative record pertaining to the Equal Opportunity Employment Commission, as another example, says something about the power of minority interests in this country, even though the formal approach would not study minority politics per se. Later we will use a modified formalistic approach to study the largest agency of government, the Department of Defense (Chapter 4). This will make clear how each of the four aspects of the formalistic approach *does* provide *some* evidence for the question, "How is power distributed in America?"

Evidence Based on the Study of Political Decisions

A second type of evidence on the question of power distribution is based on the study of decisions. This was discussed in Chapters 1 and 2. When we discussed the concept of implicit power, for example, we examined Robert Dahl's famous decision-making study, *Who Governs?* (1961). The decision-making study project of which Dahl's work was a part also generated two other books: Raymond Wolfinger's *The Politics of Progress* (1974), and Nelson Polsby's *Community Power and Political Theory* (1963). In the latter, Polsby set forth six basic principles of the decision-making approach to politics, and these six principles illustrate more fully what pluralist writers mean by a decision-making approach:[2]

1. The researcher focuses on a few or sometimes only one public decision. (Due to the number of interviews required and the great amount of sifting of documents and field work, any given decision-making study is confined to only a few illustrative cases.)
2. The researcher attempts to take a neutral stance. (He or she does not, for example, put words into people's mouths by asking questions like "Who is the most powerful person running this community?"; this is because such questions assume someone does in fact run the community, whereas this ought to be the object of research—not the assumption of research.)
3. Since only a few issues can be studied, these should be ones generally accepted as important. (Even elite theorists acknowledge lesser issues are pluralistic.)
4. Issue areas should be studied over time. (This is because coalitions of interests and personalities constantly shift, the pluralists say.)
5. The researcher should focus on leadership roles (such as the roles of initiating proposals, staffing and planning, communication, intra-elite organizing, financing, and public sanctioning of decisions;[3] one notes whether role incumbents change over time, another indicator of pluralism).

6. The researcher should study the various resources used in fulfilling these leadership roles:

a. Money and credit.
b. Control over jobs.
c. Social standing.
d. Control over information.
e. Knowledge and experience.
f. Popularity, esteem, and charisma.
g. Legality, officiality, and legitimacy.
h. Ethnic solidarity.
i. The right to vote.
j. Time.
k. Personal energy.

(Because of the widespread distribution of these various sources of power, pluralists expect power to be widely dispersed.)[4]

As indicated, the decision-making approach is biased toward the study of overt exercise of power and pluralist interpretations of politics.

Why does the decision-making approach tend in this direction? First, it gives a lot of attention to interest groups, because these are prominent in the politicking that leads up to a government decision. The emphasis on interest groups fits in with the common pluralist idea of politics as the conflict of many group interests. Second, the decision-making approach focuses on the pivotal role of the person who actually makes the decision. As in Dahl's study of New Haven, this is usually the official or legislator. This also fits in with the pluralist concept of government as a countervailing power to business or at least a neutral umpire enforcing "the rules of the game." Third, the decision-making approach calls attention to power based on many resources (money, votes, time, and the like). This suggests the fragmented or pluralistic nature of power distribution. It contrasts with radical assumptions that "resources" such as the vote are mainly symbolic in nature.

In summary, the decision-making approach is also biased. It is biased toward finding (1) that power ultimately resides with elected or appointed officials, not business people; (2) that interest groups are the main and most conspicuous influences on decision-makers; and (3) that there are a great many interest-group pressures because the resources of power are so diverse.

These conclusions contrast with the biases of the formalistic approach. The formalistic approach was biased toward finding (1) the official decision-maker is free from private forces; and

(2) votes are the preeminent political resource. It had these biases because the formal rules and laws of government suggest politics does or should operate this way.

But though the decision-making approach has biases, this is not to say they are insuperable. It only means we should be careful about accepting the implications of this method. The study of particular case decisions does provide a unique immersion in the details of politics and a sense for how politics works. Even though it has weaknesses, we will have occasion in a later chapter to use a modified decision-making approach to discuss one of the most important recent decisions in American politics: the decision to escalate the war in Vietnam during the mid-1960s. This approach adds something to our understanding that reliance on the formalistic approach alone could not give.

Evidence Based on People's Reputations for Power

Both the formalistic and decision-making methods focus on evidence of *overt* power. In the former the evidence lies in the outcome of explicit struggles over governmental laws and regulations and organizational structure. In the latter case the evidence is based on governmental decisions generally. But in Chapter 1 we raised the prospect that *implicit* power might be even more important than those things shown by overt decisions and legal structures. That is, suppose we are concerned with nondecisions, the symbolic aspect of politics, and the concept of political hegemony. These subtle aspects of power, all discussed in Chapter 1, are not readily visible in formal legal structures of government or in overt political decisions.

But how can one study nondecisions and other implicit forms of power? On this question the critics of decision-making approaches are divided. They might agree that pluralism and the focus on explicit decisions was biased for reasons discussed in Chapter 2.[5] But they share no real unity on the question of what alternative means might be used to study the broader, implicit bases of political power.

The general strategy of the critics of formalistic and decision-making approaches was to look for some *indirect* indicator of power. While one could not *see* the effects of implicit power directly (that is, the factors that made people predisposed to follow the interests of power-holders, as through socialization), it might be possible to find some political weather vane that would point out what the net effect of these invisible, implicit power forces are. The critics found three possible indicators to play this function of political weather vane: (1) people's reputations for power; (2) the social backgrounds of key decision-makers; and (3) the distribution of benefits in society. They did not agree on which was best.

People's reputations for power was among the first of the proposed alternatives. Its advocates said it would be a good reflector of both the overt aspects of authority and influence over decision-making and of the implicit aspects of power such as socialization to acceptance of dominant ideologies. This *reputational approach* was briefly discussed in Chapter 1 in connection with Floyd Hunter's classic study, *Community Power Structure* (1953).

In a later work, *Top Leadership USA* (1959), Hunter applied the reputational approach to the national level. By studying leaders' reputations for power, Hunter believed he could show how "a power structure exists in concretely definable terms at the national level." [6] The distribution of reputation for power by social class could be taken as a measure of the distribution of power, Hunter argued. More specifically, this reputational approach required eleven steps:

1. A large number of national associations were identified (Hunter studied 1,093); an expert panel was used to refine this list to the most important in terms of purpose, size, and reputation for influence (yielding a list of 106 associations in Hunter's work).

2. The leaders of these influential associations were contacted and asked to identify five national leaders whom each considered to be at the top of influence in national policy-making; these leaders were also asked to rate their own influence and the power of other associations.

3. Thirty association secretaries were then interviewed in person to corroborate the results of the first two steps.

4. For all cities over 100,000 population, the secretaries of the Chamber of Commerce and of the Community Chest/United

Fund were contacted and asked to list the five most influential individuals in their communities.

5. A sample of leaders listed in step 4 above was asked their opinions about the adequacy of the overall list of national leaders, and asked their opinions on policy matters.

6. A composite list of 500 top national leaders was then compiled; these individuals were then contacted and asked whom they knew on the list.

7. A sample of at least three leaders in thirty cities was then interviewed in person to determine their role in national policy development; special studies were made of concrete decision-making areas such as housing policy and textile tariff policy.

8. A sample of one-third of the 500 top national leaders was interviewed in person in a third cross-country research trip.

9. A fourth cross-country interviewing trip was then conducted to interview corporate management persons involved in the selected decision-making issues.

10. National elected and appointed officials were then interviewed on the selected issues.

11. Supplementary research was conducted to gather related documents, speeches, four annual polls for nominations of top national leaders, and a survey of literature in the field.

In Chapter 6 we will present the findings of Hunter's study. In general, however, Hunter felt this method proved the existence of a relatively cohesive top structure of power in America. His work was often cited as evidence for the elite-theory position discussed in Chapter 2.

As mentioned in Chapter 1, the reputational approach was much criticized by adherents of the decision-making approach. They said it biased the people who were interviewed. By asking "Who has influence?" one assumed that *someone* must be a "top leader." Besides, pluralists argued, most respondents probably knew little about the national distribution of power. They said Hunter was only documenting what associational leaders *thought* about power structure, and this could easily be wrong.

Advocates of the reputational approach sought to rebut their critics. They denied their approach was based merely on subjective impressions of who holds power, on two counts:

1. The reputational approach can be used in conjunction with a decision-making approach (as on the tariff issue studied by Hunter). The study of the interaction of reputations for power and decisions may be more illuminating than the strict decision-making approach.

2. Reputation for power may be self-fulfilling. True, the reputational approach may reflect the effect of national myths, propaganda, and popular desires about how politics *should* be. But people commonly act on the basis of their *perceptions* of reality, even when these perceptions are based on "myths."

   For example, during a prison riot some news media and politicians may focus on certain individuals as spokespersons. Even when these inmates have little prior influence among the other rioters, the very fact that authorities treat them as leaders to be negotiated with tends to make them, in fact, the leaders. Similarly, the individuals whom the media thinks are the representatives of a given ethnic community (perhaps because of their outspokenness or militance, even when a public-opinion poll would reveal little support for them in the community) will be treated as such. Soon they will be the "representatives" because they are the ones who deal with city hall, have their views discussed in the newspapers, and so on.

   Certainly perceptions cannot be dismissed out of hand as "incorrect information" or "mere myths." In the reputational approach the respondents are leaders of national associations. Even the pluralist critics of the reputational approach acknowledge the importance of these associational interest groups in politics. Perceptions by group leaders play a large role in determining who actually holds power.

Besides, the advocates of the reputational approach argued, the associational leaders are highly involved in political life—more so than, say, college professors. In their own way they are experts on power and one cannot assume they speak from utter ignorance.

These rebuttals did not convince the critics. And not only pluralist, decision-making-oriented scholars criticized the reputational approach. More radical scholars did as well. In particular, many radical scholars found the reputational approach too vague. True, Hunter provided some evidence for the existence of a national business-oriented leadership elite which was relatively cohesive (they knew each other and interacted on specific policy issues). But Hunter's approach left vague the exact nature of this elite. Specifically, Hunter largely ignored the relationship between his "top leaders" and the emphasis of most elite theorists on the concept of social *class*. Those interested in class analysis believed another indirect indicator of power was better than Hunter's emphasis on people's reputations for power: They preferred to look at the class and social backgrounds of key decision-makers.

Evidence Based on the Sociology of Leadership

Looking at the social backgrounds of decision-makers is called the sociology-of-leadership approach. Like the reputational method, it is an indirect approach to the study of power. The sociology-of-leadership approach assumes that both overt and implicit aspects of power are indicated by the relative concentration or dispersion of top office-holders by social class. If officials are concentrated in the upper class, the distribution of power may be presumed to be elitist. If decision-makers come from many social classes, politics is pluralistic.

As discussed in Chapter 2, C. Wright Mills's *The Power Elite* (1956) was based largely on the sociology-of-leadership approach. For many years it was taken as the modern classic statement of elite theory for America. It had broad influence on American political science and elicited many sharp defenses of pluralism and the decision-making method of studying power. In recent years, however, the elitist-pluralist debate has waned. Many political scientists have seen that there was some truth on both sides of the debate. Now they often seek to develop some third position that is neither elitist nor pluralist, but still provides a good framework for understanding how power works in America. In Chapter 12 we will present one such theoretical framework we believe is better than either elitism or pluralism. But for the moment it is worth understanding why leading elite theorists of the 1950s and 1960s felt the sociology-of-leadership approach was the best way of gaining evidence on how power is distributed in America.

Though recent elite theorists have had less influence on political science than C. Wright Mills, they have often spelled out more clearly just what the sociology-of-leadership approach is. In his *Who Rules America?* (1967), G. William Domhoff described the sociology-of-leadership approach as a four-step process:[7]

1. The concept of "upper class" is defined in a measurable way. Indicators of upper-class status are the following:
   a. Being listed in the *Social Register*.
   b. Attending an elite preparatory school.
   c. Belonging to an elite men's club.
   d. Being a millionaire entrepreneur or a $100,000-a-year corporate executive.
   e. Belonging to the immediate family of such a person.
2. Once the membership of the upper class is identified, the researcher seeks to show the share of the upper class in the economy: its share of control of corporate directorships, its share of personal income, and so on. (This aspect overlaps with the distribution-of-benefits approach to be discussed next.)
3. Similarly, the researcher shows the extent to which the upper class dominates the boards of directors of universities, the mass media, policy associations, and so on.
4. The same is shown for domination of high government positions.

To the extent that economic, associational, and governmental leadership is concentrated in the upper class, American politics is assumed to be elite-dominated.

Is the social background of leaders a good barometer of the distribution of power? Again, pluralist critics have said "No!" Suppose one *did* find that upper-class people held a disproportionate share of top economic, associational, and governmental positions. Could not this simply reflect the effects of education, merit, access, and other upper-class attributes which do not in themselves presume upper-class control? Does not control require coordination, shared viewpoints, and cooperation among the alleged elite? And is not the American upper class very *divided* politically? (For example, note the tensions between liberal-tending Jews and conservative-leaning Anglo-Saxons). In the end, what difference does it make if many leaders come from the upper class or upper-middle class?

The pluralists argued that if it did make a difference, one would have to look for it in the study of actual decisions. Class power could not, they said, be logically deduced from the social backgrounds of leaders. Social backgrounds prove nothing about the beliefs or political behavior of individuals, the pluralists argued.

Besides this, there were many other criticisms of the sociology-of-leadership approach. Could the *Social Register* (established in 1881) really be considered a good indicator of upper-class status? After all, many cities have no *Social Register* in the first place, and today many upper-class individuals refuse to be listed because listing seems to violate present-day democratic values. Similarly, preparatory schools and men's clubs have become significantly less exclusive since World War II. Critics would prefer often to reject the whole notion of social class for these reasons. Class lines are just too blurred in America, they say.

The merit of the sociology-of-leadership approach hinges on demonstrating upper-class dominance of top positions and then showing that class does make a difference in people's political beliefs and behavior. (These points are treated in Chapters 6 and 8, respectively.) Besides arguing that class *can* be defined and that it *does* make a difference, advocates of this approach have also sought to soften criticism by incorporating decision-making studies into the sociology-of-leadership method. Domhoff's research on foreign-policy-making, for example, and its relation to the upper class has been absorbed into current basic textbooks on American government.[8] Other scholars, primarily radical in orientation, have accepted the criticism of the sociology-of-leadership approach, however. They find it a bit *too* indirect an indicator of power. It does not necessarily show it makes a difference even if one does show that upper-class people hold a disproportionate number of top positions and even if it can be shown they have different beliefs from the general public. Why not study "what difference it makes" directly? This is what the distribution-of-benefits approach, discussed next, is all about.

Evidence Based on the Distribution
of Benefits in Society

The distribution of benefits in society is the third proposed indirect way of measuring the effects of both overt and implicit power. It is sometimes called distributional analysis. Its proponents take literally the idea that politics is "who gets what." The distribution of wealth, income, education, health benefits, occupationally prestigious positions, and so on is taken as a good indication of the distribution of power in society. In distributional analysis the researcher is concerned with how such benefits are distributed among the various social classes. So this approach, like the sociology-of-leadership approach, is compatible with Marxian and other class analyses of politics. (It need not involve class analysis, however.)

The distributional method is relatively simple. The researcher seeks out data on the distribution of income, education, and other values. One may find, for example, that the top 5 percent of income-receivers in the United States receive a disproportionate share (about 20 percent) of all personal income. Or one may find that the top fifth of the population receives a disproportionate share (about one-half) of all years of educational training beyond eighth grade. To the extent benefits are narrowly concentrated, power is presumed to be concentrated, as well.

Like all other approaches to the question of power, the distributional approach has been the subject of many criticisms and rebuttals:

1. *Criticism:* The distribution of benefits reflects economic processes, not governmental processes.
   Rebuttal: This is only because the economy and politics are closely related. For example, retailers have greater power than customers, and landlords have greater power than tenants, because the law of contracts results in benefits to retailers and landlords (customers and tenants find it very difficult to redress grievances). More important, the economy is not "nonpolitical." The distribution of economic benefits is supported at every turn by government laws and practices. This distribution is not "natural." It is underwritten

by the government. Any examination of power must consider economic *and* political power at the same time.

2. *Criticism:* The distribution of benefits may reflect chance more than power.
   Rebuttal. By definition the effect of chance on a large group tends to cancel out. Though chance may determine an individual's fate, its net effect on society is nil. Therefore chance need not be an important consideration in studying the distribution of power in society.

3. *Criticism:* The distribution of benefits may not reflect the distribution of power because the powerful may choose to help the less powerful.
   Rebuttal: Self-interest is the rule in politics, not altruism. To the extent a minor degree of noblesse oblige exists, the distributional method will actually *understate* the degree of elitism that exists in society.

The work of Graham Wootton, a noted writer on interest groups, illustrates some of the controversy surrounding distributional analysis. In his *Interest Groups* (1970), Wootton follows a variant of the decision-making approach. He suggests power can be measured by four criteria: (1) the number of people an actor can influence; (2) the extent to which these people are forced to change; (3) the cost of these changes to these people; and (4) the number of issues which an actor can influence.[9] Unfortunately, these four criteria are almost impossible to measure in practice. Can the head of General Motors influence more people, force them to move more ground at a higher cost on more issues than, say, President Ford? One cannot say. The facts are unobtainable. Both leaders are part of the same complex power system. They cannot be taken from this system, placed on a scale, and weighed in terms of their relative power.

For a start, one cannot separate the power of individuals from the power of their positions. Nor can one really assign "costs" to changes resulting from the exercise of power. And in any decision-making approach the effects of nondecisions, socialization to political symbols, and acceptance of hegemonic ideologies remains largely unnoticed and unmeasurable. The attempt to measure these four criteria creates more problems than it solves.

In the end, Wootton recognizes this. He states that differences in group influences may be attributable to differences in their endowments and resources: money, occupational position, education, and so on. That is, Wootton is led from a decision-making approach straight back to a focus on the distribution of benefits and resources as a way of indirectly measuring power. Even decision-making studies may be led to distributional analysis in the end. But this is not forced, as Wootton's own work shows. His studies are often based on a quite different approach: the historical method.

Evidence Based on History

The historical approach is the traditional method of studying politics. The decision-making, reputational, sociology-of-leadership, and distributional approaches all tend to look at power at one point in time (usually the current time). In contrast, traditional political theorists from the conservative Edmund Burke to the radical Karl Marx have made the historical approach the basis of their analysis of the workings of power.

That the historical method cannot be reduced to a precise set of methodological steps does not mean that it is unscientific. Its proponents would argue that it is the only scientific approach of all those discussed in this chapter, because it alone emphasizes politics as a process over time. This dynamic aspect is a more accurate way of understanding how power works. It may be misleading, for example, to look at the textile tariff issue at one point in (recent) time, as Floyd Hunter did. It may be more helpful to study the historic evolution of the tariff question. Hunter's study shows the great power of North Carolina textile industrialists. But the historical method could place this in a larger context. It could show how their power is part of a rearguard defense in the path of a long-term decline of the textile industry. Both the decision-making and historical approaches reveal something about power in America. Advocates of the historical method, however, feel their approach yields the richest insights and greatest feel for the subject. This author is inclined to agree, and the historical method has been emphasized heavily in Chapters 8, 9, 10, and 11 of this book.

Summary

In this chapter we have briefly outlined the major ways of seeking evidence on the question: How is power distributed in America? Some of the methods discussed leaned more toward emphasis on overt power and some toward implicit power (these concepts were the focus of Chapter 1). Similarly, some methods seemed more compatible with pluralist theory (such as the decision-making approach), while other approaches (distribution-of-benefits and sociology-of-leadership, for example) were more compatible with elite-theory interpretations of politics.

Rather than search for the "one right method," we will examine each of the approaches discussed in this chapter. While the final chapter puts forward political economy as an alternative to either pluralism or elite theory, the chapters that follow assume that *each* type of evidence is relevant to our study of power in America. If we seize upon only one type of evidence (such as the class backgrounds of leaders), our conclusions will share the biases and problems of that approach. This does not mean the evidence is worthless, only that it must be understood in the context of all the other types of evidence. All types of evidence contribute to the synthesis of interpretations presented in the final chapter. We will begin the next chapter with a consideration of the formalistic approach.

Notes

1. *Congressional Quarterly Weekly Report,* 12 October 1974, p. 2896.
2. See Nelson Polsby, *Community Power and Political Theory* (New Haven: Yale University Press, 1963), chs. 6 and 7.
3. Ibid., p. 119, citing the work of Norton Long and George Belknap.
4. Ibid., pp. 119–20.

5. See, for example, William E. Connolly, ed., *The Bias of Pluralism* (New York: Atherton, 1969); Charles McCoy and John Playford, eds., *Apolitical Politics: A Critique of Behavioralism* (New York: Crowell, 1967).
6. Floyd Hunter, *Top Leadership USA* (Chapel Hill: University of North Carolina Press, 1959), pp. xiii–xvi.
7. G. William Domhoff, *Who Rules America?* (Englewood Cliffs, N.J.: Prentice-Hall, 1967), pp. 143–46.
8. See, for example, Dennis J. Palumbo, *American Politics* (New York: Appleton Century Crofts, 1973), pp. 599–600.
9. Graham Wootton, *Interest Groups* (Englewood Cliffs, N.J.: Prentice-Hall, 1970), pp. 79–86.

4. The Structural Approach: Power in the Military

The formalistic approach was the first of several methods of seeking evidence about power in America discussed in Chapter 3. By studying the laws and organizational structures that shape government, we can tell much about how power works in America. The formalistic approach presents us with information of four important sorts: (1) constitutional and legal parameters on government; (2) description of the organizational structure of government; (3) the institutional history of governmental branches; and (4) the legislative record of these branches.

The formalistic approach pursued systematically would generate thousands of pages of description of what government *is* as a legal system. Many basic textbooks on American politics take basically this tack. They describe the federal system, the presidency, the Congress, the Supreme Court and the judicial branch in general, the administrative departments of government, and so on. (Of course, the formalistic approach is no longer used in pure form, and present-day texts also discuss informal and extra-governmental inputs to politics as well.)

In this chapter we will assume the reader has already read a basic political-science textbook that describes the general structure of American government and the role of the various branches. We will focus here, in greater detail than a basic text could, on one specific arm of government, the Department of Defense. We have selected this department because it is the largest administrative agency of the U.S. government. It is directly or indirectly responsible for the income of one out of ten Americans. Historically, the Department of Defense has been a model department of government. It has been the management model for other branches of government from Calhoun's modernization of the War Department after the War of 1812 to the administrative "revolution" of Robert McNamara during the administration of John F. Kennedy. While we will be looking at just one case, it is probably the most important case.

In examining the formal structure of power as it relates to the military, we hope to cast a little light on the issues presented in Chapter 2. We will attempt to emphasize how some of this sort of evidence about power supports the pluralist viewpoint, some supports elite theory, and some does not really fit into either category. We will look at each of the four sorts of information the formal approach gives us (as listed in the first paragraph) and then conclude this chapter with a summary of our findings. And when we consider our findings we will have to remember that this approach cannot tell us all we want to know. In particular, as discussed in the preceding chapter, the formal approach neglects the important role of implicit aspects of power.

Constitutional and Legal Constraints on Power

On August 29, 1786, a mob in rural western Massachusetts undertook a briefly successful revolt against the tax policies of the government in Boston. Shays' Rebellion showed Hamilton, Madison, and other nationalists the inability, under the Articles of Confederation, of the federal government to intervene in such revolts, even to protect federal property.[1] Because of the need to deal with such rebellions and to defend the frontier, the Federalists sought to write a provision into the Constitution of 1789 allowing a permanent standing army. The anti-Federalists saw this as a dangerous centralizing policy. They preferred the pluralism of relying on many state militias. Extreme Federalists, in contrast, wished to disarm the states and abolish the militias.

During this period public opinion was strongly against the idea of a standing army. But because the need for a strong force seemed so great, the Federalists were able to get a favorable compromise. The new Constitution did not abolish the state militias and did not even establish a permanent national army. But the Constitution did allow Congress to establish such an army and navy in the future (Article 1, Section 8). And the president of the United States was given authority over the state militias in times of emergency (Article 2, Section 2). On this basis the forces of centralization eventually prevailed.

The Constitution placed the military under the civilian control of the president, Congress, and the states. Within this context of civilian control, the Supreme Court has upheld war powers of sweeping dimensions. In wartime the Court has never refused an increase in war powers desired by any president or Congress.

On the other hand the Constitution laid the basis for military independence, to a degree. The compromises of 1789 allowed the new military establishment to play the states off against national control, presidential authority off against congressional oversight, and the president off against the departmental secretaries.[2] Even though control over the military was centralized at the federal level, a kind of pluralism continued in military affairs because of the checks and balances of the federal system itself.

Over time the legal authority at the national level in military matters came to completely overshadow that of the states. The turning point was 1903. In that year the state militias (by then called the National Guard) were placed under joint control of the federal government and the states, even in peacetime. The states lost all control over the militias in wartime. Today, when one considers the structure of the military establishment, one refers almost entirely to organization at the national level.

The Formal Structure of Power

In principle the military is organized in an entirely unpluralistic, hierarchical chain of command. This chain has four tiers: (1) the armed forces, at the bottom; (2) the civilian departments of the Army, the Navy and the Air Force; (3) the Department of Defense; and (4) oversight through the Executive Office of the President and various congressional committees. Thus ultimate authority is vested in the hands of elected national leaders, responsible to the people.

The Armed Forces and Service Departments

In principle all personnel in the armed services are responsible to superiors who in turn are part of a chain of command headed by the president. Taking the army as illustrative, the armies of the United States and the generals who head them are actually at the bottom of the command structure. This is illustrated in Figure 4–1. This lowest level includes the U.S. Army Forces Command (such as the First, Fifth, and Sixth U.S. Armies; this command also supervises the National Guard units of the states), other field commands (such as the European Command, headquartered in Germany), and the various support commands (such as commands concerned with training, communications, and intelligence).

The generals heading these commands are responsible to the army chief of staff. In 1976 this was General Frederick C. Weyand. Various special bureaus report directly to Weyand. These include the head of the antiballistic missile system and the head of the Women's Army Corps. Weyand is also assisted by several staff agencies, including personnel, logistics, reserve forces, intelligence, and engineering.

Above the chief of staff, most personnel are civilians. General Weyand reports to the secretary of the army. In 1976 this was Martin R. Hoffman. As chief of staff, Weyand also is the army representative to the Joint Chiefs of Staff (discussed later). This makes him one of the principal advisers of the president, the National Security Council, and the secretary of defense. This role means the chief of staff potentially could by-pass the formal chain of command to communicate directly with the president. Franklin Delano Roosevelt, for example, frequently ignored the civilian superstructure of the military establishment and instead relied on direct communication with his military advisers in the Joint Chiefs of Staff.

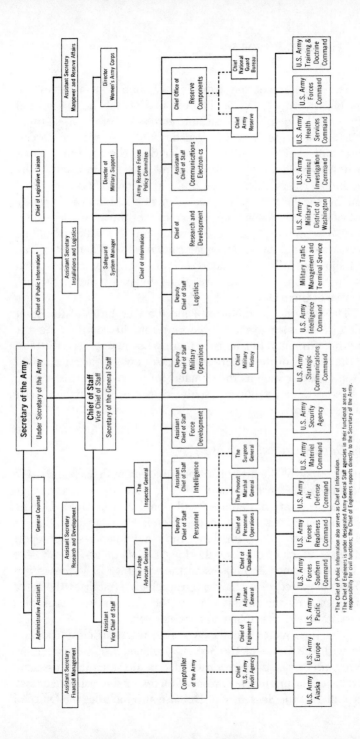

Figure 4-1 The Organizational Structure of the U. S. Army. *From Office of the Federal Register, United States Government Manual: 1973/74 (Washington, D.C.: USGPO, 1973), p. 171.*

The secretary of the army is a civilian who oversees the work of the army generals. To help him do this he has several staffs, each headed by an assistant secretary. For example, there are assistant secretaries for logistics and for reserve forces. These staffs are substantially smaller than their military counterparts under the control of the army chief of staff. Often the civilian overseers must depend on the information supplied them by the larger, more directly involved staffs of the army chief of staff. Also, some of the secretary of the army's key aides are regular military officers. These include the chief of public information and the chief of legislative liaison, both of whom are major-generals. The major-general in charge of army relations with Congress is in turn aided by nine chief assistants, only two of them civilians.

The secretary of the army (and the secretaries of the other armed services) plays an important role in coordinating the army departments. But he is ordinarily not a key force restraining the desires of the generals he oversees when they are united on some matter such as the demand for a new weapons system. Such constraint on power usually comes at the higher levels discussed below.

The Department of Defense

The secretary of the army is responsible to another civilian—the secretary of defense—as are the other service secretaries. In 1976 the secretary of defense was Donald H. Rumsfeld. The department of government he oversees is diagramed in Figure 4–2. Though this diagram shows the many agencies that report to the secretary of defense, the Joint Chiefs of Staff (JCS) are in fact the principle advisers to the secretary of defense. The JCS is composed of a chairman, the chiefs of staff of the three armed services, the commandant of the U.S. Marine Corps, plus an assistant and a secretary to the chairman.

The JCS, which has its own staff, works in close cooperation with the Office of the Secretary of Defense. This office includes nine assistant secretaries of defense, including assistant secretaries for intelligence, reserve forces, and legislative affairs. The Office of the Secretary of Defense also includes the Office of

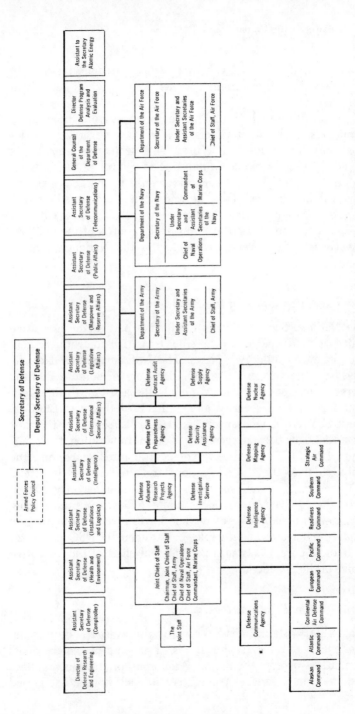

Figure 4-2 The Organizational Structure of the Department of Defense. *From Office of the Federal Register,* U.S. Government Manual: 1973/74 *(Washington, D.C.: USGPO, 1973), p. 149.*

Program Analysis and Evaluation, which became a model to other branches of government for its use of systems analysis in management.

Thus the formal structure of power runs from the military commands to the Joint Chiefs of Staff to the secretary of defense and the president. The president's secretary of defense is intended to be the prime *administrative* control on the military, and the staff of the secretary of defense is charged with the responsibility for overseeing the staff work of the armed services themselves. Later in this chapter we will look at how effective this has been. In terms of general *policy* control of the military, however, the key overseeing agency is the National Security Council (NSC).

The Executive Office of the President

The National Security Council, which is part of the Executive Office of the President, is the chief executive control over general policy on military matters. The NSC is composed of the president, the vice president, the secretary of defense, and the secretary of state. Its officers include the assistant to the president for national security affairs. In 1976 this was Lt. Gen. Brent Scowcroft, who succeeded Henry Kissinger to the post after Kissinger became secretary of state. In addition, the chairman of the JCS, the director of central intelligence, and the ambassador to the United Nations are often invited to attend NSC meetings. Established by the National Security Act of 1947, the NSC has become the major American forum for determination of military policy. The lower levels of the military establishment are, in principle, constrained by NSC policy directives. Figure 4–3 is an organizational chart of the Executive Office of the President.

Congressional Committees

The military establishment's power is also constrained by its dependence on Congress for funds. Two sets of congressional committees oversee the military: the appropriations committees and the armed services committees in each house. The armed

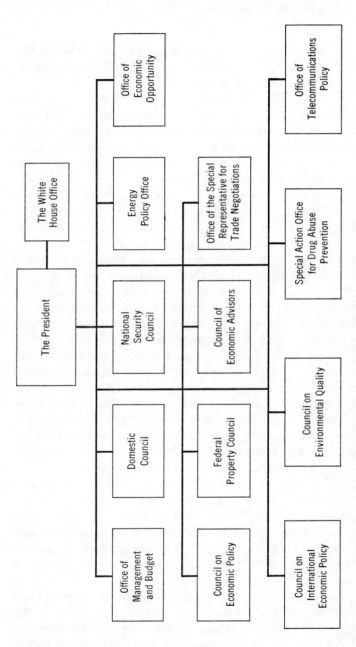

Figure 4-3 Organization of the Executive Office of the President. *From U.S. Government Manual: 1973/74 (Washington, D.C.: USGPO, 1973), p. 78.*

services committees *authorize* which programs are to be funded. The appropriations committees set the specific *amounts* allocated to authorized programs.

Prior to 1960 the appropriations committees were very powerful in their control of what funding various military programs would receive. Since then, however, the armed services committees have increased their influence by specifying dollar limits for particular defense programs (hitherto they had simply authorized lump-sum budgets).

Two-thirds of the defense budget by-passes the armed services committees and goes directly to the appropriations committees. This includes routine payments for personnel salaries, retirement benefits, and operating costs. The armed services committees largely ignore this and concentrate instead on nonroutine matters, primarily new weapons proposals.

The armed services committees were formed under the Legislative Reorganization Act of 1946, consolidating previous committees. For over a decade they emphasized policy on military housing, the draft, manpower, and military organization. In 1959 a rider (amendment) to a military construction bill gave the armed services committees more power. It enabled them to set dollar limits on appropriations for new aircraft, missiles, and ships.[3] After the rider went into effect in 1961, these committees became increasingly powerful in military matters. By the 1970s the armed services committees initiated all authorizations for research and development, testing, evaluation, weapons procurement, construction, and salary levels.

Traditionally, the seniority system in Congress has favored the more conservative representatives from the safe, solidly Democratic districts in the South. For years the armed services committees were chaired by two powerful southerners: Senator John Stennis (D, Miss.) and Congressman Edward Hébert (D, La.). Stennis and Hébert were often accused of being more advocates for, than overseers of, the military. Representative Otis Pike (D, N.Y.) charged, for example, that "the House Armed Services Committee doesn't control the Pentagon; the Pentagon controls the House Armed Services Committee."[4] And Senator Richard Schweiker (R, Pa.), who served on the Senate Armed Services Committee, stated: "There's a growing gap between the military community and the public. And, if we had done our homework as overseer, we would have narrowed the gap by now." [5] Stennis and Hébert denied these charges. They believed their policies were rooted in a genuine concern for national defense. They were predisposed to support much of what the military establishment wanted anyway. (This illustrates the issue of implicit power, discussed in Chapter 1.)

In January 1975 one of the three most liberal Congresses since World War II assembled. In a caucus choosing committee chairpeople, House Democrats—augmented by many new liberal members—created a revolution in the seniority system. They ousted Hébert as chairman of the House Armed Services Committee. Hébert, whose hawkish military policies were unpopular with liberal members, brought much opposition on himself by, among other things, talking condescendingly to the new members as "boys and girls" when they interviewed him. In his place the Democrats chose Melvin Price (D, Ill.). Price, age 70, was the second most senior member and equally conservative. The new liberal Democrats hoped, however, that he would at least be more fair in his role as chairman.

On the Senate side in 1975, three freshman liberals were added to the Armed Services Committee. Nonetheless, on both sides of Congress, the majority of Armed Services Committee members were little different from previous years. The net effect to date seems to be a slight shift toward more critical control over the military and a slightly increased role for the Democratic Caucus in determining the most important committee issues. The liberalization in the House seems particularly significant because, since 1967, the Senate had been the more aggressive of the congressional houses in cutting military budgets.

In general, however, the congressional committees which oversee the military are composed of atypical representatives. Its members are somewhat more conservative than average and more likely to support military programs. On the other hand, they have frequently opposed certain new weapons systems. They have also investigated various military scandals such as those involving weapons-procurement contracts. These committees and their chairmen have been very powerful over the years, in that the House and Senate have customarily gone along with their recommendations. Until 1971, for example, the Senate had not overruled the chairman of the Defense Subcommittee of the Senate Appropriations Committee for twenty years! And in the House, no amendment to the defense appropriations bill had been adopted since 1959 without the full support of the chairman of the House Appropriations Committee's Defense Subcommittee.[6] In the wake of antimilitary sentiment resulting from the Vietnam War, this now seems to be changing. But it remains to be seen whether, as memories of the Vietnam War fade, the conservative patterns of permissive oversight will return or not.

One structural reform of Congress suggests an increasingly important oversight role, however. A traditional weakness of the committee system of oversight has been the tiny size of the committee staff in relation to the huge number of Pentagon experts supporting budget requests. This led one member of the House Defense Subcommittee to lament, "What happens is the enormity of the federal bureaucracy is such—particularly in the Defense Department which is one of the big ones—that decades ago we lost any real control over monitoring their activity."[7] The Congressional Budget Reform Act of 1974 has now established a major staff agency to help committees like those overseeing defense to deal with this problem. The new Congressional Budget Office which this act created will make a detailed study of defense and other budgets and will undertake cost analyses of new proposed programs, feeding their conclusions and analyses to the Armed Services as well as Appropriations committees. It is still too early to conclude what effect this system will have on the military establishment, but liberals hope it will constitute a major constraint on military power.

An Institutional History of Military Power

In principle, as the previous section showed, power in the military is subject to democratic political controls at the top. The president exercises control through appointment of the secretary of defense and through control over the National Security Council. Congress exercises oversight through its Armed Ser-

vices committees and its Defense Appropriations sub-commit-
tees. While the formal system allows no direct role for interest-
group forces, it is pluralistic in the sense of democratic checks
and balances over the military branch. (In Chapter 5 we will
use the decision-making approach to look behind this formal
pluralism to understand some of the informal aspects of politics.
By looking at an important decision involving the military establishment, we will be able to better assess whether the distribution of power in the military is as democratic as it appears
from a constitutional point of view.)

We can also gain a clearer understanding of the political
issues hidden in the formal structure by looking at history. The
institutional history of the military establishments tells us much
about the general tendencies of power in American politics. It
helps explain why the formal structure has come to be the way
it is. It also tells us something about which group interests have
been favored and which have been neglected.

In the Beginning . . .

The Constitution established clear civilian control over the military. In the early years this was facilitated by the very small
size of the Department of War. (It was not renamed the Department of Defense until after World War II.) Following the
Revolution, in 1784, the secretary of war supervised only four
civilian employees: an assistant, a secretary, and two clerks. The
entire civilian staff of the military numbered less than two
dozen individuals. This pattern, which continued until after the
War of 1812, reflected the Founding Fathers' opposition to
standing armies.

When the Jeffersonians came to power in 1801, they proved
to be utterly opposed to even the small military establishment
allowed by the Federalists. Between 1800 and 1804 expenditures for both the Navy and War departments were cut by two-
thirds. The Jeffersonians also halted shipbuilding for the navy.
More important, they strengthened civilian controls over the
military, which was deemed necessary because of the erosion of
control over the military under President John Adams (1797–
1801). This did not prevent cabinet officers from continuing in

a political role, however. Notable was the political faction that formed around Secretary of the Navy Smith, whose influence led to the ouster of Secretary of the Treasury Gallatin in 1813.

From the War of 1812 to the Civil War

The Jeffersonians faced the issue of civilian control squarely and resolved it as the Constitution dictated. The cabinet secretaries were more important political figures then than they are today, however. Perhaps the most famous was Secretary of War John Calhoun (1817–1825), later to become the South's leading spokesman prior to the Civil War. Under Calhoun the War Department underwent an administrative revolution.

The War of 1812 had been a nightmare for the Jeffersonians. It showed widespread incompetence in military administration. The failure of the military led to substantial reforms. Revolutionary War figures were removed from positions of control. Jeffersonian philosophy was largely abandoned as the "New Republicans" embraced government centralization. The New Republicans, like Calhoun himself, felt that Jefferson's ideas about decentralization of power stood in the way of building a modern military establishment that would make impossible a repetition of the disaster of 1812. Centralization took the form of creation of the General Staff in the War Department and of the Board of Navy Commissioners in the Navy Department. One historian has written that "a new generation of federal executives took charge of the departments of state—men who scarcely remembered the Revolution." [8]

Calhoun reorganized the War Department along centralized lines. Many principles which are today commonplace were then established for the first time. In his army regulations of 1818, Calhoun stabilized lines of command and regularized hierarchical responsibilities. Top aides were to be chosen only on the basis of merit. Each officer was to be responsible for the expenditures of all those under him. A modern, centralized bureaucracy was created. This provided a direct model of government organization. Later, the navy and the post office were reorganized along similar lines.

Calhoun, Clay, Crawford, Quincy Adams, and other New

Republicans favored a strong army and navy. Under their leadership the Jeffersonian policies were reversed and the military establishment grew somewhat larger. Even so, comparing the period of Federalist control (1797–1800) with the era of New Republican influence (1820–1831), the budget of the War Department only increased by 24 percent. The navy budget only increased 18 percent. This must be compared to a 90 percent increase in the total federal budget. Though somewhat more favored after the War of 1812, the military establishment was under tight constraint during the entire period down to the Civil War. After 1812, civilian employees of the military constituted 4 percent of total civilian employment. During the next three decades this figure fell to 3 percent. It reached a low of 1.5 percent in 1851 and was at 2.5 percent in 1861, on the eve of the Civil War.

The inability of the military establishment to increase its proportionate role in government showed the continuing effect of popular disapproval of standing armies. Standing armies were considered to be among the prime evils of European tyrannies. Public disapproval mounted in the Jacksonian years. A select committee of Congress even recommended the abolition of West Point in 1837. They charged it with being an instrument of class division in America. In part, this reflected the unpopularity of the fact that southerners held the principal leadership positions in the military in the half-century before the Civil War.[9]

Distrust of the military led to tighter civilian control. In 1836 the secretary of war (a civilian) was given much clearer supremacy over the military head of the army. The secretary of war took final power over all financial matters. This placed the military bureaus under his direction rather than under the Commanding General of the Army. This system of dual control increased civilian control over the armed services, but it led to many conflicts between the parallel civilian and military administrative hierarchies. Civilian control was also increased in 1843 when Congress took formal control over appointments to West Point.

In response to public distrust and increasing civilian constraints on power, and in response to the negative lessons of the

War of 1812 (which showed the ineptness of the armed services), America's officer corps became increasingly separated
from politics and society. Instead, it developed professionalism.
These changes revolved around "an elite of young officers during the closing stages of the War of 1812 which shared a common view of the army's role, emphasizing the cadre plan, preparation for a future war, and formal military education." [10]
West Point influence grew more and more important, in spite of
congressional mistrust. Egalitarian criticism from the Jacksonians only served to develop heightened group awareness and
separation in the officer corps.

From the Civil War to World War I

After the Civil War the social isolation of the military increased.
This isolation was connected with increasing professionalization
and centralization on the one hand, and with the development
of a conservative military outlook on the other. The conservative identifications of the military took on added importance as
it assumed a critical domestic role in restraining labor unrest
after the 1870s.

Samuel Huntington wrote of this period: "The prevalence
of business pacifism made the dominant feature of post-1865
civil-military relations . . . the complete, unrelenting hostility of
virtually all the American community toward virtually all things
military." [11] The late nineteenth century was a period of ascendant capitalism in America. Conservative theorists like Herbert
Spencer, John Fiske, and William Graham Sumner believed that
war was unprofitable and should be opposed. This attitude remained dominant until the Spanish-American War began to
generate new viewpoints within the business community.

In the post-bellum period, the military turned inward toward ever more professionalism and separation. Professional
institutions were created: the war college, military professional
associations, military journals, and separate social facilities for
officers. The higher military ranks became monopolized by
graduates of the military academies. Eventually these tendencies were manifested in a distinctive military outlook on politics.
"Prior to the Civil War," Huntington wrote, "the fundamental

values of Army and Navy officers did not differ significantly from those of the bulk of the American population." [12] By World War I, however, the military officer corps had developed a markedly conservative stance. Their conservative beliefs included an emphasis on the inevitability of war and the necessity for discipline, obedience, loyalty, and unquestioning respect for superiors.

In one area the military establishment was able to break out of its relative social isolation. That was the area of its domestic role. Negative attitudes toward the military establishment assured its relative stagnation at about 2.5 percent of the federal civilian work force. But between 1871 and 1881 its share of federal employees leaped from 2.5 percent to 16 percent. In part this increase reflected the inclusion of civilian labor at army arsenals and naval yards as federal employees. But it also reflected the new role of the military in controlling labor.

Business pacifism did not mean military force should not be used *within* the United States. All segments of society, with few exceptions, supported the use of the military in defending the frontier and in carrying on wars against the Indians, for example. But in the 1870s a more controversial internal role became apparent. In 1877 the worst labor riots in American history occurred. During these riots, for example, the entire property of the Pennsylvania Railroad in Pittsburgh was burned to the ground. More disturbing, the state-controlled militia proved unreliable. Some militia units even sided with the rioters. After 1877 the business community and other interests demanded the construction of armories and the reorganization of the National Guard. Many armories built during this period are still standing and in use across the East and Midwest.

Reform of the state militias eventually culminated in 1903 in their being placed under the joint control of the states and the regular army. And, starting with President Hayes, troops were increasingly used to put down labor conflicts. As Walter Millis has noted, "It was renewed interest in the National Guard, generated by strikes of 1877, which set it on the path to assuming what it now proudly considers its real function. . . . There were demands for quadrupling the regular army and establishing garrisoned posts in the industrial East." [13]

To these demands for growth and change in the military were added other reform demands growing out of the Spanish-American War of 1898. This war, like that of 1812, opened to public view the administrative shortcomings of the military. In spite of Jacksonian-era reforms, military officers in the staff departments, often having gained their positions by political influence, were relatively independent of the secretary of war. The secretary became a mere moderator among the competing interests of the various military bureaus. Overall, the system was grossly inefficient. Influenced by the example of the growing German military establishment, Congress passed the Army Reorganization Act of 1903 to remedy the situation.

The Reorganization Act of 1903 established a professional general staff under the control of the secretary of war. (Similar reforms were urged for the navy, but were not successful until later.) The rank of commanding general was replaced by the chief of staff. The chief of staff, in turn, was made the chief adviser to the secretary of war and the administrative head of all War Department programs. As Paul Hammond has noted, this reform was intended to increase civilian control over the military. But it potentially made the secretary of war a mere captive of his dependency on the chief of staff. The chief of staff, as senior military officer, controlled the secretary of war's flow of advice and information, and also controlled the actual execution of the secretary's policies.[14]

World War I had a tremendous impact on the military. Controversies raged around the issues of forced conscription, the temporary nationalization of the railroads and shipping, establishment of high income taxes to finance war costs, and economic controls on production and wages. The war also brought America's first domestic propaganda agency, the Creel Committee. This group mobilized thousands of journalists and publicists in a patriotic drive to sell the official position on the war to the American people.[15] The activities of the Creel Committee and other groups carried the seeds of opportunity for the military to grow out of its relative isolation and unpopularity. The military came to see in World War I the means for ending its separation from American society.[16]

To make permanent its wartime popularity, the military

·launched three major programs directed at influencing the public:

1. *The Reserve Officer Training Corps (ROTC):* A system was established to train high school and college students as reserve officers. Within a decade, over 300 units had been established, enrolling 125,000 students.
2. *Training:* The regular army was given authority over training the state National Guard units.
3. *Public relations:* Each army regiment was assigned a geographic area within the United States. Regiment officers and recruiters were expected to build a close relationship with local leaders. The army officers were expected to display "salesmanship," to be "good mixers," and to join local clubs like the Chamber of Commerce, Kiwanis, and Rotary. "In short," Huntington wrote, "they were to blend with middle-class business America." [17]

These efforts did not prevent demobilization, which followed World War I. The size of the civilian military establishment fell back to its prewar share. The army deemphasized "mixing" and drew back into professionalism and relative isolation.

Between World Wars

The years between the world wars contrasted sharply with the rapid ascendancy of the military during and after World War II. The between-wars period was one of sharp demobilization. The officer corps felt the lesson of World War I had been the need for a peacetime draft and a large peacetime army. Though Congress authorized 288,000 men in 1920, the Appropriations committees only allowed enough funds for 150,000. Even this figure was cut further in 1927. Against the navy's strongest objections, the State Department triumphed with the ratification of the Nine-Power Treaty, which limited naval construction through 1935. The new air corps remained severely limited, as well. It proved inadequate even to fulfill its 1934 task of carrying the mails. The tone of these years was represented by the congressional investigations of the Nye Committee. This committee sought to expose munitions-makers as "the merchants of death" and a prime force in the drive toward war. And the Neutrality Act of 1937 formalized the public mood of isolationism.

In contrast, World War II brought the military unprecedented power. As in no previous war, in World War II the military made the most important policy decisions. And these proved popular with the American people. When the Joint Chiefs of Staff was formed in 1942, it became President Roosevelt's primary source of military advice. Its influence virtually excluded the civilian secretaries of war and navy, undermining the earlier struggles to establish the principle of civilian control over the military. In 1945 Admiral William Leahy stated that "the Joint Chiefs of Staff at the present time are under no civilian control whatever." [18]

By the end of the war military planners had broad authority over economic mobilization, foreign policy, and other matters never before within their jurisdiction. This increase in powers was enhanced by the relative disarray of civilian planning efforts.[19] Under the Executive Order of February 28, 1942, reorganizing the War Department, civilian control was further diminished in favor of reliance on military planners. "In every case," Paul Hammond wrote, "the pattern was to transfer functions and responsibilities out of the civilian offices to staff or command units of the military." [20] In the Department of the Navy, civilian control was eroded even more.

Demobilization and the 1950s

As the powers of the military establishment increased, an intense controversy arose over unifying the service departments under a single Department of Defense. This reform had been urged partly to reassert civilian control and partly to deal with interservice rivalries. For example, the U.S. Army Air Force squabbled with U.S. Navy aviation about jurisdiction over antisubmarine warfare. All the services clamored for the attention of President Truman. Each had its own ideas on postwar planning objectives. The unification controversy ended with the passage of the National Security Act of 1947, laying the basis for the present military establishment.

The National Security Act rejected two alternative institutional frameworks for military decision-making. It rejected wartime methods of relying primarily on the Joint Chiefs of Staff, and it rejected the traditional mode of relying on the civilian cabinet officers. Instead it created a compromise, embodied in the National Security Council (NSC). The NSC was a mixed military-civilian decision-making body bringing together the chairman of the Joint Chiefs, the secretary of defense, the secretary of state, and the president.

To accomplish this the National Security Act also established the secretary of defense as a new post, superior to the service department secretaries (army, navy, air force). On the other hand the 1947 act failed to give the secretary of defense the large-scale staff he needed to displace the Joint Chiefs and service departments in policy formulation. The secretary of defense was still ultimately dependent on his ability to maintain the cooperation and staff assistance of the military branches. This was remedied in amendments to the National Security Act in 1949, creating the Department of Defense. At the same time the service secretaries were dropped from direct participation on the NSC.

While the 1949 amendments went far toward consolidating civilian control over the military, several qualifications must be noted:

1. *More powerful JCS:* The amendments also strengthened the Joint Chiefs of Staff and increased its size.
2. *JCS direct legislative role:* The service departments were left with the right to initiate recommendations to congressional committees even when the secretary of defense opposed this.
3. Limited secretarial powers: The secretary of defense was denied the authority to abolish or transfer military combat units. (The main issue here was the possible reorganization of naval aviation.)

Increased military influence was shown in other areas in the postwar period. There was a significant increase in the number of military officers occupying normally civilian positions, especially in foreign policy. Secretary of State George

Marshall and President Dwight Eisenhower were the best-known officers representing this trend. But part of their appeal lay in the very divergence of their moderate political views from the mainstream of professional militarism.[21]

Another area of increased influence lay in the rise of what Eisenhower called "the military-industrial complex." New organizations were formed to join corporate and military interests. In 1944 Secretary of the Navy Forrestal, a former Wall Street investment broker and later the first secretary of defense, organized the National Security Industrial Association to "insure that American business will remain close to the services." Similarly, the Armed Forces Chemical Association and the Armed Forces Communications Association were created for the same reasons. And the Army Ordnance Association became the American Ordnance Association, admitting civilian business members for the first time, while unprecedented numbers of retired military officers joined the boards of defense industry corporations.[22]

The armed services came to depend increasingly on private industry for development of new defense systems, whereas in earlier years such development had been undertaken directly by the services. Commenting on the air force, which led in this trend, Pentagon efficiency expert A. E. Fitzgerald wrote that the air force "deliberately avoided creation of an in-house capability for the missile age because it wanted to create a big, well-heeled constituency of scientists, organized labor, and industry. It knew that such a constituency would push successfully to keep defense spending high and the Air Force in business." [23] In a major study of the armed services, Adam Yarmolinsky concluded that the increased importance of the private defense contractors frequently reduced junior officers to being mere liaison agents and clerks for industry.[24]

In addition to the unofficial "civilian control" represented by the growing influence of private industry, the 1950s also saw the slow increase in powers of the secretary of defense. An executive reorganization plan in 1953 and the Defense Reorganization Act of 1958 both increased the size of the secretary's staff and the scope of his powers. He gained the power to reorganize combatant functions, subject to congressional veto. On the other hand, the 1958 act also doubled the size of the JCS and increased the powers of its chairman. So although civilian authority was increasing, so was the staff function of the military.[25]

The most dramatic contest involving the issue of civilian control in the 1950s was the clash between President Truman and General Douglas MacArthur. MacArthur was an ardent supporter of an aggressive Korean War policy. He advocated war with China and a policy of military victory at the very time Truman was pressing for truce talks at the United Nations. Truman viewed MacArthur's pronouncements as insubordination. On April 11, 1951, MacArthur was relieved of his command. Later hearings by the Senate Armed Services Committee and by the Foreign Relations Committee generally confirmed the presidential charges of insubordination. Nonetheless, Mac-Arthur was made into a martyred hero and Truman's Republican opponents heaped denunciations on the president for his actions. The Truman-MacArthur clash illustrated the dangers of allowing military leaders to gain a popular following, and later presidents were sensitive to this issue.

The more assertive role of the president, the expanded powers of the secretary of defense, and the delegation of power to private military contractors—all these do not necessarily mean the power of top military officers was diminished. The service secretaries have declined in power, but the power of the Joint Chiefs of Staff has increased. Paul Hammond's study of the JCS concluded that it is characterized by "insistence upon taking exclusive jurisdiction over questions . . . , the refusal of the JCS to alter its military character by including nonmilitary experts in the Joint Staff or as advisers to the Joint Strategic Survey Committee, the difficulties in communication between the JCS and the assistant secretaries of defense, or with anyone else as a matter of regular procedure. . . . Since its establishment the JCS has maintained a barrier against anyone and everyone, including the service chiefs, the secretary of defense, and all the defense reorganization studies. Its tactics have undoubtedly been successful." [26]

In summary, the JCS are in principle subject to the policy mandates of the civilian-dominated National Security Council.

But the staff resources of the JCS far overshadow those of the secretary of defense. Under these circumstances the NSC has been a forum for policy discussion, not the overlord of the JCS. To this forum the JCS comes at least as well prepared to make its case as does the secretary of defense. Reformers have called for the establishment of an independent, civilian-dominated general staff under the secretary of defense to remedy this problem, but this proposal has gotten nowhere.[27]

Moreover, this centralization within the military—concentrating power in the JCS—came at a time when Congress was *decentralizing* its own powers of oversight. As discussed earlier, since 1961 the Armed Services committees have increased in power vis-à-vis the Defense Appropriations subcommittees. In effect, this framented the powers of oversight and created more conflict among the congressional overseers. In a study of this change, Edward Kolodziej concluded that the implementation of these committee changes has "demonstrated that the power, prestige, and public image of the armed services committees could be enhanced without a substantial improvement in Congress' overall understanding of defense policy and with a net decrease in its capacity to exert influence in this area."[28]

McNamara and the 1960s

In Robert McNamara the administration of John F. Kennedy believed it had discovered the secretary of defense who could reassert civilian control over the JCS. McNamara came to the Department of Defense after briefly heading the Ford Motor Company. In his new job he sought to implement a form of systems analysis similar to that which he had undertaken at Ford. This required the military staff to prepare cost-benefit analyses to justify their weapons and other requests. McNamara's new system proved immensely unpopular with the generals, who tended to regard it as taking power away from them and placing it in the hands of McNamara's young systems analysts.[29]

Having incurred military disfavor over his tight new accounting methods, McNamara came into open conflict with the JCS over Vietnam War policy in 1967. McNamara testified to Congress that the bombing of North Vietnam had not undercut infiltration of men and supplies into the South. The chairman of the JCS, in contrast, believed that the bombing was a key to favorable settlement of the war. President Johnson sided with the JCS and expanded the number of bombing targets in North Vietnam.

A second confrontation between McNamara and the JCS occurred over the plan for a demilitarized zone separating North and South Vietnam. The JCS opposed this as a move of static rather than aggressive warfare. McNamara, however, was able to implement construction of the zone. On the other hand, the JCS were allowed to continue an aggressive policy below the demilitarized zone.

In principle the JCS is subject to the secretary of defense, who in turn is responsible to the president. In practice, though, the lack of unity among the civilian branches and agencies often gives the JCS much room to maneuver. Not only did the JCS convince President Johnson to ignore McNamara on the bombing issue, it was also able to convince Congress to restore budget cuts McNamara had called for. This prevented McNamara from implementing his policy of "mutual deterrence" and "*sufficiency* of forces" (as opposed to the JCS-supported concept of military *superiority*).

The 1970s

When the Republican administration under Nixon took office in 1968, the political climate became even more favorable to the JCS. As the *Congressional Quarterly* noted, Melvin Laird, McNamara's Republican successor, "took the reins of power away from Pentagon civilians and put them back in the military's hands." [30] Laird virtually dismantled the power of the systems analysts McNamara had encouraged. Their authority, manpower, and funds were cut sharply.

Once overall spending levels for the various services were set, Laird tended to let the services themselves determine spending on particular programs. The JCS also found in Laird a more sympathetic advocate with Congress. For example, Laird staunchly supported the military on the controversial issue of expanding the antiballistic missile (ABM) program in

1969. Laird "handled Congress masterfully, never losing a battle over a major weapons system." [31]

In 1970 Laird again showed his sympathy with the JCS. In that year Laird's own blue-ribbon advisory panel on military organization urged him to strip the JCS of their functions in overseeing operations. Instead the JCS would have been confined to policy planning and staff support. A different, new agency would have been created for the direct overseeing of operations. Laird chose to ignore these recommendations, instead accepting the JCS's desire to retain its full powers.

Neither McNamara nor Laird was very successful in holding down the rapidly growing costs demanded by the military-industrial complex. Giant cost overruns still occurred in spite of McNamara's "total package procurement" plan or Laird's "fly before buy" policy.[32] To encourage further favorable treatment the defense industries dramatically stepped up the level of political contributions in 1972. This was catalyzed by the Democratic candidacy of George McGovern, who favored sharply increased controls over defense spending and much lower budgets for the armed services. The defense industries gave some $2.5 million to the Republican campaign in 1972, double their 1968 donations. This reflected a 6-to-1 ratio of contributions to Republicans over Democrats.

The last days of the ill-fated Nixon administration brought a cabinet shake-up in which James R. Schlesinger succeeded Melvin Laird as secretary of defense. Schlesinger was in some ways a more outspoken friend of JCS views, but he was less adept at representing these views to Congress. His public suggestion that U.S. troops might be used to end the Arab oil embargo earned him the public rebuke of Senate Majority Leader Mike Mansfield. Congressman Edward Hébert, then the powerful and conservative head of the House Armed Services Committee, warned Schlesinger that without learning the art of compromising with Congress he too might have as little luck as McNamara.[33] Schlesinger's outspoken skepticism toward détente with the USSR, his advocacy of planning for limited nuclear war, and his criticism of the secretary of state for wanting to give Pershing missiles to Israel all were policies that were unpopular in Congress. On the other hand, Schlesinger tried to hold a rein on military spending. He attempted to begin the process of trimming the large number of American nuclear weapons in Europe. He opposed the navy's quest for new aircraft carriers and the army's for three additional combat divisions. By 1975, however, Schlesinger's hard-line defense views had brought him into recurring conflict with many members of Congress, with Secretary of State Kissinger, and, indirectly, with President Ford. In a cabinet shake-up in November 1975, Schlesinger was replaced by Donald Rumsfeld. At this time it is too early to assess how Rumsfeld's role as secretary of defense will affect power in the military establishment. He has stated, however, that his policy views are not very different from those of his predecessor.

Summary

The institutional history of the military suggests the complexity of the power relationships tying together the president, Congress, the secretary of defense, and the military establishment. Each of these four centers of power has tried to increase its respective influence over national security matters. Taken in broad historical context, the growing power of the military branch is striking. The Founding Fathers frowned on a standing army and accorded it only a tiny fraction of the government's resources. Since World War II, in contrast, the military has been the largest department of government.

Moreover, within the military establishment, power has been centralized. This is reflected in the rise of the general staff concept and the JCS. The powers of the top military officers seem to have been eroded little if at all by the growth of the civilian Department of Defense. This is particularly true since the relative failure of McNamara's attempts to control the military in the 1960s. On the other hand, Congress in recent years has exhibited a more critical attitude toward military requests than in the past.

Clearly, the *potential* for civilian control has increased. The president, through the National Security Council and the Office of Management and Budget; the secretary of defense, through his expanded staff; and Congress, through its reformed committees—all could undoubtedly curtail the power of the military establishment. Usually, however, the civilian branches do not all agree. As noted earlier, the constitutional checks and balances allows the military to play one civilian branch off against the other.

At the same time, there has been an increase in the importance of private industry as a major interest-group force. Pluralism has prevailed insofar as politics in the military has not been reduced to the hierarchical chain-of-command indicated by the formal structure of power. But elitism has also been a factor insofar as the JCS has come to play a far more independent role than ever contemplated by democratic theorists. And many of the changes we have outlined in this section seem to have less to do with pluralist or elitist tendencies than with the management trends of all large, modern organizations. This is illustrated by the increasing importance of staff and budgeting experts in *both* the JCS *and* the civilian branches which oversee them. Apart from issues of the relative power of the JCS, the secretary of defense, the congressional committees, and so on, however, one fact stands out. The military establishment as a whole has increased its role and power enormously in the postwar period. This is examined in greater detail in the next section.

The Legislative Record

Congress has traditionally been friendly to military and defense objectives. But it is in Congress that the defense sector has had to claim national priority in the face of vigorous competing claims from the civilian departments. It is therefore in the legislative record of the military that one finds an indication of its power vis-à-vis other political forces in American politics.[34]

From Demobilization to Korean War Buildup: 1945–1951

Though World War II left military power and prestige at a high point, this was not enough to prevent rapid demobilization in 1946. The military suffered a series of defeats in Congress. It was unable to get Congress to "freeze" workers in war-essential jobs. It failed to get universal military training. Congress placed the development of atomic energy under civilian (Atomic Energy Commission), rather than military, control.

Yet the postwar Congress was far more sympathetic to military viewpoints than had been the case in the decades before World War II. It extended conscription to peacetime service. Over Truman's opposition, Congress passed a large shipbuilding program for the navy. And the air force enjoyed special prestige in Congress. By 1950 it had obtained authorization and funding for its central objective, a 70-wing air command. The first peacetime budgets following the war reflected far more expenditures than the prewar years.

The cold war aided military objectives. Crises in Greece and Turkey in 1947, and in Czechoslovakia, Berlin, Greece, Italy, and Palestine in 1948, convinced many congressmen of the need for high peacetime defense spending. The draft, which had lapsed in 1947, was reestablished in 1948. A slow rearmament campaign began, though still far less than desired by the armed services.

Discontent was acute in the navy. A "revolt of the admirals" occurred over cancellation of the navy's plans for a supercarrier in 1949. This conflict between the admirals and the president ended in disgrace for the navy and a stronger role for the civilian secretary of defense.

In 1950 the outbreak of the Korean War led to rapid rearmament. In the new fiscal year Congress tripled its original military budget. Secretary of Defense Johnson, blamed for American losses and resented by military officers for his economizing, was forced to resign. Congress unprecedentedly changed the laws to make it legal for a military officer—retired General George Marshall—to become the new secretary of defense. (Republicans had objected that this would undermine civilian control over the military.) Over the objections of a majority of Atomic Energy Commission members, Truman ordered and Congress funded the development of the hydrogen bomb. Congress also accelerated the stockpiling of defense-related raw materials. Stockpiling continued in 1951 and 1952 in spite of charges it was fueling inflation. In other readiness measures, Truman acquiesced to the demands of the JCS that Germany be allowed to play a major troop role in the North Atlantic Treaty Organization (NATO). And Congress passed the Universal Military Training Act of 1951. Though never fully implemented, it represented a temporary victory for the JCS concept of universal conscription.

In summary, 1951 was a banner year for the military. A record defense budget was passed, with only minor cuts. The navy received its supercarrier. Naval building and modernization programs were accelerated. Seventy-seven new military bases were authorized. The Senate set a goal for a greatly expanded 95-wing Air Force; in the next couple of years this was further increased. Hydrogen-bomb development continued at an intense level. On every front the military saw its long-established goals being realized.

Economizing with Ike: 1952–1960

As the Korean peace talks dragged out, the war became less popular. In Congress attention became focused on charges of waste and profiteering. The mood again became less favorable. Universal Military Training was killed. Military pay increases were held down to low levels. The navy lost its bid for a second supercarrier.

President Eisenhower, though a former general, was critical of unrestrained growth in the defense sector. He gave greater priority to a balanced budget. Moreover, his tremendous military prestige aided those seeking to limit defense increases. Eisenhower put forward the idea of economic rather than military confrontation with communism.

Where Truman had planned a $2 billion increase in the defense budget, Eisenhower projected a $4 billion cut. Congress accepted this. The air force was the big loser, cut back to 114 wings from the larger number projected for 1954. But this reflected a great overall advance for the air force when compared with the "victory" of getting 70 wings only a few years earlier. Military spending did increase in spite of Eisenhower economizing. Between fiscal year 1951 and fiscal year 1952, the level of military spending increased from $20.5 billion to $39.8 billion. In fiscal year 1953 the figure was $44 billion.

In the election year 1956 the attempts at economizing almost disappeared. In part the Republican leadership wanted to disprove Democratic charges of defense neglect. (Such charges would prove critical in the election of the Democratic candidate, John F. Kennedy, in 1960.) Thus in 1956 Eisenhower proposed a $1 billion increase in military spending. A Democratic Congress promptly upped this to $3 billion. The air force was given a 137-wing command. Though construction of the new B-52 bombers was funded, Eisenhower impounded the funds.

After the election, the economizing mood returned. The Democrats did an about-face, cutting Eisenhower's budget sharply. The air force was trimmed back to 128 wings. The army was cut from 19 to 17 divisions. The navy's new bomber was cancelled. Overall, however, military spending increased somewhat. Perhaps this was prompted by the Soviet launching of the Sputnik satellite—the world's first—and crises in Quemoy (off China) and Lebanon. High manpower levels were continued and pay increases given. By fiscal year 1960, military spending had crept up to $46 billion dollars, an unprecedented peacetime high. Fifty percent of the total federal budget was going to the military in spite of nearly a decade of relative peace!

The Vietnam War and Reaction to It: 1961–1976

In 1961 John F. Kennedy had come into office on a platform committed to expanding military programs. In the context of international crises in Vietnam, Laos, the Congo, Cuba, and Berlin, Kennedy had campaigned on the issue of an alleged (and actually nonexistent) "missile gap" with the Soviet Union. In 1961 he called for an increase of some $6 billion over Eisenhower's projected budget. Congress appropriated an even greater sum. Much of the new military monies were spent to develop limited-war capabilities later used in Vietnam. Some went into the navy's massive Polaris missile program. But other money was simply impounded by Kennedy's efficiency-minded secretary of defense, Robert McNamara.

Congress showed itself ready to override McNamara's budget-trimming. Over his objections it approved the RS-70 (formerly B-70) bomber program in 1962, for example. The Minuteman and Polaris missile programs were increased every year. The defense budget edged upward.

But the military sector did not fare as well under Kennedy as it had hoped. In 1963, for instance, Congress was convinced to go along with McNamara's efficiency-oriented cutbacks of the TFX fighter, the RS-70 bomber, and the Nike-Zeus missile. Congress also closed 33 military installations at McNamara's recommendation. The JCS sought but failed to get a 1963 bill preventing the president from replacing its members. The JCS were also reputedly unhappy with the 1963 Nuclear Test Ban Treaty. Perhaps most important, other sectors increased in government spending at a much more rapid rate. The share of the military in the total federal budget began to fall a few percentage points with every new fiscal year.

The Vietnam War ended this slipping of priority for the military. Largely because of the war, military spending during fiscal year (FY) 1966 increased $7 billion. There was another sharp increase the following year. Though non-Vietnam-related programs were mostly held to current levels, even here some increased. Congress overrode McNamara's objections to give the JCS the new manned bomber it had long sought. The navy was allowed to begin development of its nuclear frigate plans. And an antiballistic missile (ABM) system was begun.

By 1967 the defense and security budget had risen again to 45 percent of the total federal budget. The ABM, nuclear-frigate, and manned-bomber programs were expanded. Fast-deployment cargo ships were approved for use in limited wars. Between FY 1961 and FY 1969 the defense budget increased from $39 billion to $72 billion. At the end of eight years of Democratic rule, Johnson could point to (1) a 66 percent increase in combat divisions; (2) a 140 percent increase in attack and fighter plane payloads; (3) a 185 percent increase in nuclear weapons on alert; (4) a 326 percent increase in nuclear warships; and (5) a 900 percent increase in helicopter capacity to deploy land troops in small wars. In addition, the Polaris, Minuteman, and ABM missile programs had increased dramatically.

As the war in Vietnam wore on it became increasingly unpopular. Economic troubles at home generated demands for military spending cutbacks. Nixon, trying to hold the line, cut Johnson's FY 1970 defense budget by only $3 billion. This was largely taken out of the ABM program and ammunition for Vietnam, use of which was charged as having been excessive. This cut was a far cry from the enormous "peace dividend" many liberals hoped would come from the winding down of war-related spending.

The peace dividend never materialized. Congress was convinced to channel funds into increased military payrolls and new weapons systems. The ABM system was again expanded. The army received a new tank. The air force received the controversial and costly C-5A cargo plane, development funds for the B-1 bomber, and the F-15 fighter. The navy received the new F-14 fighter. By 1971 Nixon felt able to request a $9 billion increase in defense spending, and Congress allowed $4 billion of it. Congress also turned aside attempts to cut American troop strength in Europe. In 1972 it approved the new Trident missile submarine system. The FY 1973 bill, providing $74.4 billion for the Defense Department, was the largest single appropriation ever made for any purpose by Congress.

In 1974 President Nixon requested further increases of $5 billion, in spite of the close of American troop involvement in Vietnam. This was tied to significant cuts in domestic spending. Much of the increase for the military was necessitated by the rapidly escalating personnel costs of the new volunteer army system Congress had passed as a substitute for the enormously unpopular conscription system. In FY 1975 Congress appropriated $83 billion, a further increase. No major weapons system was denied. Nixon's successor, President Ford, campaigned heavily in 1976 on the issue of further major increases in defense spending. Ford called for a budget of $108 billion for defense in FY 1977. Noting that U.S. military spending had fallen behind that of the Soviet Union in every year since 1970 (in contrast to earlier "superiority"), most congressmen seemed to accept the election-year mood of a tough national posture. Ford's unprecedented request was accepted with only minor cutbacks, setting an FY 1977 budget fully $14 billion higher than the previous year.

The postwar legislative record of the military shows that group to be at the peak of influence in *absolute* terms. It has been able, with the help of recurring international crises and wars, to expand steadily and greatly. It has been able to aid in the defeat of many major liberal attempts to curtail its spending levels. Unlike the situation after World War I, the post–World War II period has seen no return of the military to prewar low spending patterns. On the contrary, it has been successful in obtaining virtually every major weapons system it has sought from Congress.

The limits of military power become apparent only when one considers its influence in *relative* terms. Many of the seeming increases in the military were eroded by inflation. In terms of uninflated real dollars, U.S. military spending actually declined between 1965 and 1975.[35] Defense spending had dropped to only 28 percent of the federal budget. Though Ford's proposed increases reverse these trends somewhat, overall they still suggest that the military has been less successful than domestic interests in the struggle for the federal dollar. Thus the military was winning most of its political battles in absolute terms, but in relative terms it was losing the war of the budget.

Summary

In this chapter we have used an essentially formalistic approach to the study of power. This approach emphasizes the constitutional and legal parameters of government, the government's organizational structure, and the institutional history and legislative record of the government branches. While it tends to neglect the issue of implicit power discussed in Chapter 1, it does shed some light on the elitist-pluralist debate outlined in Chapter 2. Some of the evidence revealed by this approach supports a pluralist position, some an elite-theory position, and some fits in neither category.

Pluralist theory suggests that power in America is quite fragmented. Decisions emerge from the conflict of a great many interests, public and private, no one of which is dominant. Moreover, the system is open and the coalition of interests dominant at the moment is unlikely to be dominant in a later period. Several aspects of military politics illustrate the pluralist view:

1. *The vitality of the constitutional checks and balances among the branches of the federal government:* The continuing conflicts and shifting alignments of the president, the secretary of defense, the JCS, and Congress continue to manifest themselves. The admirals wanted a supercarrier in 1949 and General MacArthur wanted a free hand in 1951, but the president opposed both and strengthened his control and that of the secretary of defense, instead. In the 1950s Eisenhower wanted to limit the rate of increase in military spending, but Congress frequently gave the defense establishment more money anyway. During the Vietnam War, Congress became increasingly critical, but the president and the military conspired to conceal from Congress information on such matters as American military involvement in Cambodia. Again and again one finds instances of the various branches of government conflicting in shifting coalitions against one another.

2. *The vitality of competing interests in the political struggles over federal spending:* Not only was the military strikingly neglected in the period before World War II, but its postwar position of relative preeminence (with over one-half of the federal budget) has declined to one of much reduced importance (with less than one-third of the budget). In a short period of time the military sector was displaced from its dominant position. This is quite in contrast to elite theorist C. Wright Mills's dire predictions about the "military ascendancy." It suggests, rather, that the top levels of power in America are open and constantly shifting.

3. *The vitality of democratic controls over the military:* Both the president and Congress have significantly improved their powers of oversight of the military. The powers and staff of the secretary of defense have grown enormously, and the service departments, after a series of sharp confrontations, were made subject to his authority. Similarly, the reformed congressional budget system, expanded staffs of the armed services and defense appropriations committees, and the auxiliary congressionally directed staffs in the General Accounting Office and Library of Congress, as well as the new Congressional Budget Office, promise an increasingly effective level of democratic oversight.

While we have examined the Defense Department as a case in point, similar observations of other departments of government could be cited to buttress pluralist theory.

Yet there is much in military politics that supports the elite-theory view of how power works in America. Elite theory suggests that there is a tendency for power to become concentrated over time, for democratic controls to become more symbolic than real, and for a few established interests to become dominant for long periods. This viewpoint is supported by the following evidence:

1. *Centralization of power has occurred in the military establishment.* From Calhoun's administrative reforms establishing clearer hierarchical relations to the pre–World War I general-staff concept to the unprecedented powers of the JCS during and after World War II, the concentration of power has been almost unabated. The JCS have been able to maintain direct access to the president, by-passing the secretary of defense when necessary. Likewise, they have maintained direct access to Congress, even when the secretary of defense (acting for the president) disapproves. The JCS have also been able to exclude the integration of civilians with their own top planning staffs. And their staffs, in spite of the growth of parallel staffs in the Department of Defense and in Congress, far overshadow their civilian counterparts in size and capabilities. This in turn leads to a relative monopoly of information and staff work which deters would-be political opponents.

2. *The power of the military establishment has become allied with business, the elite group most cited by elite theorists.* Eisenhower's 1960 warning against the military-industrial establishment did not imply that a military-industrial elite controlled American politics. But there seems little doubt that military-industrial relations entered a new era after World War II. This new era was marked by the formation of new military-industrial associations, by the infusion of top military personnel into private management, and by the increasing reliance by the military on private corporate development of military systems. In spite of corporate competition for contracts, the overall political effect has been the predicted one. A large and powerful coalition of defense-related economic groups has arisen to defend the military's spending requests. The antiwar groups have proved evanescent and it is doubtful whether

any new public interest groups will prove capable of countervailing this coalition in a way pluralists hope for.

3. *Democratic reform efforts seem to hold little promise at present for changing these patterns.* Even McNamara was frequently rebuffed by Congress, and his attempt to control the military establishment was a relative failure. Subsequently secretaries of defense have been highly favorable to JCS goals, even outspokenly so. And in spite of a relatively liberal Congress, liberals have again failed to curtail military spending. Sharp new increases are in the offing, the new budget reforms notwithstanding. While the percentage of the budget the military gets has declined relative to the expansion of welfare, health, and similar costs, the military's share remains enormous and growing. It acquires virtually all the new weapons systems it seeks in spite of urgent domestic needs.

The study of military politics also suggests other kinds of evidence that do not fit neatly into the pluralist or elitist viewpoints. Later, in Chapter 12, we will suggest another way of interpreting American politics that is not elitist or pluralist and which *can* use this evidence. For now, however, we will simply call attention to these other findings about power which emerge from the formalistic approach:

1. *The systemic nature of power:* The success of the military sector, like other sectors, is tied to the economy. In wartime and crises the military budget surges ahead of economic growth, while in peacetime and recessions it lags behind. In broad terms, however, the military budget is associated with the general trends of tax revenues, which in turn reflect the general growth or contraction of the economy. The increase in military spending between World War II and the Vietnam War was as much a result of economic expansion in the country as it was a result of strictly political considerations.

2. *The influence of functional role:* The conservativeness of the military sector is not a direct function of its ties to business, elite theory notwithstanding. Conservative military viewpoints long antedate the rise of the military-industrial establishment. The development of a distinctively conservative military view corresponds chronologically with the adaptation by the military of a

domestic-control role. Specifically, it corresponds to the period during which the military sector was used to control labor disturbances. This control role had precedents going back to the time of Shays' Rebellion. During this period, when a conservative view was crystallizing among the military, business pacifism was at a high point. Rather than reflecting business values, military politics in its conservative aspects reflect the functional role the military plays in society. This role emphasizes the values of strength, discipline, and obedience.[36]

3. *The importance of institutionalized politics:* Political systems become self-perpetuating. Soon after the conservative belief-sets of the military consolidated in the late nineteenth century, many new military institutions formed. These included war colleges, military journals, separate social facilities for officers, and a new elite role for the service academies. These conservative orientations became fixed in college traditions, editorial policy, the norms of social clubs, and so on. Socialization to dominant norms became intense and comprehensive. Self-selection of individuals predisposed toward military values became another reinforcing aspect of the system. The values of the period during which a political subgroup becomes institutionalized has a long-lasting effect on the politics of that group. For example, the air force, institutionalized relatively later in American history, is relatively more liberal by tradition. (Of course the conservative influence of functional role, discussed in point 2, remains an important constraint.)

In summary, when we look at the evidence suggested by the formalistic approach to power we find three sorts: (1) some evidence suggests power is fragmented among many competing groups (the pluralist view); (2) some evidence, on the contrary, suggests power operates at a relatively elite level with a minimum of significant group competition (the elite-theory view); and (3) other evidence suggests the difficulty of any group interpretation of politics (whether the many-group approach of pluralism, or the elites-versus-masses approach of elite theory). Instead, the *systemic* nature of the *political economy* seems the most important aspect of politics. In Chapter 5 we will use the decision-making approach (discussed in Chapter 3) to study further how power works in American politics.

Notes

1. Richard H. Kohn, *Eagle and Sword: The Federalists and the Creation of the Military Establishment in America, 1783–1802* (New York: Free Press, 1975), pp. 73–75.
2. Samuel Huntington, *The Soldier and the State* (Cambridge, Mass.: Harvard University Press, 1967), pp. 163–64.
3. Congressional Quarterly, Inc., *The Power of the Pentagon* (Washington, D.C.: Congressional Quarterly, 1972), pp. 3–5.
4. Ibid., p. 3.
5. Ibid., p. 5.
6. Ibid., p. 9.
7. Ibid., p. 8. Rep. Donald Riegle (R, Mich.).
8. Leonard White, *The Jeffersonians* (New York: Macmillan, 1951), pp. 11–12.
9. Huntington, *The Soldier and the State*, p. 205.
10. William B. Skelton, "Professionalization in the U.S. Army Officer Corps During the Age of Jackson," *Armed Forces and Society* 1 (Summer 1975): 465.
11. Huntington, *The Soldier and Society*, pp. 226–27.
12. Ibid., p. 257.
13. Walter Millis, *Arms and Men: A Study in American Military History* (New York: G. P. Putnam's Sons, 1956), pp. 143, 144–45.
14. See Paul Y. Hammond, *Organizing for Defense: The American Military Establishment in the Twentieth Century* (Princeton: Princeton University Press, 1961), pp. 10–12, 22.
15. See Millis, *Arms and Men*, p. 235.
16. Huntington, *The Soldier and the State*, pp. 282–84.
17. Ibid., p. 285.
18. Ibid., p. 336.
19. Hammond, *Organizing for Defenses*, p. 107.
20. Ibid., p. 123.
21. Huntington, *The Soldier and the State*, p. 373. However, on the general increase in the role of professional military personnel in foreign policy after World War II, see D. F. Bletz, *The Role of the Military Professional in U.S. Foreign Policy* (New York: Praeger, 1972).
22. Ibid., p. 362.
23. Adam Yarmolinsky, *The Military Establishment: Its Impact on American Society* (New York: Harper and Row, for the Twentieth Century Fund, 1971), pp. 55–56.
24. Ibid., p. 57. For further discussion, see S. C. Sarkesian, ed., *The Military-Industrial Complex: A Reassessment* (Beverly Hills, Cal.: Sage Publications, 1972); R. Kaufman, *The War Profiteers* (Garden City, N.Y.: Doubleday, 1972); S. Gottlieb, "State Within a State: What Is the Military-Industrial Complex?" *Dissent* 18 (October 1971): 492–502; V. V. Aspaturian and R. H. Ferell et al., "The Military-Industrial Complex: USA/USSR," *Journal of International Affairs* 26 (1972); R. N. Kharasch, *The Institutional Imperative* (New York: McKay, 1973); and S. Rosen, *Testing the Theory of the Military-Industrial Complex* (Lexington, Mass.: Heath, 1973).

118   Power in the United States

25. Congressional Quarterly, Inc., *Congress and Nation,* Vol. I (Washington, D.C.: Congressional Quarterly, 1965), p. 1949.
26. Hammond, *Organizing for Defense,* p. 351.
27. Ibid., p. 390.
28. Edward A. Kolodziej, *The Uncommon Defense and Congress, 1945–1963* (Columbus: Ohio State University Press, 1966), p. 382.
29. A seminal work is C. J. Hitch and R. McKean, *The Economics of Defense in the Nuclear Age* (Cambridge, Mass.: Harvard University Press, 1960). See also A. Enthoven, "Systems Analysis and the Navy," in F. Lyden and E. Miller, eds., *Planning, Programming, Budgeting: A Systems Approach to Management* (Chicago: Markham, 1967), pp. 265–91.
30. Congressional Quarterly, Inc., *Congress and Nation,* Vol. III, p. 249.
31. Ibid., p. 250.
32. See Seymour Melman, *Pentagon Capitalism* (New York: McGraw-Hill, 1970); S. Melman, *The Defense Economy* (New York: Praeger, 1970); S. Melman, ed., *The War Economy of the United States: Readings in Military Industry* (New York: St. Martin's, 1971); James Clayton, ed., *The Economic Impact of the Cold War* (New York: Harcourt, Brace and World, 1970); Kenneth Boulding, ed., *Peace and the War Industry* (New York: Aldine, 1970); Sidney Lens, *The Military-Industrial Complex* (Kansas City, Mo.: Pilgrim Press, 1970).
33. *Congressional Quarterly Weekly Report,* 23 March 1974, p. 738.
34. This section draws on Congressional Quarterly, Inc., *Congress and Nation,* Vols. I–III.
35. *Congressional Quarterly Weekly Report,* 27 March 1976, p. 692.
36. See Huntington, *The Soldier and Society.* See also R. Joseph Monsen and Mark W. Cannon, *The Makers of Public Policy: American Power Groups and Their Ideologies* (New York: McGraw-Hill, 1965), p. 296.

5. The Decisional Approach: The Vietnam War

In American political science the study of governmental decisions has become the dominant approach to understanding power. Unlike the formalistic approach, discussed in Chapter 4, the decision-making approach emphasizes the informal as well as formal aspects of politics. It centers on the concept of *influence* (discussed in Chapter 1). The decision-making approach is a method of studying power which has been very controversial because of its alleged bias toward pluralist theory. (Recall that pluralist theory was discussed in Chapter 2 and the decision-making method in Chapter 3.) This approach is concerned with tracing the historical development of a political decision or event. In so doing particular attention is given to who initiates policy, who responds to initiatives and how, and what the policy outcome is. From such information political scientists infer the distribution of power in governmental affairs.

A complete decision-making case study would require book-length treatment. In-depth interviews would be conducted with all major figures in the decision. An intensive field study of organizational settings pertinent to the case would be undertaken. While no pretense is made that this chapter is such a full-length treatment, it is possible to present a case study that indicates the general nature of the decision-making approach. Through it, further light can be shed on how power is distributed in America.

The case we will study is President Johnson's decision to escalate the war in Vietnam during the mid-1960s. This case has been selected for three reasons. First, it continues our treatment of the military in politics. Because of this we can see better how the decision-making approach *does* go beyond the limits of the formal approach discussed in the previous chapter. Second, foreign and military policy is usually perceived to be relatively nonpartisan and free from domestic economic influences. This helps to balance the later chapters, which focus on the political role of business. Third, this case not only involved matters of the highest importance but it was also subject to unusual exposure to public view. This was associated with the unprecedented release of government documents in the *Pentagon Papers* in 1971.[1]

Much of this chapter recounts the history of the escalation decision. The many actors in this event are identified and their influence partly revealed in the description of their roles. We will follow the decision-making approach in letting the reader become immersed in the details of our case. But at the end of the chapter we will return to the main themes of this book. We will look back over the details of the escalation decision and discuss various alternative theories to account for it. The relative validity of pluralist and elite theory perspectives will be considered. And we will consider the kinds of evidence from the decision-making approach that fit neither viewpoint. (In reading the detailed account which follows it may help the reader to try to anticipate what generalizations about power might be drawn from this decision-making case.)

The Actors

From late 1964 through the spring of 1965, the groundwork was laid for escalating American troop involvement in the Vietnam War. By the end of 1965 involvement had increased from 23,300 men in an "advisory" capacity to 184,000 men in combat and other war-related functions. This decision was a crucial step in a series of determinations which eventually brought over half a million American citizens to fight in Vietnam. The war proved to be the most unpopular in American history. How did this happen, who made the decisions, and what does this tell us about the distribution of power in this country? Approaching these questions from the point of view of decision-making, we will begin by examining the background and role of the major participants in the escalation decision.

The President

On October 21, 1964, during his successful campaign against Senator Barry Goldwater, Lyndon Johnson told an audience at Akron University that he would not send young Americans to fight in Asia. In his memoirs Johnson explained his later shift away from this policy. "My generation had lived through the change from American isolationism to collective security in 1940–1941," he wrote. "I had watched firsthand in Congress as we swerved in 1946–1947 from the unilateral dismantling of our armed forces to President Truman's effort to protect Western Europe. I could never forget the withdrawal of our forces from South Korea and then our immediate reaction to the Communist aggression of June, 1950. As I looked ahead, I could see us repeating the same sharp reversal once again in Asia. . . ." [2]

President Johnson was a man long accustomed to the concepts of the cold war. "I am not going to be the President who saw Southeast Asia go the way China went," he once stated. Tom Wicker of the *New York Times* observed, "A whole lifetime of political and human experience was distilled in that sentence." [3] In 1964, however, Lyndon Johnson was running for the presidency. He and his staff were preoccupied with the campaign. As David Halberstam noted in *The Best and the Brightest*, this "allowed the bureaucracy to plan for the war." Even in early 1964, he continued, "the play was being held closer and closer, and there were fewer and fewer decision-makers." [4] For the moment Johnson was content to leave it that way.

The Secretary of Defense

Robert Strange McNamara had come to the Kennedy administration from the presidency of the Ford Motor Company. He had gained the reputation of being a brilliant administrator who could control the military. McNamara proved an energetic leader who made frequent trips to Vietnam. By default Secretary of State Dean Rusk had been pushed to the side. McNamara became the major adviser to the president on Vietnam. It was he who could play the balancing role between the civilians and the generals in a time of growing divisions. Of him Halberstam wrote, "No one could doubt his good intentions, his ability, his almost ferocious sense of public service, yet something about him bothered many of his colleagues. It was not just Vietnam, but his overall style. It was what made him so effective: the total belief in what he was doing, the willingness to knock down anything that stood in his way, the relentless quality, so that other men, sometimes wiser, more restrained, would be pushed aside." [5]

The Secretary of State

A quite different man, Secretary of State Dean Rusk was not prone to challenge the military or McNamara. A professional diplomat of long career, Rusk's beliefs were toughened with time. He advocated containment even to the point of armed force. His moderate liberalism was tempered by a strong measure of anticommunism. In this sense Rusk was similar to Lyndon Johnson. Added to mutual southern backgrounds, this made the two men close. Of Rusk, Johnson later recalled, "He stood by me and shared the President's load of responsibility and abuse. He never complained. But he was no 'yes man.' He could be determined, and he was always most determined when he was telling me I shouldn't do something I felt needed to be done." [6] Though soon eclipsed by McNamara as Johnson's adviser on Vietnam, Rusk's hard-line approach to war issues continued to be an important factor in late 1964 and early 1965.

The Special Assistant to the President for National Security

McGeorge Bundy, also a holdover from the Kennedy administration, came from the Eastern establishment. After attending Groton, Yale, and Harvard, he had become first a professor of government and then a dean of the college at Harvard. There he met Jack Kennedy and began a relationship which led him to Washington to function as a key administrative aide on national security affairs. Though not intimate with Johnson and Rusk, his work earned their respect. McGeorge Bundy had the reputation of being bright, witty, and a supreme administrator. "Clerk of the World," Marcus Raskin called him. Like many others who figured in the decision to launch an American ground war in Asia, Bundy was a "hard realist." He shared the cold-war conventions of the postwar generation. Through his office in the basement of the White House (sometimes called the Little State Department), Bundy's influence surpassed that of Rusk and rivaled McNamara's. All three—Bundy, Rusk, McNamara—were men whose decisions had led Kennedy to establish American commitments in Vietnam. As Tom Wicker observed, "They had a vested interest in its [the war's] success, on which largely depended their own reputations." [7]

The Joint Chiefs of Staff

The JCS had favored an increase in American ground troops since at least 1961. Its reports on the Vietnamese situation were perpetually optimistic. They hinted that if only a few more major programs could be committed to Vietnam, the war might soon be won. Internally the JCS were split by air force emphasis on extended bombing. A skeptical army preferred counterinsurgency on the ground. Externally, however, the JCS presented a united front which frustrated even McNamara's efforts to obtain the more pessimistic truth. Eventually, in late 1963 and early 1964, McNamara had sought a joint Defense Department-CIA independent study of the situation in Vietnam. The JCS were able to block this, but the CIA went ahead on its own.

Eventually a far more pessimistic appraisal was submitted, but to little effect. "Once again," Halberstam wrote, "the military was able to hold onto its version of reality, this time against the best efforts of the Secretary of Defense." [8] By January 1964, the JCS were vigorously pressing for a wider war free of past restrictions. The seeming incapacity of the South Vietnamese regime to cope with the expanding National Liberation Front strengthened the hand of the JCS. The more restrained position of McNamara was undermined.

General Wheeler. Earle G. Wheeler (West Point, 1932), a veteran of World War II, became chairman of the JCS in 1964. An army professional, Wheeler wanted desperately to avoid the type of partial commitment and limited war which Korea had represented. Like other JCS members, he wanted a clear American commitment to a major war effort. Unlike the president, Wheeler understood this would involve a major American combat presence over several years. Even then, a sizable American force might be necessary for decades. Wheeler never clearly communicated this to the president. His greatest importance in Vietnam policy came only after the decision to escalate had been taken.

General Westmoreland. William C. Westmoreland was commander, U.S. Military Assistance Command, Vietnam (MACV). As such he held responsibility for the day-to-day conduct of the war. Westmoreland had come to this command from the superintendency of West Point. He had fought in both World War II and Korea. Westmoreland was pessimistic about the conduct of the war prior to the decision to escalate. He was skeptical of the effectiveness of air force bombing. He lacked confidence in South Vietnam's army. For Westmoreland the war could—and had to be—won on the ground using American forces.

The Ambassador to Vietnam

Prior to being appointed ambassador to Vietnam in 1964, General Maxwell Davenport Taylor had had long associations with the Far East. He had been in Tokyo from 1935 to 1939, after which he served briefly in Peking. He had been the commander of the Eighth Army in Korea in 1953. Later he headed all U.S. army forces in the Far East. It was he who had held the post of chairman of the JCS before Wheeler.

Popular with the Kennedy's, Taylor had gained a somewhat partisan reputation as a result of his book, *The Uncertain Trumpet* (1960). This work attacked Eisenhower's "massive-retaliation" policies. Instead Taylor emphasized the need for "limited-war" capabilities, such as those later needed in Vietnam. Thus Taylor's perspective meshed well with Kennedy's own emphasis on limited-war forces. Under Kennedy, Taylor had successfully pressed for the establishment of the advisory U.S. military presence in Vietnam which preceded the escalation.

In 1964 Taylor was associated with the enclave strategy. He believed that American goals would be maximized by a defensive strategy centered on concentration of forces in advantageous areas. Westmoreland, in contrast, favored a more aggressive strategy of search-and-destroy operations. More optimistic than Westmoreland, Taylor did not see the need to increase combat troops. Westmoreland, in contrast, believed that additional troops were essential to the war.

The Assistant Secretary of State for Far Eastern Affairs

William P. Bundy, McGeorge Bundy's older brother, became assistant secretary of state for Far Eastern affairs in 1964. Coming by way of the Defense Department from a CIA background, William Bundy was a civil servant dedicated to supporting presidential war policies. Though not at the center of power, Bundy was closely connected to the top. At the Department of State his role was to secure the cooperation of the Department of Defense. In this context he advocated a hard military line. Skeptical if not contemptuous of the peace movement, William Bundy's views found their way into innumerable documents that filtered up to Rusk, McNamara, and McGeorge Bundy. These reinforced the anticommunist military strategy that was being formulated at these higher levels. He was, Halberstam wrote, "a classic insider's man. His name would probably be on more pieces of paper dealing with Vietnam than anyone else's, yet he was the man about whom the least was known, the fewest articles written." [9]

The Assistant Secretary of Defense

John McNaughton was another of the important insiders virtually unknown to the public. Assistant Secretary of Defense McNaughton was McNamara's representative and advocate. A midwesterner who had become a Harvard law professor before coming to the Kennedy administration, McNaughton was a rationalist, a meticulous quantifier, a bureaucrat. He was capable of putting forward views that were not his own in a forceful and dispassionate manner. He was therefore associated often with the defense of hardline policies. Yet he was also an important advocate of arms control. His latent antipathy toward the military tempered his relations to the JCS. His attitudes toward Vietnam were on balance pessimistic. Already in 1964 he had commissioned Daniel Ellsberg to prepare a secret study on how to disengage from Vietnam gracefully should the war effort there collapse. His views reinforced McNamara's own reservations about the war, but McNamara remained virtually the sole recipient of McNaughton's doubts.

Other Actors

Among the other actors who might be mentioned was Admiral Ulysses S. Grant Sharp, Commander in Chief, Pacific (CINCPAC)—a firm supporter and early proponent of the need for escalation. Another actor was CIA director John McCone, a former business executive for whom anticommunism was an ingrained reflex. McCone's hawkish policies on Vietnam were frequently put forward.

Summary

What are the collective attributes of the decision-makers—Johnson, McNamara, Rusk, McGeorge and William Bundy, Wheeler,

Westmoreland, Taylor, McNaughton, Sharp, and McCone? At the most obvious level, all were white males who, at an average age of fifty-four, were quite different from the American population at large. With few exceptions their social backgrounds were what C. Wright Mills and elite theorists would predict.

Of the top echelon of men who advised President Johnson on Vietnam, McNamara had risen through the corporate ranks to become president of the Ford Motor Company before becoming secretary of defense. The Bundys were representative of the elite of Boston's old families and had been educated accordingly. Rusk, though not personally wealthy, had become president of the Rockefeller Foundation (1952–1960) prior to becoming secretary of state. He was now at home as a member of New York's elite Century Club. McCone, of course, was a right-wing millionaire from iron and shipbuilding. He was a member of no less than nine elite men's social clubs. Of the remainder, four were military men (Wheeler, Westmoreland, Taylor, and Sharp). Each was a graduate of the military academies and in 1964 all except Taylor were still career men. Taylor had been chairman of the board and chief executive officer of Mexican Power and Light (1959–1960), and later head of that new institution of New York's elite, the Lincoln Center.

Of Johnson's top advisers only McNaughton lacked an elite background. McNaughton was the son of a small-town newspaper publisher, and had gone on to become a professor of law at Harvard. It was also McNaughton who, more than the others, was critical of the hard line on Vietnam. But he played a lesser role and his criticisms were not widely known.

Johnson's decision-makers in 1964 and 1965 held opinions about the war that were strikingly more hawkish than those of the general public. From the fall of 1964 through March of 1965, when the escalation occurred, only 12 to 29 percent of Americans favored increased military action or carrying the war to the North. (The percentages varied according to how the question was asked. There was *not* a tendency for the proportion of hard-liners to rise over time.) Earlier, during the spring and summer of 1964, virtually all the major decision-makers were seriously considering military escalation. But of the American public, only 8 to 12 percent favored military action or took

a "fight-or-get-out" attitude.[10] It was only later, *after* the escalation decision had been made, that a majority of Americans
supported the increased ground war or professed a passive
"don't know" attitude. This tendency of the public to support
governmental actions after the fact illustrates the power of
elites over public opinion. (Recall the discussion of this point
by Edelman in Chapter 1.) Far from reflecting public opinion,
these leaders helped to shape it in a temporarily new direction.

The Background to the Decision

A year after Ho Chi Minh proclaimed the Republic of Vietnam
in 1946, civil war erupted in what was then Indochina. As the
dominant power in the area, the French had negotiated with
Ho Chi Minh but these talks had broken down. The French had
refused Ho Chi Minh's demands that Cochin-China be included
in the proposed regional federation. Instead the French installed
Bao Dai—the emperor of Annam and who had been the leader
of the puppet government under the Japanese during World
War II—as head of southern Vietnam. The United States recognized the Bao Dai government in February 1950, and began
channeling economic and military aid to it through the French.
Later the U.S. Military Assistance Advisory Group (MAAG)
was created in Saigon. An alliance with Bao Dai and the French
was formalized in 1950 under the Mutual Defense Assistance
Agreement. By 1952 the United States was paying approximately one-third of all war costs. After the Korean Armistice,
this aid was further increased.

Between 1946 and 1954 Ho Chi Minh had waged a long
war against the French. It culminated in the spectacular and
historic French military debacle at Dien Bien Phu in 1954. This
defeat led to French withdrawal under the terms of the Geneva
Agreement, which partitioned Vietnam along the 17th parallel,
with Ho Chi Minh governing the North and Bao Dai the South.
The Geneva Agreement also called for elections in 1956 to lead
toward reunification. Between 1954 and 1956, however, American and French support for Bao Dai's premier, Ngo Dinh Diem,
intensified. Diem overthrew Bao Dai and refused to participate
in the reunification elections. Instead he proclaimed South Viet-

nam a republic with himself as its president. In 1956 and 1957, then-Vice-President Richard Nixon and Diem exchanged visits and the commitment of the Eisenhower administration to South Vietnam deepened.

From 1958 on, both communist and noncommunist opposition to Diem intensified in the South. In 1960 the United States responded by increasing the MAAG group from 327 to 685 persons. Communist terrorist activities nonetheless increased further. In December 1960 the National Liberation Front was formed as an insurgent government in the South. Diem charged the North with direct aggression.

As the new U.S. president, John F. Kennedy pledged continuing support for the Diem regime. As the military situation in the South continued to escalate, Kennedy sent General Maxwell Taylor to investigate. Taylor's report prompted Kennedy to give new assurances of further support to South Vietnam. In November 1961, Kennedy secured the approval of the National Security Council (NSC) to increase the number of military advisers in South Vietnam. By the end of December 3,000 persons were involved in these activities. This figure rose to 11,300 a year later. In October 1963, there were 16,000 advisers; by July 1964, 21,000. The escalating American presence in Vietnam required its reorganization. In February 1962, MAAG was replaced by the Military Assistance Command, Vietnam (MACV).

As this increase occurred, criticism of the Diem regime became sharper in American media. Publicity was given to charges of corruption and lack of popular support. Diem was criticized for representing a tiny Catholic minority in a Buddhist land. Diem's "strategic hamlet" program for isolating the population in paramilitary camps did not lessen fears of concentration camps and tyranny. The Kennedy administration itself came into increasing conflict with Diem. A major issue was Diem's refusal to allow military aid to the Montagnards and other groups within South Vietnam which were anticommunist but not reliably pro-Diem. By April 1963, Diem's differences with the United States had led him to call for the reduction of the American military force in his country.

In the summer and fall of 1963, violent Buddhist and student demonstrations culminated in the overthrow of Diem by a military junta under General Duong Van Minh. It was later alleged that this coup was encouraged by the United States. Though hailed in America as a sign of progress, the overthrow actually led to a series of unstable governments. After Kennedy's assassination, President Johnson promised greater military commitment to South Vietnam. This promise was reiterated by McNamara and Taylor in their May 1964 inspection trip to Vietnam. Following these promises, General Khanh and other South Vietnamese leaders began calling for carrying the war into North Vietnam. It was a decision on this matter which faced Johnson, McNamara, Rusk, and others in the fall of 1964 and the spring of 1965.

Summary

The background to the escalation decision suggests a number of generalizations about power in America. First, American involvement in Vietnam was bipartisan. It stretched from Truman through the Eisenhower years to Kennedy and Johnson. Second, this bipartisan commitment to South Vietnam was deeply imbued with the ideology of anticommunism. Increased military actions were justified to the American public on this basis (and not, for example, on the basis of economic interests). Third, economic self-interest and business pressure did not appear as dominant factors in the escalation decision. Insofar as they were important it was in terms of implicit power relations mediated through the pro-"free enterprise," quasi-religious rhetoric of anticommunism.

The Decision-Making Case Study

Vietnam became a sensitive issue after the rise of the military junta in 1963. Johnson and his top advisers tended to become more guarded about information and decisions pertaining to the war. For example, Chester Cooper, a governmental adviser whose war views were pessimistic, "found that it was more and more difficult to reach McGeorge Bundy on the subject as the questions became graver and the failures more apparent." [11]

Part of this guardedness derived from the political tight-rope President Johnson was walking in his reelection campaign. On the one hand, Johnson wished to portray himself as a moderate, contrasting his restrained views with the "radical" tendencies of Senator Barry Goldwater, his opponent. In a speech to the American Bar Association, for example, Johnson suggested that "some . . . are eager to enlarge the conflict. They call upon us to supply American boys to do the job that Asian boys should do." [12] And in a famous speech shortly before the election, Johnson proclaimed, "We are not about to send American boys nine or ten thousand miles away from home to do what Asian boys ought to be doing to protect themselves."

On the other hand, Johnson was covertly sanctioning the escalation of the war. Later, in his autobiography, Johnson innocently wrote: "A good many people compared my position in 1964 with that of the Republican nominee, Senator Barry Goldwater of Arizona, and decided that I was the 'peace' candidate and he was the 'war' candidate. They were not willing to hear anything they did not want to hear." [13] Yet this statement was a self-deception at best.

Throughout 1964 the Democrats never ceased to exploit the peace issue in a manner which suggested Goldwater was a warmonger and Johnson was the best hope for peace. [14] Almost unknown to the public, however, only four days after Kennedy's murder, Johnson had already issued National Security Memorandum 273 (NSAM 273) authorizing covert military action against North Vietnam.

The Precipitating Event

NSAM 273 was widely publicized in terms of its rhetoric of "Vietnamization" of the war. Much attention was given to its provision for a 1,000-man reduction in troops in Vietnam. (This was more an accounting artifact than a reality, however, attributable to the method of troop rotation.) [15] More significant were the secret provisions for escalated paramilitary activities against the North. While ostensibly reaffirming existing Vietnam policy, NSAM 273 deemphasized the nonmilitary priorities for South Vietnam that had appeared in Kennedy's planned text of the subject. Instead Johnson added an authorization for "selected actions of graduated [escalating] scope and intensity" against North Vietnam.[16]

On the basis of this authorization the CIA prepared an operations plan, Operations Plan 34a (OPLAN 34a). Implemented in February 1964, OPLAN 34a activities called for about twenty "destructive undertakings" plus psychological warfare from February through May 1964. Two later phases were to involve more intense military operations. These raids were to be "nonattributable" commando operations using American materiel and American direction, but with South Vietnamese manpower. Johnson approved these plans on January 16, 1964.

The 34a operations became the precipitating factor in the Tonkin Gulf incident. On July 31, 1964, as part of covert raids on the North, a torpedo boat shelled an island off North Vietnam. Though officially "nonattributable," these raids were perceived by the North as American aggression. The following day Admiral Sharp ordered the destroyer *Maddox* on a patrol in which it electronically simulated an attack on North Vietnam for purposes of pinpointing radar locations. While the joint occurrence of these two actions (the raid and the patrol) risked retaliation, no effort was made to coordinate them. The North Vietnamese, believing the *Maddox* patrol was linked to the coastal shelling, ordered its boats to attack. This attack in the Gulf of Tonkin was splashed across American headlines as a new Pearl Harbor. It seemed to represent an unprovoked attack by Ho Chi Minh and an escalation of the war. The public knew nothing of the secret and provocative raids which had preceded the attack.

The Gulf of Tonkin Resolution

On early Sunday morning, August 2, 1964, President Johnson was informed of the attack on the *Maddox*. A few hours later he called a meeting of Rusk, Wheeler, Vance (McNamara's deputy secretary), and several intelligence experts. This meeting resulted in a presidential order to double the Tonkin Gulf patrol. The destroyer *Turner Joy* was added with air support and authorization to respond to attack "with the objective not only of driving off the force but of destroying it." [17]

On August 4 the second Tonkin Gulf incident occurred. The controversy surrounding it is intense. Many argue that the incident was fabricated in order to justify American escalation of the war. Ostensibly, however, on the evening of August 4 the *Maddox* monitored radio broadcasts in which North Vietnam again ordered an attack. At the same time its radar detected two patrol boats some 36 miles distant. When the contacts had approached to 12 miles, the *Maddox* opened fire. After this a torpedo was observed passing within 300 feet of the *Turner Joy*. At about the same time American aircraft launched attacks on the North Vietnamese vessels. After about an hour's activity the two North Vietnamese boats were reported sunk. There were no American casualties and no damage.[18] Subsequent messages from the field indicated confusion about whether an attack had actually taken place.

Informed of this second incident, McNamara asked Wheeler to make sure Sharp "was willing to state that the attack had taken place." There would be no retaliation, he said, until it was "damned sure that the attacks had taken place." [19] After Sharp confirmed the incidents, a National Security Council meeting was convened. Here Johnson called for retaliation and authorization was granted. The only opposition came from Dean Rusk. Rusk, fearful of Chinese involvement, amended the retaliatory plans to omit bombing two bases near China's borders.

On the evening of August 4, Washington time, congressional leaders were called and informed of the Tonkin Gulf incident. Johnson informed them of his need for a congressional resolution sanctioning his actions. Present were nine Senate and seven House leaders. Each was asked by Johnson for his reactions. Each endorsed the retaliation and the proposed resolution. This group included the entire congressional leadership of both parties plus the heads of the Foreign Relations committees. The Republican presidential candidate, Goldwater, was then contacted. He too approved the actions. No one, it seemed, wished to appear soft on communism in an election year.

At 11:36 P.M., President Johnson went on national television to explain the Tonkin Gulf incidents. They were, he said, examples of unprovoked aggression of a repeated nature. Justifiably the United States was committed to retaliation. The following day Johnson bolstered his hard-line image, stating in a speech that "there can be no peace by aggression and no immunity from reply." [20]

On August 5 Johnson was presented with a draft of the Southeast Asia Resolution (also called the Gulf of Tonkin Resolution). This had been written by Rusk and his undersecretary, George Ball, in consultation with congressional leaders. Later this resolution would be used as congressional authorization for an escalated land war. It was passed in the House without opposition and by the Senate with only two dissenting votes. The Tonkin Gulf Resolution authorized Johnson to "take all necessary steps, including the use of armed force, to assist any member (of SEATO) requesting assistance in defense of its freedom."

Although Fulbright and some other leaders understood that this resolution sanctioned force even to the point of a de facto declaration of war, there was great confusion on the floor of Congress. Many if not most congressmen assumed that their votes upheld only limited reprisals for specific attacks of the sort those on the *Maddox* were alleged to be. Johnson signed the resolution into law on August 11, 1964.

Preelection Restraint

In the short run Johnson temporarily suspended naval patrols. This may have reflected William Bundy's advice that the patrols be disassociated from the 34a raids in order "to maintain the credibility of our account of the events of last week." [21] At the same time Johnson sought to convey the impression to Hanoi and the American people that American policy had not changed. He denied that the war was being escalated. As Tom Wicker of the *New York Times* wrote: "The Tonkin Gulf response was deliberately designed not to be taken by Hanoi as an escalation—which was the last thing the President wanted to order or be accused of in the middle of a campaign against Goldwater." [22]

Nonetheless, the covert 34a activities against the North continued during August. Now each had to be endorsed by the personal signature of McGeorge Bundy and other "303 Committee" members. (This top-level executive group had been formed after the Cuban crisis to oversee secret paramilitary activities. It was composed of representatives of the president, departments of State and Defense, and the CIA.) Many voices argued for the continuation of these actions. The JCS continued to press for their program of intensified raids. John McNaughton argued strongly for them as well. On August 11, in a memorandum to McNamara, William Bundy argued for continuous military pressure on the North. Three days later Wheeler sent McNamara another memorandum emphasizing the positive value of military reprisals.

By the middle of August the JCS had achieved some of its goals. Field commanders were authorized to pursue North Vietnamese forces into North Vietnam waters and air space. In mid-August Rusk let it be known that the State Department opposed a new Geneva Conference until South Vietnamese morale and stability improved. The JCS took advantage of this to suggest that an escalating air campaign against the North would be the best means to this end.

The building pressure for military escalation stood in stark contrast to Johnson's posture in the 1964 election campaign. During this time he correctly gauged public opinion as hostile to escalation. He therefore kept most of these activities secret. Nonetheless, the calls for escalation had become sufficiently intense in August that Johnson scheduled a top-level strategy meeting for September 7, 1964. In anticipation, John McNaughton prepared "A Plan of Action for South Vietnam," which called "for actions that would provoke a DRV (North Vietnam) response that could be used as grounds for a U.S. escalation." [23]

It was in this context that Johnson, Rusk, McNamara, Wheeler, Ambassador Taylor, and CIA Director McCone met on September 7. In this meeting the JCS proposals were discussed. Though his views as articulated by McNaughton were clearly similar to those of the JCS, McNamara set a different tone for the meeting. He expressed his understanding that at present "we are not acting more strongly because there is a clear hope of strengthening the GVN (South Vietnam)." [24] Certainly this was the view of Rusk, who argued that all alternatives short of bombing should be exhausted before adopting the JCS plan. McCone reinforced this mood of caution by noting the dangers involved in escalation.

Thus the September 7 meeting did not mark the decision to escalate the war. But underneath the cautionary views was an underlying shared assumption that escalation would indeed occur if lesser alternatives failed to stabilize the situation. Given the low probability that that would occur, the strategy meeting must be understood as a virtual if implicit commitment to escalation after the elections. Only the JCS seemed oblivious to the political considerations and called for immediate air bombing. The others, while not disagreeing in principle, did not share the JCS sense of urgency. For them, the time was not yet right.

Even so, the September 7 meeting did result in a small intensification of the war. Naval patrols were resumed in the Gulf of Tonkin. Covert paramilitary raids were again undertaken. And "tit-for-tat" reprisals were authorized to respond to any attacks on U.S. and "special" South Vietnamese forces. These policies (effective from mid-September to mid-December 1964) were formalized by President Johnson in National Security Action Memorandum 314 (NSAM 314, August 10, 1964).

As expected the NSAM 314 policy was less than successful. On September 18, six days after the resumption of patrols, American destroyers fired on radar-identified attackers and scored several hits. No return fire was received. This was precisely the sort of incident against which William Bundy had warned. Johnson promptly suspended naval patrols until the following February.

On October 4, however, Johnson authorized more covert coastal raids. This seemed to elicit an intensification of North Vietnamese infiltration into the South. Taylor called Johnson's attention to this negative effect on October 16. Then, on November 1, 1964, the National Liberation Front attacked the American air base at Bien Hoa, South Vietnam. The JCS and Ambassador Taylor immediately called for bombing the North under the "tit-for-tat" guideline of NSAM 314. Acting just a few days before the 1964 elections, Johnson, on the advice of Mc-

Namara and Rusk, refused to escalate the war. Nonetheless a new task force under William Bundy was established to reevaluate American policy on reprisals and escalation.

A Promise of Escalation

The William Bundy group submitted its report on November 21, 1964. It called for "strong U.S. pressures against the North and resistance of negotiations until the DRV was ready to comply with our demands." [25] At the same time the JCS renewed their call for an escalating air war. The National Security Council met to consider the Bundy report on November 24. Although it favored the Bundy conclusions, there was some dissent. Rusk favored vigorous efforts at negotiations even if this were to mean more compromise of objectives. No firm decision was reached at this time.

The NSC met with Ambassador Taylor on November 27. The next day it arrived at a policy to be recommended to the president. Ostensibly a compromise plan, the NSC recommended: (1) an initial phase of increased pressure on the North, including resumed naval patrols; and (2) a second phase of air strikes if, after thirty days, the initial pressure appeared inadequate. The NSC members hoped the second phase of air escalation might lead the North into negotiations which the United States could enter on strong terms. Of this expectation the *Pentagon Papers* comment, "In retrospect, the Principals [the NSC leaders] appear to have assumed rather low motivation on the part of the DRV. Either this, or they were overly optimistic regarding the threat value of U.S. military might, or both." [26] In effect, though negotiations were contemplated, a renewal of the Geneva Conference was explicitly opposed. A hard negotiating line on war demands was laid down. The proposed escalation promised to be but the first step in a more protracted and intense conflict, not a step toward early negotiations on favorable terms.

On December 1, 1964, Johnson met with the NSC members to approve their plan in principle. At this time only Phase 1 was authorized (increased pressure and patrols). In holding back on the air war, Johnson was guided by two considerations.

First, there was a need to consult with and prepare American allies for a radical shift in policy. Second, and more important, it was necessary to provide time for the South Vietnamese leadership "to get themselves together." Johnson regarded this as a prerequisite to any further American action. Thus, when an American officers' quarters was bombed in Saigon on Christmas eve—and Taylor again urged air war—Johnson still held off.

In his autobiography President Johnson cited two additional reasons for this delay. First, his advisers nearly unanimously counseled him that the government in the South was so shaky that it could not withstand a major attack from the North (which the escalation might trigger). Second, escalation might provoke National Liberation Front attacks on the many Americans and their dependents in the South. Before escalation, an evacuation program for dependents would have to be undertaken.[27]

These reasons did not reflect any real opposition to escalation. Each was a particularistic, tactical consideration. Underlying them was a strategic consensus on the rationale for escalation. Escalation was seen as a desirable vehicle for forcing the North to negotiate on American terms.

Meeting with Taylor on December 3, President Johnson instructed the ambassador to make clear to Saigon (the regime in the South) that the air escalation they wanted depended on their reforming their government. On December 9, 1964, Taylor met with Premier Huong and General Khanh in Saigon. He presented a list of nine specific governmental changes desired by Washington. Huong and the generals agreed. They had no choice since they faced National Liberation Front control of the countryside outside Saigon and the prospect of their own imminent collapse if they were not bolstered by American strength. The American pledge of military escalation was aimed at encouraging the South's dissident generals to rally behind Huong's civilian regime.

Khanh's Coup

Gearing up for escalation, American ambassadors briefed the governments in Thailand and Laos. The Canadians were contacted. William Bundy discussed the new military strategy with officials in New Zealand and Australia on December 4 and 5. Prime Minister Harold Wilson of Great Britain was advised on the plans on December 7, 1964.

Thus, in the weeks before Christmas 1964, joint United States–South Vietnam planning for the air war escalation was well under way. The remaining obstacles were being removed rapidly. Only a few voices of criticism were raised. Rusk's undersecretary of state, George Ball, wrote a critical memorandum. New Zealand leaders expressed reservations in their discussions with Bundy. Some intelligence units within the CIA remained skeptical. But these were exceptional, cautionary flags in a race toward air war that nearly everyone—certainly all the top decision-makers—agreed had to be run.

In the middle of this well-oiled machinery for war, a monkey wrench was thrown. The plans for escalation ground temporarily to a halt. The cause was a move by General Khanh and younger officers to oust the civilians from power on the night of December 19, 1964. The details of this crisis are not important here, but the effect was to introduce a long period of delay. During this time President Johnson, operating through Ambassador Taylor, sought to use the threat of holding back on increased military involvement as a way of forcing the military to accept civilian rule. This Johnson rightly deemed important to forestall mounting domestic criticism of the Vietnam War. This criticism, articulated by antiwar Senator Wayne Morse, was shared by a growing number of Americans. Johnson's pressure at first seemed to have some effect on Khanh. The eventual outcome, however, was the completion of the coup and the establishment of outright military rule on January 28, 1965.

Johnson was guided by his fear of collapse of the government in the South. Counting on escalation as a new hope for a solution to the conflict, Johnson could only protest the coup. In fact the United States was deeply committed to the new regime and to escalation. Khanh was therefore able to call Johnson's bluff and refuse to accede to the democratic trappings the Americans wished to impose for the sake of domestic opinion.

For example, only the day before the coup, McGeorge Bundy and Robert McNamara had written a memorandum to

Johnson which acknowledged the need to shore up the Saigon regime but concluded, "We are both convinced that none of this is enough, and that the time has come for harder choices." [28] The National Liberation Front, they believed, was making rapid gains. It was encouraged by a perceived lack of American will and power. It was time to support the South through escalation. Of the top decision-makers, only Rusk opposed this. Rusk favored the then-current policies, without either escalation or withdrawal.

Shorn of democratic pretense, American defense of Saigon became more unpopular than ever. Historically, however, American citizens have rallied behind presidential military moves *after* they had been taken. The proposed escalation was interpreted in this light. For this reason public opinion was not a crucial factor in the decisions of this period.

A Policy of Escalating Reprisals

On the basis of acceptance of the Khanh government, American policy-making moved quickly. On February 7, 1965, the National Liberation Front (NLF) undertook a major attack on an American "advisers" barracks at Pleiku. Johnson took this as cause to decide upon the policy of retaliation long urged by the JCS and others. He met with the NSC the same day (February 6, Washington time). With the support of McGeorge Bundy, Taylor, and Westmoreland, President Johnson ordered reprisal air strikes against the North, even though Soviet Premier Kosygin was visiting there. Even George Ball, representing the State Department, concurred.

Of those present the only dissent came from Senate Majority Leader Mike Mansfield, who had been invited to the meeting along with House Speaker McCormack. Mansfield feared direct Chinese involvement or at least a healing of the Sino-Soviet split. Johnson rejected these views. "We have kept our gun on the mantle and our shells in the cupboard for a long time now," he said. "And what was the result? They are killing our men while they sleep at night. I can't ask our American soldiers out there to continue to fight with one hand tied behind their backs." [29] Johnson's feelings were strengthened by intelligence reports which cast doubt on the validity of Mansfield's fears about China.

What Johnson authorized was a long-prepared reprisal plan the JCS titled "Flaming Dart." Flaming Dart was implemented within fourteen hours after news of the Pleiku attack. Forty-nine Navy jets bombed the Dong Hoi guerrilla barracks in North Vietnam. Further strikes were conducted the following day. Anticipating escalation, American dependents were evacuated from Saigon.

Late on the evening of February 6, a study group led by McGeorge Bundy and John McNaughton returned from talks with Taylor and Westmoreland in Saigon. The Bundy report pictured a "deteriorating" situation. It concluded that the best means to aid the Khanh regime was a policy of "sustained reprisal." This policy explicitly committed the United States to a long war in Asia. McNaughton wrote: "Measured against the costs of defeat in Vietnam, this program seems cheap." [30]

On the morning of February 8, Johnson met with the Bundy brothers, McNamara, Wheeler, McNaughton, McCone, Ball, and others. All supported the Bundy reprisal plan. Only the JCS disagreed, preferring reprisals to be intense immediately rather than gradually escalating.

With this consensus achieved, Mansfield, McCormack, and their Republican counterparts (Senator Everett Dirksen and Representative Gerald Ford) were admitted to the room. McNamara and Ball briefed them and President Johnson summarized "our position." The war consensus was drawn tighter among the top decision-makers.

On February 10, 1965, the NLF attacked the American base at Qui Nhon, killing twenty-three Americans. Johnson again called an NSC meeting which again consensually decided upon further air strikes. Disagreement came only from George Ball and Vice President Hubert Humphrey. They argued only that retaliation should await Kosygin's departure. Except for deleting one target near Hanoi, this dissent was overruled. A new series of raids was authorized.

Thus a threefold policy emerged from the February 10 meeting. First, sustained air actions would be taken against the North. Second, the "pacification" (counterguerrilla) program would be intensified in the South. And third, North Vietnamese "aggression" would be publicized, using the United Nations as a forum. On February 13, Taylor reported to Johnson that "our decision had been received in Saigon with 'deep enthusiasm.' " [31] Under the new policy President Johnson authorized the JCS to begin their operation titled "Rolling Thunder." This was a program of "measured and limited" but nonetheless sustained bombing of North Vietnam.

Escalation on the Ground

The policy of escalation got off to a slow start. Rolling Thunder had to be delayed until March 2, 1965, due to political turmoil in South Vietnam culminating in Khanh's ouster. During this period Rusk launched a major public-relations drive to justify American policy. By obfuscating intentions *not* to negotiate until the situation in the South improved, he deflected mounting demands that Johnson declare his willingness to negotiate a peace.

Among the top decision-makers, debate centered on the meaning of "limited" in the policy of "limited but sustained" bombing. Taylor and McGeorge Bundy favored intensification of attacks in a systematic, progressive way. Taylor believed this would pressure the North to cease intervention, while Bundy saw improving South Vietnamese morale as the rationale. For Taylor such intensification was an alternative to ground war in the South, about which he had many misgivings. But the JCS and Westmoreland influenced Johnson to view the two as complementary.

On March 24, McNaughton presented Johnson with a memorandum urging extreme measures against the North, and intervention of U.S. combat troops in the South. On April 1, McGeorge Bundy advocated a lesser version of McNaughton's proposals. This plan allowed slow escalation of Rolling Thunder against the North and allowed the Marines to play an aggressive role in the South. This "compromise" plan was approved by the NSC on April 2. It became official policy under NSAM 328 on April 6.

Thus the inauguration of an American combat role did not come as part of a great internal debate among the top decision-makers. Rather it was a corollary to a consensual policy of air-war escalation. Only one dissent might have been important. CIA director McCone had been impressed with evidence showing that air bombing to date had been counterproductive. It had only served to strengthen North Vietnamese commitment to the war. McCone wrote a memorandum stating that without an all-out air bombing of the North, the NSAM 328 policy on combat troops in the South would only serve to mire American forces down in endless ground warfare. This memorandum did not reach the president, however, until after NSAM 328 had become policy. By then McCone himself had been replaced as CIA director by Admiral Raborn. Acting on Raborn's advice, Johnson called a temporary halt to the bombing. When negotiations failed to materialize in a few days, Johnson used this as justification for an intensified stage of bombing.

Almost unnoticed, the ground war began to escalate as well. Two Marine battalions were sent to Danang on March 6, bringing American troop totals to 27,000. Some 20,000 more troops had been added by the beginning of May. By the end of June 1965, 28,000 more had arrived. This emerging trend toward escalation on the ground surfaced in top-level debate. In mid-April 1965, Ambassador Taylor became increasingly upset about "what he regarded as Washington's excessive eagerness to introduce U.S. combat forces into South Vietnam." [32] He was also upset that Washington refused to escalate the air war faster. In a cable to McGeorge Bundy on April 18, Taylor expressed his oposition to the combat troop build-up.

The Honolulu Conference

Taylor's dissent formed the background to the Honolulu Conference of April 20, 1965. This conference was attended by Taylor, McNamara, Westmoreland, Wheeler, Sharp, McNaughton, and William Bundy. Here a compromise agreement was hammered out which overruled Taylor's objections. It called for a "plateau" on air strikes in the North coupled with a build-up of ground forces in the South. This decision reflected the emerging understanding that the bombings were not succeeding in driving the North to the bargaining table on American terms.

As this became readily apparent, the rationale for the bombing shifted. Where once bombing advocates cited the need to force negotiations, now they emphasized interdicting supply routes to the South. Increasingly, the war in the South came to seem the key to the Vietnamese conflict. The Honolulu Conference constituted a compromise only insofar as the increase of ground troops in the South was labeled part of a build-up of "enclaves" advocated by Taylor. It was not yet an explicit program for a major American combat role. Johnson endorsed the conference's compromise.

In June 1965, Johnson granted Westmoreland's request for authority to use American troops to assist South Vietnamese units in emergencies. Shortly thereafter Johnson also authorized the use of American combat troops apart from South Vietnam units if the South Vietnamese government so requested and Westmoreland considered their use "necessary." By the end of June American troops were participating in their first major search-and-destroy operations. They rapidly became an integral part of the ground war in the South. In July, McNamara, after visiting Saigon, reported a deteriorating situation to Johnson. The president then announced the sending of 50,000 more combat troops to Vietnam with additional units to follow.

Thus, during the spring and summer of 1965, it had become evident that an escalated bombing program had been countered by North Vietnam infiltrating a whole regiment into the South. Taylor found himself no longer able to argue against escalated American ground warfare under these circumstances. Much as he might want to avoid an American Dien Bien Phu, Taylor saw the need for an American response to Hanoi's own counter-response. Honolulu had seemed to Taylor a compromise, committing American troops to a presence in Vietnam but not to an aggressive combat strategy. This "enclave" strategy was short-lived, however. In retrospect it seemed a mere rationale for escalating the ground war without saying so. It was only a matter of a short time before NLF pressure, the demands of Westmoreland for a freer hand, and Johnson's own get-the-job-done temperament combined to discard the enclave strategy in favor of an explicit American combat role.

This was accomplished in June and July of 1965. A few, such as George Ball of the State Department, were reluctant to see Johnson follow this path. But after Honolulu—a conference in which the military decision-makers were the predominant influence—men like Ball were left with a *fait accompli.* The major American troop escalation had already been decided upon. In May and June there was full evidence of the presence of North Vietnamese army units in the South. Westmoreland insisted that the American troops already in the field be used to aid the dangerously weak Saigon regime. For Ball to argue against this seemed an argument for acceptance of defeat.

Johnson, who had seen what the Republicans had done to his party over the issue of "losing China," was not about to "lose Vietnam" to the Communists. At the same time, however, Johnson was fearful of public reaction against having "American boys do what Asian boys should be doing for themselves," as he had put it in his election campaign. Thus Johnson authorized a major American combat role, but he sought to keep it secret as long as possible. When a leak by a minor State Department briefing officer released the story for American headlines, Johnson sought to deny it. The White House falsely claimed the American mission was unchanged. This credibility gap, as the press called it, was to grow into a major domestic issue as the Vietnam War wore on.

Summary

What can the decision-making approach tell us about power in America? It has clear limits (recall Chapter 3). In selecting a case like the escalation decision, critics can always claim the case is atypical. Hundreds of other decisions might have been selected, possibly leading to different results. Even if one accepts the representativeness of the case chosen, it has not been possible to undertake a full decision-making study. We have not interviewed the top decision-makers, we have not surveyed the historical background in detail, we have not traced the decision over a long period of time.

Even if we look at decision-making studies of the Vietnam escalation which *have* done the best in this regard, it is still impossible to "measure" the many influences which motivate top decision-makers. We do not know, for example, the weight to be given to the effects of Johnson's schooling, his religion, his career history, the historic experiences of his generation, the effect upon him of the media and of public opinion, and so on. That is, the decision-making approach neglects the indirect or implicit aspects of power discussed in Chapter 1.

We may speculate upon these things as Halberstam does brilliantly in his book, *The Best and the Brightest*. In the end, however, we have no "scientific" assessment of the causal factors of a decision. There is no possible quantitative measurement of power in terms of "scope of outcomes," "number of actors influenced," or the "value of outcome to actor." A decision is a subtle matter. It is infinitely complex and motivated by factors only sometimes apparent even to the decision-makers themselves. The decision-making approach always leaves room for many interpretations of the same event.

Pluralist and Elite-Theory Interpretations

Nonetheless, the study of the Vietnam escalation decision does point to some conclusions about power in America. We noted earlier, for example, that the decision-makers were unrepresentative of the American people—in social background, connections to business and wealth, in age, sex, and race, and in the toughness of their views on the war. But though their opinions were more hard-line than those held by the public, American commitment to fight in Vietnam was a bipartisan policy of long standing. As such, Vietnam strategy could be and was discussed in the vocabulary of anticommunism. Justification largely ignored the rhetoric of protecting American economic interests or placating business pressures. The case bears out some of the expectations of *both* the pluralists and the elite theorists.

For those who picture America as pluralist in power structure, comfort might be found in emphasizing that this key decision was *not* made by a conspiratorial group of behind-the-scenes actors. Business people did not appear as string-pullers

manipulating government leaders. Rather, the decision to escalate the war in Vietnam was made by an elected leader and his
appointees. The decision, while unpopular, was still supported
by most Americans after it became known. Those participating
in the decision represented diverse backgrounds: business (Mc-
Namara), academia (McNaughton and McGeorge Bundy), the
military (Wheeler, Westmoreland, Sharp, Taylor), and professional political and administrative life (Rusk, Johnson). Although elite theorists might expect those with business backgrounds to be the most "imperialistic" on the war, the individual
among the top decision-makers who most openly expressed dovish opinions was George Ball, and Ball came to the State Department from a career as an investment banker.

Pluralists may thus contend that decision-makers from diverse backgrounds hammered out a difficult decision which they
were entitled to make. They may be seen as being free from
conspiratorial selfish interests intervening behind the scenes.
The decision was later supported by the American people. In
this interpretation of power, democratic principles are upheld.
While the specialization of labor assures that such decisions
must be made by a relative few, there is no elite dominance.
There is no rule in the interests of a select class of interests.

Yet elite theorists are not without their own comfort in
analyzing the Vietnam decision. This decision, after all, was
made by a surprisingly small number of men. These men, in
the main, shared a socially elite or business-connected background which, while not fully homogenous, had very little
diversity. This may account for their attitudes on escalation of
the war being well "in advance of" (which is to say not supported by) American public opinion prior to escalation. Because these hard-line views were not those of the public, Johnson intentionally campaigned in 1964 to portray himself as a
peace candidate opposed to escalation. After his election he
sought to keep the decision process and its outcomes secret.
This was true not only during the deliberations themselves, but
even after the decision was being implemented on the battle-
field. While the public came to support this *fait accompli* temporarily, it hardly illustrates the democratic process as normally
understood.

Alternative Theories

Classic democratic theory is clearly not upheld in the case of the Vietnam escalation. But can the elite theorists really claim that this decision shows an elite acting in the interest of a select class of interests? Many wish to argue that the decision is elitist only in the sense that all bureaucracy is elitist. That is, perhaps there is something like Michels's "iron law of oligarchy" at work (recall Chapter 2). A small group may make a decision, even a bad and unpopular decision, but that need not make it a *class* elite. They may simply represent the few who necessarily form the peak of organizational life, struggling to maintain their position as best they can muddle through the turbulent currents of politics.

This theory of the Vietnam decision emphasizes politics as a reflection not of the democratic process (pluralism) or of elite interests (elite theory), but rather as a reflection of the nature of the bureaucratic system. But "the nature of the system" is a vague concept for political analysis. It means different things to different people. For some it has to do with the characteristic *social psychology* of bureaucrats. Others see a kind of *bureaucratic pathology* at work. Still others emphasize the *ethnocentrism* of American bureaucrats. These different emphases are not mutually exclusive.

The social psychology of bureaucrats is emphasized in Irving Janis's book, *Victims of Groupthink* (1972). Janis analyzed the Vietnam and other foreign-policy miscalculations. In each he found patterns predicted by social psychological studies of groups under stress. For such groups, including the top Vietnam decision-makers, there is a tendency to seek psychological comfort by mutual acceptance of a comforting definition of the situation. The group chooses a way of looking at things which upholds group values. Then vigorous social pressures are brought on group members to conform to the consensus.

For example, in the case of the Vietnam escalation, the comforting common view defined the Indochina war as a Korean-type conflict involving Northern aggression by an enemy thinking in rational (cost-benefit) terms. In this definition of the situation, the decision-makers simply had to make the benefits of aggression too costly to pursue rationally. This consensus represented what Janis calls "groupthink."

The bureaucratic mentality associated with "groupthink" displays three main characteristics. First, the top decision-makers tended to uncritically accept black-and-white characterizations of the Communist and non-Communist sides to the conflict. Second, they distanced themselves from the conflict. This was done by depersonalizing the war by abstract discussion of "body counts," "surgical air strikes," and "pacification." Third, dissenting group members were brought under pressure to conform. Johnson, for example, branded George Ball as "Mr. Stop-the-Bombing." Similarly he ridiculed the peace proposals of the liberal Americans for Democratic Action before a secret session of key decision-makers.[33]

Morton Halperin, a former NSC staff member, described a similar bureaucratic mentality in *Bureaucratic Politics and Foreign Policy* (1974). Halperin discussed three types of bureaucrats. First, the president reflects "uncommitted thinking." This sort of thinking is oriented toward keeping options open and making decisions which gain the support of as wide a group of advisers as possible. Second, those concerned with broad national security issues reflect "ideological thinking." They simplify problems by relating everything to a particular ideology, like anticommunism, which helps determine their decisions. Third, agency staff, as within the JCS, reflect "grooved thinking." They have a programmed response to situations like military threat. This response enhances the role of the departments they work for.

Halperin described how the bureaucratic mentality affects decision-making. Information reported to senior officials is biased according to departmental interests. In the Vietnam decision, for example, the air force routinely exaggerated the effectiveness of their bombing programs.[34] Information is also biased according to personal self-interest. For instance, George Ball supported the initiation of bombing against his own convictions, which he withheld. He did this to stay "in the mainstream" and not sacrifice future influence over Vietnam decision-making.[35] Information sources themselves may thus become stereotyped and irrationally ignored. Ball became cast as a devil's advocate whose objections were discounted before he expressed them. As Halperin observed, permitting this kind of typecast dissent preserves the fiction that the decision was preceded by controversy. Finally, the top decision-maker will often try to respond to his or her advisers by a compromise that gives something for everyone. In the Vietnam escalation, the compromise was the Honolulu Conference plan: increased air war *and* increased ground war *and* the possibility of an enclave holding strategy *and* the hope for negotiations later.[36]

The consensual, interest-enhancing bureaucratic pattern of decision-making is incremental in nature. It proceeds a step at a time, often on the basis of biased information. Townsend Hoopes, a deputy assistant secretary of defense in 1965, put much of the blame for the Vietnam decision on incrementalism. During the Eisenhower, Kennedy, and especially Johnson years, Hoopes noted, there had been a radical decline in the long-term, policy-making function (the Policy Planning Staff) within the State Department.[37] Incrementalism thrives on the kind of bureaucratic environment of cozy consensus that existed in this decision, Hoopes argued.[38] Lack of long-term planning went hand-in-hand with lack of strong exponents of serious alternative policies. Matters become all the worse when the cozy bureaucratic consensus is ethnocentric and insists on imposing a black-and-white ideology (anticommunism) on a culture whose situation does not fit these terms.[39]

Alexander George is among those who have viewed the closed bureaucratic circle as the basic problem in foreign-policy-making. True, advisers and advocates under Johnson took different positions on the escalation. They debated them before the president. But the full range of relevant alternative options was not considered. In particular, with George Ball typecast into a minor role, no serious study was given to preparing for a face-saving exit from Vietnam. The "debate" took place within the narrow limits of a consensus. The "alternative" options all assumed escalation. To avoid this bureaucratic syndrome, George argued, the president must institutionalize "multiple advocacy" in the foreign-policy bureaucracy. Important spokespersons must be assigned the role of defending *each* of the *full* range of relevant options, not just those within the bureaucratic consensus.[40]

Conclusion

As with pluralist and elite-theory interpretations of the Vietnam escalation decision, there are problems with the "bureaucratic-nature" theory, too. On the positive side, bureaucratic-nature theory is highly descriptive. The bureaucracy *did* seem to operate in the incremental, consensual, information-distorting manner this theory predicts. This theory also dispenses with the need to emphasize behind-the-scenes group influences, whether elitist or pluralist in nature. Since such influences did not seem important, bureaucratic-nature theory avoids some of the problems of the pluralist and elite-theory perspectives.

But bureaucratic-nature theory only explains *how* power operates. It does not explain *why* the result in this case was *what* it was. The fact that the top decision-makers shared a hard-line anti-Communist consensus is treated as mere happenstance. Marxist theorists, in contrast, might say that that consensus was a direct reflection of the *implicit* power of capitalist drives for world hegemony and the defeat of anticapitalist movements around the globe. Even though capitalists themselves were not lurking directly behind the scenes, elite theorists say, they were nonetheless the "real" powers at work. This is because the top decision-makers were under their implicit power. That is, the top decision-makers had been socialized to accept capitalist culture and capitalist world-views.

Bureaucratic-nature theorists like Janis and George argue that it is *not* necessary to change capitalism to change the outcome of decisions. They suggest bureaucratic reforms to improve organizational rationality. Basically, they propose to institutionalize comprehensive planning procedures and devil's advocates to assure that the bureaucracy treats seriously and fairly the full range of policy options. But elite theorists say that this is self-contradictory. If bureaucratic nature is as Janis, George, and others say it is, then the bureaucracy will find ways to make its nature known regardless of the proposed reforms.

The nonconsensual options in comprehensive plans will receive only pro forma consideration. The devil's advocates will continue to be typecast and discounted, just as George Ball was. Basic political patterns will not disappear merely because organizational structure is altered slightly.

In summary, bureaucratic-nature theorists see the Vietnam escalation decision rooted in flaws in organizational structure and communications flow. Elite theorists, in contrast, say that these flaws are not basic *causes* at all. Rather the distortion of information and other flaws are *caused by* the same thing that caused the decision to have the outcome it did. That is, anti-communism and capitalist culture, combined with the bureaucratic elite decision-making process, assured that a hard line would be emphasized within the air force and other departments (causing "flawed" or distorted information on war prospects) *and* at the top levels of decision-making (causing a consensus on escalation).

The decision-making approach really cannot settle this dispute. What it settles is only shifting the focus to the importance of *implicit* power. This illustrates what was said in Chapter 1. If aspects of capitalist culture, like anticommunism, indirectly distributes power in favor of capitalist interests, perhaps an elite-theory view can be sustained. But the information we need to know cannot be found in the direct study of decision-making. Therefore in the next few chapters we will look at some other approaches to the study of power which *do* claim to tell us something about the indirect or implicit side of power.

Notes

1. *The Pentagon Papers: The Defense Department History of United States Decision-Making on Vietnam* (Boston: Beacon Press, 1971), Senator Gravel Edition, 5 vols. The present case study draws upon this work and related documentation.
2. Lyndon Baines Johnson, *The Vantage Point: Perspectives on the Presidency, 1963–1969* (New York: Holt, Rinehart, and Winston, 1971), p. 152.

3. Tom Wicker, *JFK and LBJ: The Influence of Personality on Politics* (Baltimore: Penguin, 1969), p. 208.
4. David Halberstam, *The Best and the Brightest* (New York: Random House, 1972), p. 306.
5. Ibid., p. 219.
6. Johnson, *Vantage Point*, p. 20.
7. Wicker, *JFK and LBJ*, p. 199.
8. Halberstam, *Best and Brightest*, p. 307.
9. Ibid., p. 393.
10. See John Mueller, *War, Presidents, and Public Opinion* (New York: Wiley, 1973), pp. 81–83. See also Ralph Stavens, "Washington Determines the Fate of Vietnam," in R. Stavens, R. Barnet, and M. Raskin, eds., *Washington Plans an Aggressive War* (New York: Random House, 1971), p. 105.
11. Halberstam, *Best and Brightest*, p. 361.
12. Quoted in Rowland Evans and Robert Novak, *Lyndon B. Johnson: The Exercise of Power* (London: Allen and Unwin, 1967), pp. 531–32.
13. Johnson, *Vantage Point*, p. 68.
14. See Theodore H. White, *The Making of the President 1964* (New York: New American Library, 1965), ch. 10.
15. Stavins, "Washington Determines Fate of Vietnam," p. 94n.
16. Peter Dale Scott, "Vietnamization and the Drama of the Pentagon Papers," in Noam Chomsky and Howard Zinn, eds., *The Pentagon Papers*, Vol. 5 (Boston: Beacon Press, 1972), pp. 216 ff.
17. Public Papers of the Presidents of the United States: Lyndon B. Johnson, 1963–1964, Vol. 2 (Washington, D.C.: USGPO, 1965), pp. 926–927.
18. *Pentagon Papers*, Vol. 3, pp. 184–85.
19. Ibid., p. 185.
20. Johnson, *Vantage Point*, p. 117.
21. Stavins, "Washington Determines Fate of Vietnam," pp. 98–99.
22. Wicker, *JFK and LBJ*, p. 238.
23. *Pentagon Papers*, Vol. 3, p. 132.
24. Ibid., p. 193.
25. Ibid., p. 135.
26. Ibid., p. 247.
27. Johnson, *Vantage Point*, p. 121.
28. Ibid., p. 123.
29. Ibid., p. 125.
30. Ibid., pp. 127–28.
31. Ibid., p. 130.
32. *Pentagon Papers*, Vol. 3, p. 274.
33. Irving L. Janis, *Victims of Groupthink* (Boston: Houghton-Mifflin, 1972).
34. Morton H. Halperin, *Bureaucratic Politics and Foreign Policy* (Washington, D.C.: Brookings, 1974), p. 49.
35. Ibid., pp. 154–55.
36. Ibid., p. 210.
37. Townsend Hoopes, *The Limits of Intervention* (rev. ed.; New York: McKay, 1973; orig. 1969), pp. 5, 7.
38. Ibid., pp. 7, 218.

39. The ethnocentrism theme is discussed in Francis Fitzgerald, *Fire in the Lake* (Boston: Little, Brown, 1972); and in Ralph K. White, *Nobody Wanted War* (Garden City, N.Y.: Doubleday Anchor, 1970), ch. 10.

40. Alexander L. George, "The Case for Multiple Advocacy in Making Foreign Policy," *American Political Science Review* 66 (September 1972): 772–73.

6. The Reputational and Positional Approaches

Political decisions often ultimately rest on diffuse forces such as culture, socialization, and role sets. Because of their importance, political analysis must take account of the concept of implicit power. Since implicit power cannot be studied directly as by a decision-making approach (how can one study what is implicit, a nondecision?), many have suggested political scientists look to some *indirect* indicator of power. An indirect measure would tap the net effect of both overt and implicit aspects of power. Moreover, such a measure would reflect the effect of power over millions of decisions, not just the one or two cases surveyed in a decision-making study. Finally, a good indirect measure would not be limited to power in government alone. It would also take account of power in the private sector. This is desirable because "private government" has as much to do with "who gets what, when, and how" as does government proper.[1]

What is an indirect indicator of power? It is anything that measures an aggregate effect of power. Power has many generalized effects: it shapes people's reputations for influence; it enables people to hold important positions; it generates the distribution of benefits in society. Each of these has been proposed as an indirect measure of power in American politics. The first two are discussed in the remainder of Chapter 6; the distribution of benefits is treated in Chapter 7.

Indicators of Power: Reputation

The reputational approach was outlined briefly in Chapter 3. Lower-level power-holders are questioned about their perceptions of which individuals hold greater power. Progressively higher-level power-holders are then questioned, refining the list of power-holders at each step. Eventually a final list of individuals with the greatest reputation for power is obtained. Reputation is then taken as an indicator of indirect, cumulative effects of overt and implicit power. As an indicator, reputation for power has the advantage of being partially self-validating. That is, since people must act on the basis of their perceptions of reality, reputation for power by itself elicits deference, subordination, and compliance. That is, reputation for power may become indistinguishable from power itself.

Relatively few scholars have utilized this approach at the national level. An exception is the work of Floyd Hunter. The reputational method may be illustrated by a brief presentation of his work, *Top Leadership USA* (1959).

Set in the Eisenhower period, Hunter's study used the multistaged interviewing procedure outlined in Chapter 3. The purpose was to test the hypothesis that there is a circuit (as opposed to a pyramidal structure) of people who represent many influence groups and regions. While these people may sometimes disagree, they are united in a shared common interest in the corporate system. This circuit, Hunter believed, was informal and not highly visible. Nonetheless, it tied together decision-makers whose intercommunications and interactions served to formulate national policy in advance of public discussion of issues.

In order to establish the existence of such a network or circuit of decision-makers it was necessary for Hunter to devise some criterion for "top leadership." As indicated, the criterion chosen was reputation for power. Using the reputational approach, Hunter developed a list of the top 500 influential persons in America.

The base of his interviewing procedure started with Chambers of Commerce and Community Chests (United Funds). Since these are predominantly business-linked associations, his sample of top influentials was biased toward inclusion of people in business. This tendency was compounded by the fact that the Eisenhower administration included a disproportionate number of corporate representatives in comparison with later administrations.

Nonetheless, recognizing that Hunter's list of power-holders is in many ways arbitrary, the reputational method does not require that one establish the exact composition of the top 500. It is enough that the list of top influentials seem on face validity to include many who are commonly regarded as national decision-making leaders. While Hunter's list was unrepresentative in some respects (too many business people, too few academics), Hunter did develop a list of very powerful individuals. The list included, for example, such figures as Dwight Eisenhower, Sherman Adams, Roger Blough, Arthur Burns, Vannevar Bush, Harry Byrd, James Conant, Thomas Dewey, John Foster Dulles, Marion Folsom, Averell Harriman, Christian Herter, Herbert Hoover, Hubert Humphrey, Lyndon Johnson, Walter Kohler, John McClellan, John McCormack, George Meany, Richard Nixon, Sam Rayburn, Nelson Rockefeller, Francis Spellman, Arthur Sulzberger, Thomas Watson, Charles Wilson, and many others. Though now mostly forgotten, these individuals were certainly leading figures of the 1950s.

Thus, even though Hunter's list of top influentials was not fully representative, it was still representative enough to warrant further investigation. Hunter found that the top 100 leaders each had communicated with an average of 65 other top leaders. Each also stated that they had worked with an average of 40 other top leaders on at least one issue. The favored means of personal contact among the top 100 was direct, by telephone. Over half the top 100 had served on the Business Advisory Council (BAC). BAC was a highly prestigious adjunct to the Commerce Department. It served as a vehicle for transmission of ideas between the administration and the business community (BAC has now been reorganized as the Business Council and is independent of the Commerce Department). Less extensive but still substantial interaction levels were found in leadership levels just below the top 100.

In order to validate this evidence on the existence of a circuit of top power-holders, Hunter related the top influentials to a particular decision-making case, the textile tariff issue. The business-related nature of the case chosen further biased Hunter's conclusions in favor of finding business powerful. The decision-making aspect of Hunter's study was further undermined by only a 33 percent response among top influentials to his questionnaire on this issue. Of those responding, however, 73 percent had heard about the issue directly from textile industry leaders. Some 19 percent stated they had worked directly with other members of the top 100 on this issue.[2] A much larger percentage held an interest in the tariff issue and had working relationships with other group members on the basis of which they could have exercised their influence had they chosen to do so. These relationships are illustrated in Figure 6-1.

Hunter's evidence, while subject to criticism, presents a case for the existence of a relatively compact "circuit" of top decision-makers. During the late 1950s these leaders were known to each other, communicated with each other, had working relationships with each other, and on a specific test issue (textile tariffs) many collaborated together. This top leadership group was predominantly corporate and financial in institutional composition.

Hunter's work is suggestive, if inconclusive. Apart from his reputational method, however, Hunter's impressions, based on his hundreds of interviews with leaders, are also interesting. Based on statements culled from his extensive interviews, Hunter developed a specific theory of political process. In forming policy, he said, top leaders seek out others on their rough level who have similar interests, and then seek to organize them. Those who do not want to participate are not pressured to do so, but there is a general business consensus on most matters. Hence politics tends to be a matter of activating potential leaders, not convincing them. This is especially so on key issues such as taxation or fiscal policy, less so in foreign policy. In this process leaders directly affected by an issue mobilize people they know can "cue" the business community to a particular policy position.

Such mobilization takes place, however, only when a policy affects or potentially affects leaders adversely. On most issues

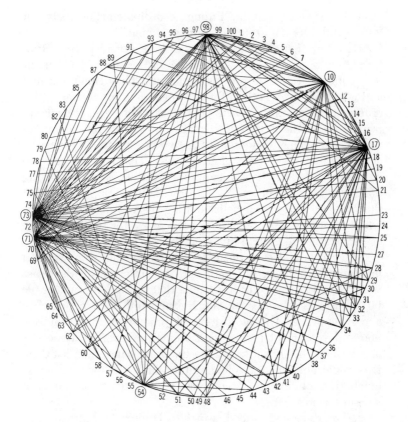

Figure 6-1 Working Relationships between Six National Leaders and Seventy-Seven Peers on the Tariff Issue, 1958. Numbers Are Code Numbers of Top Leaders. *From Floyd Hunter,* Top Leadership USA *(Chapel Hill: University of North Carolina Press, 1959), Figure 5, p. 219. Reprinted with the kind permission of the author and publisher.*

businessmen are content to let professional politicians run the routine aspects of politics. When exceptional cases come along, however, the business influentials know men specialized in contacting politicians—a lawyer here, a banker there. In this way, Hunter concluded, "politics get decided and moved, not by magic, but by men. They get moved, not altogether by men elected to public office, but through coordinate actions between formal and informal groups of interested men." [3]

If reputation can be taken as an indicator of power, Hunter's study seemed to show that there did exist an inner circuit if not inner circle of top decision-makers. They communicated and acted with each other. Businessmen were prominent in this group, as were professional politicians. The reputational approach shed little light on the relative powers of business vis-à-vis the politicians. If anything the two groups seemed inextricably intertwined in a symbiotic process. That is, since the two were not in conflict it was inappropriate to speak of one being dominant over the other. Nonetheless, Hunter emphasized that the common underlying belief uniting the top decision-makers, whether in business or politics, was a sense for the importance of protecting the growth of American economic interests.

Pluralists and elite theorists might both find some support in Hunter's findings, but both find discomforting evidence, as well. Pluralists can point to the fact that in the long run, textile tariff business interests lost out. Business did not "dominate" in a narrow sense. The motivation of promoting American economic development is a general public interest, not a specifically business or class interest. On the other hand, pluralist theorists might not expect the finding that influence operated not so much through interest groups as on a person-to-person basis among top influentials.

Elite theorists, indeed, can cite Hunter to buttress their claim that there is an identifiable national elite which is business-linked. But elite theorists must be discomforted by evidence that professional politicians rather than businessmen figured so critically among the top influentials and were crucial links holding the network of top influentials together. Taken together with the findings of Bauer, Pool, and Dexter on tariff politics in the 1950s, which also emphasized the autonomy of the professional politician and the weakness of business interest groups, it is difficult to portray politics as dominated by a business elite.[4]

In sum, Hunter's reputational approach provides tentative evidence for the existence of a coherent governing elite with striking business connections. Not only are those reputed to hold power in a working relationship with one another, they also seem to display a relatively consensual approach to working together. Other purportedly important political forces in America—unions, academics, farmers, blacks, and so on—have little representation among the top influentials by reputation. The political and the economic do display an elite leadership pattern according to this evidence, but they form parts of a consensual system. The political cannot, on this evidence, be said to reflect a host of small interests scattered across a plurality of groups in American society. Nor does the image seem to hold of the political responding to the demands of an independent, dominant business interest.

Indicators of Power: Social Background

Social background is the indirect indicator of power used in the sociology-of-leadership (or positional) approach, discussed in Chapter 3. In this section we will investigate whether this indicator leads to conclusions similar to those just outlined. Radical and Marxist social scientists have preferred social backgrounds as an index to power distribution because it is clearly related to class analysis of politics, whereas reputation is not. Nonetheless, the sociology-of-leadership approach is far from monolithic. Both conservative and liberal or radical scholars have used it. While its use does bias the researcher somewhat in the direction of class analysis, it does not necessitate elite-theory conclusions.

Many political scientists have used the sociology-of-leadership approach and have come to conclusions consistent with pluralist political theory. Among the earliest was the oft-cited work of Donald Matthews, *Social Background of Political Decision-Makers* (1954). Matthews studied 311 presidents, vice-presidents, and cabinet officers from 1789 to 1934. Contrary to what elite theorists might expect, Matthews found that the professional upper-middle class—not the upper class—dominated politics. Some 70 percent were lawyers (considering the years since 1877). On the other hand, pluralists would have to concede that very, very few top leaders (4 percent) were children of workers, farm laborers, servants, or other parents of low social status.

In *Men Who Govern* (1967), David Stanley, Dean Mann, and Jameson Doig found a similar pattern. Their study of 1,000 top administrators filling 180 top positions in the administrations of Roosevelt through Johnson also showed a pattern of dominance by the professional upper-middle class. Most top leaders came from previous executive experience in government, law, and business. "Considering how different the jobs are," the authors concluded, "it is astonishing how much alike the men are . . . ; these executives come . . . from big government, big law, and big business." [5] Since "big law" is largely corporate law, this work does underline the bias of top American leadership toward overrepresentation of business interests and underrepresentation of other interests. Nonetheless, the upper class (the capitalists) cannot be said to dominate in terms of *directly* holding key governing roles.

A third study in the same vein was conducted by Thomas Dye in 1973. Dye studied 286 top American leaders, including the president, vice president, secretaries, undersecretaries and assistant secretaries of the departments, presidential advisers, ambassadors-at-large, key congressional leaders, Federal Reserve Board members, and top military leaders. These top leaders were not generally of upper-class origin. For example, only 10 percent attended private preparatory schools and only 6 percent attended the prestigious elite preparatory schools. (Such attendance is often taken as an indicator of upper-class status, or at least socialization to it.) While not upper class, the governing elite was *not* pluralistically representative of American society at large, however. Dye concluded that "studies consistently show that top business executives and top political decision-makers are atypical of the American public. They are recruited from the well-educated, prestigiously employed, older, successful, affluent, urban, white, Anglo-Saxon, upper and upper-middle class, male populations of the nation. We had expected our top institutional leaders to conform to this pattern and we were not at all disappointed." [6]

A fourth and final corroborating study was Robert Presthus's *Elites in the Policy Process* (1974). Presthus studied a fairly broad group of 249 political leaders. This included a sample of 100 U.S. congressmen and 149 state legislators. He found that only 10 percent considered themselves "upper class." On the other side, only 9 percent labeled themselves "working class." A separate sample of top U.S. civil servants (those over GS 17) showed similar results. Presthus also found a relatively high level of mobility. Though 79 percent of legislators and 97 percent of civil servants were in upper or upper-middle socioeconomic status (by occupational status and educational level) themselves, only one-third of their fathers had that high a status. In sum, Presthus's study also showed the absence of direct upper-class dominance. But it did show a pronounced bias toward the professional-lawyer-business upper-middle class. Some 99 percent of legislators and 99.5 percent of bureaucrats could be so classed by occupational status, compared to only 31 percent of the American population at large. The leadership elite was also different in political attitude. The overwhelming majority of the political elite displayed little political alienation or cynicism, whereas about half of the American public manifests high alienation and lack of trust in government.

Social Backgrounds and Elite Theory

The foregoing studies paint a picture of power in America which does *not* support the idea of an upper-class elite that dominates politics. Perhaps the governing group is not as pluralistic in terms of social class as might be desired. Perhaps businessmen and business-related professionals are heavily overrepresented. But the evidence cannot be stretched to portray American government as literally in the hands of members of a business upper class. How, then, do elite theorists use the sociology-of-leadership approach to support their arguments?

One way is to examine social backgrounds in *historical* context. The social backgrounds of leaders at critical, institution-founding historical turning points is particularly important. That may remain hidden in blanket surveys of the type discussed in the preceding section. The historical approach to the sociology-of-leadership is associated with the work of a conservative elite theorist named E. Digby Baltzell. Though conservative, Baltzell's work has many radical implications.

Baltzell's work traced the establishment of upper-class institutions in the late nineteenth and early twentieth centuries. In *Philadelphia Gentlemen: The Making of a National Upper Class* (1958) Baltzell showed the emergence of a dominant elite in the City of Brotherly Love. He documented the coalescing of "old families" in the Rittenhouse Square section of Philadelphia, the definition of "polite society," the emergence of a "new and more conspicuously colorful world known as 'Society'" in the 1880s, its formalization in the *Social Registers* of the 1890s, in boarding schools, men's clubs, and fashionable churches.[7]

Emerging from Baltzell's social history is the image of the Philadelphia gentleman. He is of English or Welsh descent, and his family had been in Philadelphia since Revolutionary War times. One of his ancestors had money or married well, leaving Quakerism for the more fashionable Episcopal Church. His family had been in the *Social Register* since its inception. He was educated at the Episcopal academy or another elite preparatory school. Later he went to Harvard, Yale, or Princeton, going on to law school at the University of Pennsylvania. He became a partner in a prestigious Philadelphia law firm. He came to sit on the board of directors of several cultural and economic institutions in the city. He lived in Chestnut Hill or on the Main Line. He had lunch with his peers at the Rittenhouse or Philadelphia clubs.

This image was an ideal type. Few would meet it completely, but it was a standard to which all might aspire. Similar studies in other cities pointed toward similar conclusions about the emergence of a national upper class in this period.[8] (This will be discussed further in Chapters 10 and 11.)

Baltzell's work contained a radical implication. It said that not only did a national upper class exist, but it was solidified around schools, churches, and other institutions. Not only was the upper class a statistical group (those with high incomes) but it was also a cohesive, self-conscious elite (sharing underlying orientations different from the general population). On the other hand, Baltzell admitted that the elitist nature of prestigious preparatory schools, colleges, men's clubs, churches, and the *Social Register* had declined markedly since World War II. "The class remains," he wrote, "but its authority, like that of parents, has rapidly declined." As upper-class social institutions were somewhat democratized, only politics provided a common link among upper-class representatives.[9] Baltzell's second work, *The Protestant Establishment* (1964), traced the rise and decline of these social institutions.

Baltzell's work showed a tradition of upper-class hegemony now increasingly diluted by upper-middle-class influences. Radical elite theorists argued, however, that the traditional upper class provided the mainstream of the governing elite. Though numerous and influential, the upper-middle-class professionals discussed by Baltzell and others were seen as well-socialized agents of upper-class beliefs.

The radical view assumes that there *are* distinguishable class-linked differences in political beliefs, and this is examined in Chapter 8. In the following section, however, we will review the radical argument that upper-class and big-business interests dominate American politics directly *or* through upper-middle-class professionals who are socialized to serve their interests.

C. Wright Mills's work, *The Power Elite* (1956), examined the class-linked pattern of recruiting top American leaders. Mills questioned the traditional image of the political career pattern. He denied that top leaders started in local politics and went through a lengthy series of intermediate positions before reaching national-level leadership. Mills found instead that top leadership positions were filled by men whose careers were as likely to have been outside politics as within it. The typical top leader and even typical second-level leader (such as departmental undersecretaries) had never before held political office prior to becoming a top national leader in the Eisenhower administration.

Top leaders, Mills found, were not only recruited in a nontraditional manner, they came from business and upper-class backgrounds. Of the top fifty governmental leaders (president, vice-president, cabinet members, major agency heads, and top presidential advisers), Mills found only 6 percent were professional politicians.[10] Another 18 percent were professional civil servants. Fully 75 percent were political outsiders. Of the bulk who were outsiders, over three-quarters were "quite closely linked, financially or professionally or both, with the corporate world and thus make up slightly over half of all the political directors." [11]

For example, the Department of State was headed by a New York lawyer who handled Morgan and Rockefeller interests. Treasury was headed by a Midwest executive who directed over thirty corporations. The Defense Department was headed by the former president of General Motors, which was then the largest producer of military equipment in the United States. Even the second-level deputy leaders usually had fathers who were big businessmen or were themselves businessmen, bankers, or corporate lawyers by background. "As a group," Mills concluded, "the political outsiders who occupy the executive command posts and form the political directorate are legal, managerial, and financial members of the corporate rich." [12]

The social background of key appointed government leaders was all the more important due to the growing importance of the executive branch of government. Congress seemed in a political decline, unable to cope with the growing complexity of government. They were apparently able only to respond to executive initiatives. Since congressmen tended to be more upper-middle-class or middle-class professionals (not necessarily closely connected to the corporate rich), Mills felt congressional decline worsened the class distribution of power in America. Congressmen were often connected to business, but this was usually local or regional business. The top executives, in contrast, were connected to national business. Mills therefore viewed Congress as being at merely "middle levels" of power.

Mills had tried to document the *corporate-linked* career pattern of top executive leaders of government. A later scholar, G. William Domhoff, undertook similar studies showing the connection of top leaders to the national *upper class*. In *Who Rules America?* (1967) Domhoff sought to prove:

1. That a social upper class exists.
2. That it holds disproportionate wealth and receives disproportionate income.
3. That its representatives disproportionately occupy top policy-making posts.
4. That it trains or indoctrinates many others to its perspectives,

notably top lawyers and managers in upper-class-dominated institutions.

His general approach was outlined in Chapter 3.

Domhoff defined membership in the social upper class by attendance at an elite preparatory school such as Groton or Choate, membership in an exclusive men's club such as the Cosmos or Links, being the child of a millionaire or of a $100,000-a-year executive, or being the close relative of such a person. Domhoff found, for example, that over half of the directors of the largest American corporations were upper class by these criteria. Similarly, Domhoff was able to show that the Council on Foreign Relations and the Committee for Economic Development and other prestigious policy-advisory groups were heavily upper-class-connected. The social upper class was also shown to have dominated the Business Council, a key business advisory group to government. Domhoff documented how various foundations and regulatory agencies were often upper class as well. Using similar criteria, Beth Mintz documented the social and business elite nature of the U.S. Cabinet (96 percent elite backgrounds under Nixon; 92 percent under Johnson; 65 percent under Kennedy; 95 percent under Eisenhower).[13] Domhoff corroborated Mills's finding that many high government posts are populated by members of the upper class.

Domhoff did *not* assert that there was a fully homogenous national governing elite. The elite, he admitted, often displayed internal disagreements. The elite was not omnipotent and did not triumph on every aspect where its interests were at stake. At lower levels of power, such as Congress or the state governments, a relatively pluralistic politics existed. Domhoff *did* argue, however, that there was a national social elite with a high overlap with key governing positions, that its internal disputes were overshadowed by common class-linked orientations (discussed in Chapter 8), and that it reaped the benefits of America's political economy in a very disproportionate way (discussed in Chapter 7).

Domhoff was able to document very extensive upper-class participation in the top levels of American government. Nonetheless, such direct upper-class influence over government is not the rule. As indicated in the previous section of this chapter, the upper-middle class of professionals, not the upper class, is the most numerous force in the higher echelons of government. Like Mills, Domhoff hypothesized that such professionals were well-socialized agents of upper-class interests. But where Mills emphasized the socializing effect of corporate connections, Domhoff emphasized socialization to upper-class perspectives through the elite policy associations.

As a case in point, Domhoff studied "How the Power Elite Set National Goals." This was a reference to the process that culminated in the Eisenhower administration statement, *Goals for Americans*. In late 1956 the Rockefeller Brothers Fund convened a panel of some 85 persons, predominantly corporate leaders, foundation officials, and leading members of various policy and academic groups. Some labor leaders and journalists were also invited. This panel was given a broad mandate to assess American priorities.

Future Secretary of State Henry Kissinger prepared two of the reports for the Rockefeller group. The final report was presented in 1958. This in turn prompted the Republican party to establish a "GOP Goals Committee" under Charles Percy (formerly president of Bell & Howell, later a Republican senator from Illinois). Eisenhower then established a blue-ribbon commission on national goals. A President's Commission on National Goals was announced in 1960, funded by the Rockefeller Foundation, the Ford Foundation, the Alfred Sloan Foundation, the Carnegie Corporation, the U.S. Steel Corporation, and three small foundations.

The President's Commission was administered by the American Assembly, "a discussion organization of big business and their advisers." [14] The eleven commissioners included the American Assembly president, the chairman of General Dynamics, the past president of the U.S. Chamber of Commerce, the past president of Harvard University, the past president of the University of Virginia (who was related by marriage and corporate directorships to the DuPont interests), a retired general, a retired judge, the heads of the University of California and of MIT, and the head of the AFL-CIO. A majority of those asked to write papers for the commission were corporate- and elite-connected. The staff was headed by William P. Bundy, on leave from the CIA, later to be a key decision-maker on Vietnam (discussed in Chapter 5), and a member of an upper-class Boston family.

While the *Goals for Americans* report was mainly symbolic, Domhoff contended that its elite-connected manner of formulation was typical of American policy process. Domhoff's studies stress the overlap between key policy-making groups (the Business Council, the Committee for Economic Development, the Conference Board, the Advertising Council, the Brookings Institution, the American Assembly, the Council on Foreign Relations) and elite social clubs (the Links, the Pacific Union, the Bohemian, the Century, and others). On such evidence Domhoff concluded that the governing elite displays striking cohesion. "Everything we know about socialization, status, small groups, and occupational roles would lead to the conclusion," he wrote, "that these people do develop an in-group feeling, a 'we-ness,' a class awareness (dare I say class consciousness?)." [15]

Criticisms of the Social-Backgrounds Approach

C. Wright Mills himself set forth with great clarity the limits of the sociology-of-leadership approach:

We cannot infer the direction of policy merely from the social origins and careers of the policy-makers. The social and economic backgrounds of the men of power do not tell us all that we need to know in order to understand the distribution of social power. For: (1) Men from high places may be ideological representatives of the poor and humble. (2) Men of humble origin, brightly self-made, may energetically serve the most vested and inherited interests. Moreover, (3) not all men who effectively represent the interests of a stratum need in any way belong to it. . . .

For the most important set of facts about a circle of men is the criteria of admission, of praise, of honor, of promotion that prevails among them; if these are similar within a circle, then they will tend as personalities to become similar. The circles that compose the power elite do tend to have such codes and criteria in common. The co-optation of the social types to which these common values lead is often more important than any statistic of common origin and career that we might have at hand.[16]

That is, the data on upper-class individuals holding key decision-making positions are merely suggestive. Such individuals are numerous and prominent enough that their importance as a class *may* be great *if*: (1) class is important in determining political beliefs and preferences (discussed in Chapter 8); *and if* (2) upper-class influence is multiplied by the co-optation of upper-middle-class professionals. Data on social backgrounds do not tell us much about either class beliefs or co-optation.

Of course, many other criticisms may be made of the sociology-of-leadership approach:[17]

1. Indicators of upper-class status (such as membership in elite clubs, listing in the *Social Register*) are arbitrary and of declining validity in recent times; since any *one* criterion is judged adequate for inclusion in "upper-class" status, many mistakes may be made.

2. Decision-makers with corporate backgrounds need not necessarily retain loyalties to or be influenced by their former business connections.

3. Ethnic, religious, and other differences among the upper class may outweigh the alleged consensus on "basic" upper-class interests.

4. The concept of upper-class interests is itself so broad as to be almost tautological (for example, even legalization of strikes or government unemployment payments are interpreted by elite theorists not as defeats for the upper class but rather as tactical concessions serving the upper-class interest of preventing worker radicalization).

5. Little is done to show *concretely* how upper-class status leads to influence over politics. (Domhoff cites the socializing influence of the elite policy associations, but his evidence here is based on impressions from a tiny number of cases.)

6. The upper class may not be class conscious. (Domhoff's evidence is limited to data showing high intermarriage rates among the upper class, overlapping membership in elite clubs and institu-

tions, and a common expensive life style—these suggest the possibility of class consciousness but do not prove it.)

All of these are valid criticisms. They qualify how we may interpret data based on social backgrounds as an indicator of the
distribution of power. But some qualified conclusions may still
be drawn.

Conclusion

On balance, the evidence from the study of social backgrounds
provides ammunition for the elite theorists. Consequently, radical scholars have often emphasized this approach to political
analysis. The social-class homogeneity of those who occupy top
governing positions in America is striking. These are not ordinary people. By class they are distinctly upper-middle and
upper class. The higher the political post occupied, the more
likely corporate and upper-class ties will be present.

The similarity of social backgrounds is the basis for expect-
ing a politics of elite consensus. One would not expect a politics
of pluralist conflict. Hunter's reputational study pointed in this
direction, finding a relatively harmonious pattern of political
and business elite interaction with nonbusiness interests being
of distinctly subordinate importance. C. Wright Mills discussed
this in terms of a political "theory of balance" centering on "the
conservative mood." [18] The politics of elite consensus was
stressed by Domhoff in his analysis of the overlap between cor-
porate- and upper-class-linked policy associations and the socialization of upper-middle-class government leaders like Secretary of State Henry Kissinger.

Robert Presthus's study, *Elites in the Policy Process* (1974),
also suggests a politics of elite consensus. In a survey of directors of interest groups, Presthus found that three-quarters *disagreed* with the notion that interest groups are competitors with
political leaders in a struggle to shape government policy. In
fact, three-fifths of the interest-group directors said they "en-
counter no consistent opposition from any source." [19] Presthus
found that legislative, bureaucratic, and interest-group elites

were much more likely to view interest-group activities as legitimate than do ordinary citizens. In part this reflected the similar
social backgrounds of these elites.

Ultimately, however, the sociology-of-leadership approach
does not uphold adequately an elite theory of American politics.
This is because upper-class individuals and those with direct
corporate or financial backgrounds, while numerous, are still a
minority of top policy-makers. True, the distribution of positions
of power is highly skewed toward the upper end of the socioeconomic status spectrum. But anyone who wishes to speak of
an elite "dominating" politics must account for the central role
of upper-middle-class professionals—the lawyers, the professional politicians, the career civil servants.

If American politics is to be portrayed in terms of elite consensus, then we must show how key upper-middle-class professionals are socialized agents of a social and business elite. The
sociology-of-leadership approach provides impressions but not
solid evidence on this score. True, politics is often one of elite
consensus—as shown in our study of the "cozy consensus" on
escalating the Vietnam War studied in Chapter 5. But how can
we distinguish between consensual politics born of elite influence
versus consensus born of coincidence of viewpoints not dependent on elite influence?

Two basic methods have been proposed. First, we can study
whether there is a distinctive social and business-elite point of
view. That is, we may question whether Mills and Domhoff are
correct in assuming that the governing elite coheres around
certain underlying basic interests and beliefs. This leads to
asking if the upper-middle-class professionals, who are most
numerous in government, take the side of elite opinion or of
public opinion. This issue is taken up in Chapter 8.

Second, we can study whether the policy outputs of the
governmental system favor the interests of the purported elites.
Unless benefits are distributed disproportionately toward the
elites, elite theory collapses. If the alleged elites behave, not in
their own interests, but like non-elites would if they held key
policy-making positions, then it would seem to make little difference *what* the social background of policy-makers is.

The next chapter examines this question of the distribution of benefits in America. For the moment, however, we must conclude that the sociology-of-leadership and reputational approaches provide evidence that does not clearly support either pluralist or elite theory. Again, if anything there is more evidence for viewing American politics as a consensual political economic *system* supported by—but not dominated by—homogenous upper-status social backgrounds of its leaders. Again, a systems approach may be better than a group approach (whether dominant-elite-group or many-group pluralist theory). This will be taken up in Chapter 12.

Notes

1. This criterion paraphrases Harold Lasswell's classic definition of politics in *Politics: Who Gets What, When, How* (New York: World, 1972; orig. 1936).
2. In another study of general tariff policies during this period, Bauer, Pool, and Dexter found relatively low levels of interest and activity in the general business community. See Raymond Bauer, Ithiel de Sola Pool, and Lewis Dexter, *American Business and Foreign Policy* (2nd ed.; Chicago: Aldine-Atherton, 1972; orig. 1963).
3. Floyd Hunter, *Top Leadership USA* (Chapel Hill: University of North Carolina Press, 1959), pp. 260–61.
4. In contrast, Bauer, Pool, and Dexter, *American Business and Foreign Policy*, emphasized the relative independence of political leaders from direct business pressures. Instead they emphasized the diffuse influence of free-trade economic thinking among influentials.
5. David Stanley, Dean Mann, and Jameson Doig, *Men Who Govern* (Washington, D.C.: Brookings, 1967), pp. 78–79.
6. Thomas Dye, "Men in Authority: Five Thousand Top Institutional Positions in America and the Men Who Occupy Them," a paper presented to the annual meeting of the American Political Science Association, New Orleans, Sept. 4–8, 1973, p. 23.
7. E. Digby Baltzell, *Philadelphia Gentlemen: The Making of a National Upper Class* (Chicago: Quadrangle, 1958), pp. 384–85.
8. For example, see Julia Altrocchi, *The Spectacular San Franciscans* (New York: Dutton, 1969), pp. 360–61.
9. Baltzell, *Philadelphia Gentlemen*, pp. 420–21. See similar conclusions in Nathaniel Burt, *The Perennial Philadelphians: The Anatomy of an American Aristocracy* (Boston: Little, Brown, 1963), pp. 594–95.
10. C. Wright Mills, *The Power Elite* (New York: Oxford, 1956), p. 232.
11. Ibid.
12. Ibid., p. 235.

13. Beth Mintz, "The President's Cabinet: 1897–1972," *The Insurgent Sociologist* 5 (Spring 1975): 144.
14. G. William Domhoff, "How the Power Elite Set National Goals," a paper for the Conference on National Priorities, Stanford Research Institute, January 15–17, 1970, p. 9.
15. G. William Domhoff, "Social Clubs, Policy-Planning Groups, and Corporations: A Network Study of Ruling-Class Cohesiveness," *The Insurgent Sociologist* 5 (Spring 1975): 181.
16. Mills, *The Power Elite*, pp. 280–81.
17. See Allen H. Barton, "Empirical Research on National Power Structures," International Study of Opinion Makers and the American Leadership Study, Bureau of Applied Social Research, Columbia University, September 1973, pp. 51–52. For other criticism, see Earl Latham's review of G. W. Domhoff's *The Higher Circles* (1970) in *American Political Science Review* 66 (March 1972): 199–201. On radical criticisms, see John Mollenkopf, "Theories of the State and Power Structure Research," *The Insurgent Sociologist* 5 (Spring 1975): 245–64; see also Domhoff's response in "Some Friendly Answers to Radical Critics," *The Insurgent Sociologist* 2 (Spring 1972): 27–39.
18. Mills, *The Power Elite*, chs. 11 and 14.
19. Robert Presthus, *Elites in the Policy Process* (Cambridge, Eng.: Cambridge University Press, 1974), p. 366.

7. The Distributional Approach: Economic Stratification and American Politics

Another indirect indicator of power is the distribution of benefits in society. This follows the biblical dictum, "By their fruits shall ye know them." The analysis of benefits or distributional approach assumes the following: (1) self-interest is a paramount human characteristic; and (2) the powerful are disproportionately successful in obtaining benefits. Although altruism may exist, this only means that the distributional approach tends to *understate* the elitist nature of power. That is, because the powerful may distribute some benefits to the less powerful, there is a tendency for economic and other advantages to be more evenly distributed than would be the case if the more powerful exercised their full influence. Chance might be thought a confounding factor for this approach, but this is not so. By definition the net effect of chance is zero. The holding of benefits in a particular case may have a great deal to do with chance. But the aggregate distribution of benefits does not.

The analysis of benefits in society can require trudging through mountains of statistics about wealth, income, education, and other advantages. In the end we will find that benefits in America are distributed in a much more unequal way than most people believe. The seeming equality of cultural style (dress, rock music, and the like) hides a profound inequality in income and other benefits. Without detouring too long into the world of economic statistics, it *is* helpful to review the highlights of this sort of empirical analysis.

Benefits: Wealth

Lampman's classic study of privately held wealth in 1953 showed that the top 1.6 percent of all Americans owned:

5.9 percent of pension and retirement funds.
13.3 percent of life insurance reserves.
16.1 percent of real estate.
18.2 percent of other miscellaneous property.
22.1 percent of all debts and mortgages.
29.1 percent of the cash.
36.2 percent of other mortgages and notes.
28.2 percent of federal bonds.
82.2 percent of all stock.
88.5 percent of nongovernmental bonds.
100 percent of tax-exempt state and local bonds.

In all, the top 1.6 percent owned nearly *one-third* of all privately held wealth, a staggering disproportion for a country with equalitarian values.[1] Moreover, Lampman found this inequality had been relatively constant since the 1920s at least.

These findings were corroborated a few years later by James Smith and Staunton Calvert, officials of the Internal Revenue Service. They discovered that the share of top wealth-holders continued to rise during the relatively prosperous 1953–1958 period.[2] Updating this work through 1962, Smith found a slight increase compared to 1953.[3] Further support was found in studies by two Federal Reserve officials, Dorothy Projector and Gertrude Weiss. Where Lampman had found that the top 9.2 percent of the population held *half* of all privately held wealth in 1953, Projector and Weiss showed that the same proportion was held by only 4 percent in 1962.[4] The trend toward even greater inequality of wealth during prosperous times was evident.

In his most recent study of personal property, Smith found
that the top 4 percent held some 37 percent of personal wealth
in 1969. As a group they could have bought the entire national
output of the United States in that year and had enough left
over to do the same for four European countries as well! [5] The
general picture is one in which the wealthiest one-fifth of the
nation owns *three-quarters* of all private wealth, while the
poorest fifth owns less than one-half of 1 percent!

Benefits: Income

Like wealth, the distribution of income has remained highly
unequal for some time. Table 7–1 indicates the distribution of
family income from 1947 through 1974. It shows the top 20 percent receive twice their proportional share of national income.
The top 5 percent receive three times their share. The lowest
three-fifths of the nation receive less than their proportional
share. A slight equalization has occurred since 1947, however.
But in 1974 the average family income gap between a person in
the top 5 percent and in the lowest 20 percent was still enormous: $31,948 to $6,500.

What equalization has occurred has tended to benefit primarily the middle to upper-middle class, not the lowest strata.
Gabriel Kolko, in *Wealth and Power in the United States* (1962),

Table 7–1 *Percent of Aggregate Family Income Received
by Each Fifth and the Highest 5 Percent of Families from
1947 to 1974*

	1947	1950	1955	1960	1965	1970	1974
Lowest 20%	5.1%	4.5%	4.8%	4.8%	5.2%	5.4%	5.4%
Second 20%	11.8	11.9	12.2	12.2	12.2	12.2	12.0
Third 20%	16.7	17.4	17.7	17.8	17.8	17.6	17.6
Fourth 20%	23.2	23.6	23.4	24.0	23.9	23.8	24.1
Top 20%	43.3	42.7	41.8	41.3	40.9	40.9	41.0
Top 5%	17.5	17.3	16.8	15.9	15.5	15.6	15.3

Source: U.S. Dept. of Commerce, *Statistical Abstract of the United States
1974* (Washington, D.C.: USGPO, 1975), p. 392.

found that the bottom 10 percent of Americans received some 3.4 percent of all income in 1910. Data in 1968 showed the figure to be only 1 percent in recent years. In 1910 the lowest half of Americans received 27 percent of all income. In 1968 their share dropped to 22 percent.

These figures *underestimate* the maldistribution of income. Upper-income receivers have, for example, greater opportunity to underestimate their income for IRS purposes. This is partly because they are often not subject to income withholding for taxes. The IRS estimates this may involve $30 billion in unreported income by members of the top 10 percent. In addition, many benefits do not count as taxable income at all: expense accounts, cars, travel, medical facilities, company resorts, gifts, and so on. The Treasury Department estimates that expense accounts alone may involve some $5 to $10 billion in unreported actual income, mostly among top income receivers. Finally, as Kolko notes, income figures underestimate maldistribution by failing to take account of the tendency of modern corporations to withhold a larger proportion of net profits. This enables top income receivers to take their benefits as capital gains through stock price increases rather than as income taxable at higher rates. Referring to data in Table 7–1, MIT economist Lester Thurow has noted that "the distribution of total income is substantially more unequal than the census indicates." [6]

The slight trend toward equalization observable in Table 7–1 is partly due to the decline of low-paying farm sector jobs and a corresponding increase in better-paying service-sector jobs. This sectoral shift is now in the past and will not be a factor in further equalization. Thurow has also pointed out two other reasons for the slight equalization. First, since World War II, *male* incomes have been becoming more unequal, but this has been somewhat more than compensated for by wives going to work to help counter the decline in their husbands' relative incomes. [7]

Second, some equalization is due to the twenty-seven-fold increase in welfare, Medicare, and other social-assistance programs between 1945 and 1974. Such spending increased from $9 billion to $242 billion, augmenting the incomes of the elderly, the ill, and others of low income. [8] Were it not for increased social-welfare outlays and working wives, family income inequalities would have widened markedly. The proportion of working wives may now have reached a plateau for the bottom three-fifths of income-receivers. If women's liberation, a primarily middle- and upper middle-class phenomenon, draws more women into higher-status jobs, it is likely that the beneficiaries will be families in the upper strata of income-receivers and that the gap will widen.[9] With regard to social-welfare spending, candidates of both parties in the 1976 presidential elections have taken a stand for limiting expansion of government services. So both factors (working wives and social spending) in the future may well *not* continue to compensate for the trend toward increased income inequality.

Do Taxes Redistribute Income?

How can America's seemingly progressive national income tax system be reconciled with these facts on income inequality? The net impact of taxes is subject to intense debate, but nearly all studies show far less redistribution of income than is often supposed. For example, Gabriel Kolko found that in 1958 the lower 85 percent of the population all paid about the same percentage of their incomes in federal, state, and local taxes (about 20 percent), while the top 15 percent paid a somewhat higher rate (about 33 percent). On the other hand, studying the same period, the Joint Economic Committee of Congress found that those with incomes over $250,000 paid average federal taxes of only 25 percent.[10]

Leon Keyserling, former head of the President's Council of Economic Advisers, found a more unequal impact than had Kolko. Using 1960 data, Keyserling concluded that the low rate of capital gains taxation on property income more than counterbalanced the progressive income tax. Consequently, he said, the poor did pay more than their share in taxation.[11]

An authoritative study of this question was undertaken by the Brookings Institution, using 1966 data. In this study, *Who Bears the Tax Burden?* (1974), Joseph Pechman and Benjamin Okner found little effect of taxes on income distribution. Their more sophisticated computer analysis of the effects of taxation took into account many indirect effects ignored in earlier studies. Using assumptions as favorable as possible to finding the tax system progressive, Pechman and Okner found that federal, state, and local taxes reduce the share of the top 10 percent of income receivers by only 2 percent. Income shares of those in the bottom half increased by less than 1 percent. Performing the same analysis using assumptions favorable to finding the system regressive, Pechman and Okner found changes in income shares of all groups (deciles) of the population to change less than 1 percent after taxation. Almost identical conclusions were reached in a 1966 study by the Survey Research Center of Michigan.[12]

In short, the progressive national income tax does *not* lead to income redistribution because of: (1) the regressive nature of other taxes (especially state and local property, excise, and sales taxes);[13] (2) tax loopholes; and (3) nonreporting of income.[14] Moreover, many taxes on corporate income are merely passed on to the consumer in the form of higher prices.

Estate and inheritance taxes at death do not provide intergenerational equalization either. Though theoretical rates are as high as 80 percent, Kolko estimates that the average rate is only 14 percent. Estate taxes can be largely avoided by giving away assets before death, and through trusts or other loopholes.[15]

Though concern for tax reform has risen in recent years, reforms thus far make little difference for income distribution.[16] In summary, as a recent study of after-tax income distribution concluded: "Despite sizable governmental efforts toward a more egalitarian distribution during the 1960s, we find that final distributions changed very little in ten years." [17]

Benefits: Economic Position

Economic position is a third benefit whose distribution may be taken as an indicator of distribution of power in America. It, too, is quite concentrated among a small fraction of the population. Ownership of the means of production is often taken by radical social scientists as a key to interpreting American politics. It is often argued, for instance, that economic concentration in America is growing, becoming monopolistic, and that finance capital (banks) forms the pinnacle of this concentration of power.[18] Each of these assertions is discussed in the sections that follow.

Is the Concentration of Capital Increasing in the United States?

Were America to live up to the capitalist myth of a nation of relatively small producers, none able to affect prices, the economic basis for the existence of a ruling class would be absent. The first step in class analysis of government is establishing that this economic basis is substantial and growing.

This aspect of the radical argument is relatively well supported. A recent report of the Federal Trade Commission (FTC), for example, documented the growth of economic concentration. It showed the 200 largest corporations in manufacturing controlled a share of assets as large as that of the 1,000 largest firms in 1941.[19] In that year the Temporary National Economic Committee of Congress had raised national alarm over the concentration of economic power among the top 1,000 firms, then far less concentrated than today.

The merger movement increased rapidly in the late 1960s. It eased at the end of the decade but has never subsided to the earlier low levels. Table 7–2 summarizes this development.

Table 7–2   Mergers in Manufacturing, 1950–1973

Period	Number of Mergers
1950–54*	285
1955–59*	673
1960–64*	873
1965–69*	1,630
1970	1,351
1971	1,011
1972	911
1973	874

Source: U.S. Department of Commerce, *Statistical Abstract of the United States 1974* (Washington, D.C.: USGPO, 1975), p. 506.
* Average annual rate.

Commenting on these trends, Senator Lee Metcalf (D, Mont.) stated in 1975 that "the 500 biggest U.S. corporations now hold more than two-thirds of all business income. The top 111 manufacturing corporations hold more than half of all assets and get more than half of all profits in manufacturing. . . . These economic giants far too often can avoid effective public regulation because the U.S. Congress, government regulatory agencies and the general public—including representatives of consumers and workers—simply cannot get adequate detailed information." [20] Economic concentration may well become more extreme in the years ahead.

Is Concentration Creating Monopolization?

The economy may become concentrated without monopolization if enterprises merge in unrelated industries. Since diversified (conglomerate) mergers were the main type in the 1960s, one may suppose this is just what happened in America. True, some traditional mergers did occur: Douglas Aircraft and McDonnell Aviation, Atlantic Refining with Richfield Oil and Sinclair Oil. But many more mergers involved unrelated firms. Is monopolization really a factor in America?

The FTC study cited above emphasized the monopolistic nature of recent merger trends. From 1948 through 1967, 80 percent of large acquisitions by the top 200 manufacturing firms were in the same industry group.[21] The FTC said that "large absolute size is increasingly founded upon and supported by dominant market position in a wide variety of markets." [22] A later FTC report (1973) noted an increase in mergers of the monopolistic type in recent years. "On balance," it stated, "merger activity in the American economy remains at a high level. . . . Conglomerate mergers, especially of the 'unrelated' category, seem to be giving way to those characterized by horizontal and vertical relationships." [23]

Leading firms where the top four firms control 50 percent or more of sales account for 64 percent of manufacturing sales.[24] By far the largest portion of the monopolistic sector is associated with the automobile industry (which has a concentration ratio of 0.81). Over three dozen other industries had concentration ratios over 0.70 during the 1960s.[25] Thus the top four firms control over half of sales in oil refining, electrical machinery, transportation equipment, rubber, and tobacco products. Forty to 50 percent is controlled in primary metals, chemicals, instruments, aircraft, and dairy products.

The proportion of sales controlled is an arbitrary yardstick. Less concentrated industries may nonetheless be marked by price leadership. Under price leadership, lesser firms willingly follow the lead of larger firms on pricing. This leads to monopolistic practices even though monopoly profits are distributed among more firms. Testifying before a 1967 Senate committee, John Kenneth Galbraith asserted price leadership was "everyday practice in autos, steel, rubber, and virtually every other large industry shared or dominated by a relatively few large firms." [26] An earlier study by Walter Adams had found a pattern of administered prices in steel, aluminum, chemicals, petroleum, automobiles, cigarettes, airlines, and metal containers.[27]

One of the most recent proofs of the importance of administered prices occurred during the Nixon administration. Prof. Willard Mueller recounted how Nixon "conducted a truly historic economic experiment. In January, 1969, the President announced he would bring about price stability without significantly increasing unemployment. He pledged he would accomplish this without any government intervention in the marketplace. For the next twenty-seven months, despite active manipulation of fiscal and monetary policy, price inflation continued—indeed accelerated." [28] Unemployment rose steeply as well.

President Nixon thus found prices continued to rise where classical economic theory predicted they should fall. Most economists concluded that the theory was correct, but the market was not free to behave as a competitive market. Price increases were greatest in the more concentrated sectors of the economy.[29] Mueller concluded that "business enterprises with great discretion in administering prices can distort the pricing process by maintaining or even increasing prices in the face of falling demand, or by failing to decrease prices when they enjoy above-average productivity gains." [30] FTC economist Frederic Scherer has estimated that monopolistic price distortions cost the economy some $87 billion every year.[31] And governmental tax policy has encouraged this monopolistic merger activity! [32]

Is Economic Power Being Concentrated in Financial Institutions?

Radical scholars have argued that banks are gaining control over the American economy through underwriting corporate expansion and concentration.[33] A study of bank control was conducted in 1968 by the Subcommittee on Domestic Finance of the House Committee on Banking and Currency. This study found "the trend of the last thirty to forty years toward a separation of ownership from control because the fragmentation of stock ownership has been radically changed toward a new concentration of voting power in the hands of a relatively few financial corporations, while the fragmentation in the distribution of cash payments has been continued." [34] That is, the study supported the view that economic power is accumulating in the hands of banking institutions. Banks, the report contended, are "the major force in consummating mergers." This has led to increased bank interlocks on corporate boards.[35]

This trend toward bank control, however, is still limited in magnitude. Most corporations are still management-controlled. A 1963 study by Robert Larner found that only 16 percent of the top 200 nonfinancial corporations were *not* management controlled.[36] The 1968 Patman Committee report cited above found that an additional 18 to 33 percent had come under bank control, though even this may be disputed.[37] A more recent congressional committee report concluded that the Patman Committee figures underestimated bank control. Senator Lee Metcalf (D, Mont.) stated there was "a massive coverup of the extent to which stock holdings in large corporations are concentrated in the hands of a very few institutional investors." [38] And the banking industry itself is very concentrated. In 1966 the top 50 commercial banks held 44 percent of deposits; by 1971 they held 50 percent.[39]

Economic Position: Summary

The American economy is highly concentrated and is slowly becoming more so over time. Monopolization has proceeded far enough to allow corporate prices to defy the laws of competitive economics. One author writes that "about one-third of the total U.S. economy is monopolized; the remaining two-thirds is reasonably competitive. But that monopolized one-third is the country's industrial heartland and casts a long shadow over the rest of the country." [40] Through the voting power of financial institutions, control is becoming even more confined in a relatively few hands.

In terms of analysis of the distribution of benefits, economic position is therefore quite concentrated. The top 500 or so manufacturing firms and the top 50 financial institutions dominate the economy. And they are tied together by interlocking directorships, linking economic notables in a given metropolitan area, linking corporations in the same industry, and linking corporations to banks. [41] It is no exaggeration to state that less than 0.5 percent of the population control the American economy through the economic positions they hold. [42]

Benefits: Education

The distribution of economic benefits in the United States lends support to those who see America as fundamentally elitist. But what of noneconomic benefits, which one would expect to be distributed more equally? For example, from 1950 to 1970 the distribution of education among adult white males has become noticeably more equal. [43] Where in 1950 the least-educated fifth of the nation received only 8.6 percent of years of education, by 1970 they were receiving 10.7 percent. Correspondingly, the share of the best-educated fifth declined from 31.1 to 29.3 percent.

This, of course, still represents considerable inequality. One government report indicated that of high school graduates who are in the top fifth of ability in aptitude tests, fully 95 percent go on to college if their parents are among the top one-fourth of income receivers, while only 50 percent of this aptitude group whose parents are in the bottom quarter economically go to college. Thus, "high school graduates from the top socioeconomic quartile who are in the third [middle] ability group are more likely to go to college than even the top ability group from the bottom socioeconomic quartile." Moreover, the colleges those in the upper group go to are much more likely to be private four-year institutions and much less likely to be public or community colleges.[44] Class inequalities are even greater when graduate and professional training are considered. The rise of the community college system seems likely to reinforce the inequities of the existing class-based tracking system in future education.[45] The economic facts of educational life were dramatized recently when U.S. Commissioner of Education Terrel Bell resigned from his post. His reason? The inability to support three sons in college on his commissioner's salary of $37,800.[46]

Benefits: Health

Numerous studies show that the poor spend less on health, are more poorly treated, and consequently live shorter lives.[47] On the other hand, there has been a drastic reduction in class inequalities since 1930. The former high correlation of class with use of hospital services has declined sharply.[48] This equalization is due largely to the growth of government and private health-insurance systems, including Medicare and Medicaid. With the seemingly imminent passage of an American national health-insurance system, further equalization may occur in the years ahead. Health is a benefit far more equally distributed than the others we have considered.

Effects of Benefit Maldistribution: Campaign Finance

If economic benefits are quite unevenly distributed, perhaps power is as well. Certainly a reciprocal relation exists between power and the possession of economic benefits. A concentration of wealth, income, and high economic/occupational position confers power, and power enables the reaping of more benefits. But just how does this occur? What is the concrete link connecting benefits and power? One commonly given answer to this question is campaign finance. By controlling the funds candidates need to get elected, economic notables *may* be able to dominate the nomination process. Is this so?

The vast and growing expense of election campaigns provides a seeming opportunity for elite domination of politics. In 1912, presidential election expenditures were under $3 million. By 1952 the figure was $12 million. And then, in the post-Korean War period, costs soared. By 1972 presidential campaign funds were estimated to be over $83 million! When costs of *primary* campaigns are added in, the trend is even more striking.[49]

On the other hand, the number of contributors to campaigns is increasing. Herbert Alexander has estimated that some 9 million people contributed to the 1968 campaign, for example, compared to only 3 million in 1952.[50] The 1972 rate was even higher, in part because the Democratic candidate, George McGovern, relied heavily on a mail contribution campaign. Through the 1972 elections, however, it could still be said that "campaigns would be impossible without the big contributor. It is still the big contributor who finances political campaigns." [51]

Big contributors can be of critical importance even when the total amount given by small donors is greater overall. Large contributions solicited early in campaigns provide all-important "seed money" that supports the costly direct-mail, television, and other fund-raising procedures which bring in the small givers. Moreover, the small contributor rarely has any input of ideas. In contrast, large contributors are often contacted directly by a candidate and his or her aides. An attempt is made to convince the large donor that the candidacy coincides with the interests of the giver. It is at this stage that the candidate may be tempted to adopt a position closer to those of contributors.

Most contributors of amounts over $500 are businessmen. Of donors of more than $10,000, nearly all have been members of the corporate rich. The great majority are Republicans, but wealthy individuals are also important to the Democrats. Democratic large donors are often Jewish businessmen, members of certain New York Wall Street firms, some Texas oil executives, and other men of new wealth, as in Southern California.[52] Labor has not been a counterbalancing political force. Organizationally, the AFL–CIO's Committee on Political Education (COPE) and other union sources have raised some $7 to $10 million dollars for recent presidential campaigns. But as *individuals,* even the presidents of the largest American unions have been able to make only very small campaign contributions. As individual contributions have been the more important, and since wealthy individuals have been predominantly Republican, the Republican party has routinely raised far more money than the Democratic party in national election campaigns.

Recent reforms of the campaign process may have a dramatic impact on the pattern of possible elite domination just outlined. In 1971 the Federal Election Campaign Act was passed. This provided more stringent reporting requirements for campaign contributions.[53] It was an important factor in bringing to light several aspects of the scandals that culminated in the resignation of President Richard Nixon. Afterward, pressure grew for even more drastic reform of campaign finance.

The result was the Federal Election Campaign Act of 1974, later amended in May 1976. Under this legislation Congress placed unprecedented limits on campaign contributions. Wealthy individuals were forbidden to contribute more than $1,000 per candidate per race, and no more than $25,000 per year. Federal matching funds were provided up to $5 million total for the primary campaigns (with a cost-of-living clause allowing upward revision), but only for contributions of $250 or less. Public funds were also provided for the fall general elections ($20 million) and for the national nominating conventions ($2 million, with corporate contributions barred for the first time). Numerous additional reporting and spending limits were also legislated. These and more detailed regulations were placed under the supervision of a new Federal Election Commission (whose regulations might be vetoed by either house of Congress).

While the effect of the new campaign finance reforms cannot yet be assessed, news reports indicate a substantial change. Large contributors continue to play a role, but far more attention is given to public funding and small contributions. Wealthy donors can still act as recruiters for numerous $1,000 donations, but "the day of the five- and six-figure plungers is plainly over, and their exile has been the first visible result of the new law." [54] But while the effect of wealth will be much less than in the past, the campaign reforms will not create a political revolution. On the contrary, perhaps the chief criticism of the new laws is that they favor incumbent politicians. That is, incumbents have various perquisites (such as free postage) and the advantages of public office (such as announcing new federal projects for their constituents), which give them an edge over their challengers. With spending limits on challengers held to the same level as for incumbents, the incumbents may be better off.

Ultimately it is difficult to assess the effect of benefit maldistribution on political campaigns. Reforms should minimize the most serious abuses. But it is also possible to argue that full public funding could shift the political spectrum even further to the Democratic side. And radicals are quick to point out that the campaign finance reforms make it harder than ever to sustain a viable third-party alternative to the Republicans and Democrats. That is, it further stabilizes the dominance of the two major parties.[55]

Effects of Benefit Maldistribution: Business Reformism

Campaign finance seems *not* to be a direct or sure means for translating economic benefits into political power. Money does not dictate politics in a simple way. Pluralist theorists say that, in fact, money is but one of a large number of power-producing resources. Others include time, commitment, knowledge, manpower, expertise in use of media, personal charisma, and the like. Elite theorists, in contrast, say that the striking maldistribution of economic benefits in American society *must* affect the power structure much more than these other factors, many of which can be bought. But how?

Other approaches to the study of power have suggested partial answers. Just as wealth does have *some* effect on campaign finance, so it seems likely that there is *some* class effect on politics indicated by the high-status social backgrounds of people holding top national offices (the sociology-of-leadership approach) or reputed to be powerful (the reputational approach). Although such evidence suggests American politics are far less egalitarian than democratic mythology would have it, this evidence falls short of proving elite theorists' claims that a capitalist elite controls politics in America. On the other hand, the preponderance of evidence *is* inconsistent with the pluralist image of politics—the competition of many, relatively small groups, in which large corporations and financial institutions play no disproportionate role. So our analysis thus far does not support *either* elite theory or pluralist theory. (The fact that evidence lies on both sides is why the elitist-pluralist debate in political science has been so intense and long-lasting, but it also suggests the need for a new analytic framework which goes beyond elitism or pluralism.)

In this section it is contended that the maldistribution of wealth, income, and economic position *is* linked to politics in an important way. The link is not through campaign finance or any other money-buys-influence mechanism. Instead the connection lies in the process of "business reformism." The politics of urban renewal illustrate this process.[56]

Urban renewal after World War II started as a liberal reform supported by social workers, educators, veterans groups, trade unionists, civil rights advocates, consumers, mayors, churches, and other liberal groups. The initial business reaction was critical. Business spokesmen supported the objectives of slum clearance and housing construction, but not the means. Such problems were thought better handled by private enterprise in cooperation with local governments. Accomplishing the task through federal legislation was believed to be too costly and socialistic. The initial phase was thus one of reform pressure from nonbusiness sources, prompted by a postwar housing crisis following troop demobilization.[57]

In the second stage of the process of business reformism, conservative spokesmen interpreted for the business community the possibilities of the proposed reforms. Thus one found the August 1949 issue of *Fortune* emphasizing the economic benefits that were to accrue to the business community. It noted that the Chemical Bank & Trust Company had estimated the housing program would create an annual flow of about $1 billion in tax-free, federally guaranteed securities. The growth of business support was also greatly aided by the endorsement of renewal by Senator Philip Taft, the leading conservative of the day.

At the same time, the most redistributionist aspects of the

program were strongly opposed. Business groups were prominent, for example, in the successful drive to kill wartime-created rent control in 1949–1950. If the first stage of business reformism was marked by automatic business conservatism, the second was characterized by a growing awareness of the potential positive aspects of reform. In addition, action was taken to overrule the most objectionable (redistributionist) aspects of the program.

The third phase was marked by the consolidation of business opinion. The original reform program was adapted to other, more profitable purposes. In the case of urban renewal, the more profitable approach emphasized subsidies to downtown business, bank-administered FHA loans to middle-class homeowners, and clearance of substandard housing to make way for more expensive rental units. (Later this shifted to rehabilitation without rent control—the Georgetown strategy—but the effect was the same.) At the same time, public housing was kept to a bare minimum.

The 1949 Housing and Renewal Act had not provided for any type of nonresidential renewal. But by 1964 a representative of the National Association of Real Estate Boards—now in *favor* of renewal—testified that about half of all obligational authority in the proposed bill for that year would be used for commercial and industrial purposes. Similarly, the 1949 act had authorized construction of 810,000 public housing units over six years. Fifteen years later less than one-seventh this number had actually been built. In 1949, House Republicans voted against renewal by the wide margin of 34 to 131; in 1954 only 9 Republicans were in opposition.

The 1954 turning point came with the Housing Redevelopment Act, based on the work of the President's Advisory Committee on Government Housing Policies and Programs. Business representatives on this committee were twice as numerous as all other group representatives combined. As housing administrator Albert Cole said: "Most of the conclusions of the Advisory Committee . . . are included in the pending bill." [58] The head of a national realty group stated that "very much the same view [as ours] is taken." [59] The Chamber of Commerce "strongly supported" the 1954 change in urban renewal, as did the

Mortgage Bankers Association of America and other business groups testifying at the hearings.

The overall effect was to drive up rents by reducing the housing supply in the inner cities. Downtown business, real estate, and financial interests were subsidized. By the 1960s the bulk of liberal sentiment had swung 180 degrees toward disassociation from the erstwhile reform.

Business reformism is a process linking the concentration of economic benefits to political power. Money does not buy power directly, at least not in the main. But the concentration of economic interest provides the basis for long-term organization to redirect reforms. Tammany boss George Washington Plunkitt called reformers "mornin' glories" who soon passed on to other things, and there is still some truth in this.[60] From time to time, particularly in the aftermath of crises, "pluralistic" coalitions of reformers do overrule economic elite interests. But the concentration of economic benefits and position assures that the initial reform will be subject to a long process of revision, accommodation, and adjustment. As with the "regulatory" commissions and numerous other reforms, including urban renewal, the long-term picture is in accord with elite-theory expectations even though the short-term reform victories seem good illustrations of pluralist views.

The difference between the long-term and the short-term is substantial. In the next four chapters we will accordingly emphasize an *historical* perspective on the topics we have been discussing. The chapters until now have examined several indicators of power: decisions, reputation, social background, benefits. They have led us to support, in part, the elitist theory of American politics *and* to support, in part, pluralist theory. Now we will begin thinking about how to integrate what we have learned. Is there some framework for looking at American politics which goes beyond elitism and pluralism? Earlier we suggested that "political economy" might provide a basis for reconciling the different ideas examined in this book. The last chapter will deal with this. Before that, however, we will discuss three related subjects: (1) evidence for the homogeneity of elite viewpoints (that is, even though upper-status groups disproportionately occupy elite positions, can we assume they hold some common set of attitudes different from the public, on the basis of which one might expect different political dispositions?); (2) the politics of oil (a specific historical case); and (3) the history of the American political economy. After discussing the relation of the general indicators of power, which have been examined in chapters up until now, to long-term historical trends, Chapter 12 will take up the question of political economy as a possible alternative framework for interpreting American politics.

Notes

1. Robert J. Lampman, *The Share of Top Wealth-Holders in National Wealth, 1922–1956* (Princeton, N.J.: Princeton University Press, for the National Bureau of Economic Research, 1962). Lampman found that the share of top wealth appeared to rise in peace and prosperity and decline during war and depression, with no significant net trend since the 1920s.
2. Cited in Leititia Upton and Nancy Lyons, *Basic Facts: Distribution of Personal Income and Wealth in the United States* (Cambridge, Mass.: Cambridge Institute, 1972), Table 15. Smith showed that in 1962 the top 1 percent of wealth-holders controlled:
   11.2 percent of insurance equity.
   11.9 percent of trust, pension funds, and other assets.
   15.8 percent of real estate and residences.
   24.4 percent of notes and mortgages.
   47.5 percent of bonds.
   71.6 percent of corporate stock.
3. James D. Smith and Staunton K. Calvert, "Estimating the Wealth of Top Wealth-Holders from Estate Tax Returns," *Proceedings of the American Statistical Association,* Philadelphia annual meeting, September 1965. There was some tendency to remove wealth from bonds and cash savings to invest in real estate and mortgages during this period.
4. Dorothy S. Projector and Gertrude S. Weiss, *Survey of Financial Characteristics of Consumers* (Board of Governors of the Federal Reserve System, August 1966), Tables A2, A16, and A36.
5. James D. Smith, "The Concentration of Personal Wealth in America, 1969," *Review of Income and Wealth,* Series 20, No. 2 (June 1974): 172. Smith found that in 1969 the top 4 percent owned:
   12 percent of misc. wealth.
   27 percent of real estate.
   31 percent of savings bonds.
   33 percent of cash.
   40 percent of business assets.
   63 percent of corporate stock.

74 percent of other federal bonds.

78 percent of state and local bonds.

100 percent of corporate and foreign bonds.

100 percent of notes and mortgages.

Differences from the Projector and Weiss study may be due primarily to differences in estimation techniques.

6. Lester C. Thurow, "More Are Going to be Poor," *New Republic*, 2 November, 1974, p. 26. Thurow states that "while 25 percent of all income is capital income in the Gross National Product, only 4 percent of census income is capital income. Since the ownership of capital is much more unequal than the distribution of earnings (the richest 15 percent of families own 76 percent of all privately held assets and the poorest 25 percent have no assets), the distribution of total income is substantially more unequal than the census indicates."

7. In the postwar period the number of working wives increased from one in three to nearly one in two.

8. See *Statistical Abstract of the United States, 1970* (Washington, D.C.: USGPO, 1970), p. 276; ibid., 1975, p. 280. Considering federal outlays alone, the rise was from $4 billion in 1945 to $140 billion in 1974.

9. A study for the Joint Economic Committee of Congress in 1972 noted: "If the current movement toward women's lib were to open up new job opportunities for women and succeed in attracting more women into the labor force, the distribution of family income might become more dispersed by either measure (i.e., both in terms of proportionate income shares and in terms of absolute income differentials). More working wives would raise family incomes at all levels but the family incomes of the rich would grow more rapidly than those of the less well off. Wives of high income males have the greatest potential for entering the labor force since they currently have the lowest labor force participation rates." Lester C. Thurow and Robert E. B. Lucas, *The American Distribution of Income: A Structural Problem* (Washington, D.C.: USGPO, for the Joint Economic Committee of the U.S. Congress, 17 March 1972), p. 14.

10. Gabriel Kolko, *Wealth and Power in America: An Analysis of Social Class and Income Distribution* (New York: Praeger, 1962), p. 37. Paul Douglas, "The Problem of Tax Loopholes," *The American Scholar* (Winter 1967–68): 23.

11. Leon Keyserling, "Taxes From Whom, For What?," *New Republic*, 23 April 1966, p. 18. Keyserling found that those below $2,000 income paid 38 percent of their income in all taxes; those from $2,000 to $5,000 paid a rate of 38–41 percent; those from $7500–$10,000 paid a rate of 22 percent; and those over $10,000 in income paid 32 percent. By comparison the Office of Tax Analysis states that the average rate of federal taxation for incomes over $1 million was 24–25 percent during this period.

12. Joseph A. Pechman and Benjamin A. Okner, *Who Bears the Tax Burden?* (Washington, D.C.: Brookings, 1974), p. 56, Table 4–6. See also Joseph A. Pechman, "The Rich, The Poor, and the Taxes They Pay, *The Public Interest*, no. 17 (Fall 1969), p. 33. The second study was Survey Research Center, *Survey of Consumer Finances: 1967*, as cited in Herman Miller, *Rich Man, Poor Man* (New York: Crowell, 1971), p. 16. The SRC found that the share of income received by the bot-

tom 40 percent of income receivers was not affected by taxation; the middle 20 percent declined 1 percent; the upper-middle 20 percent increased 2 percent; the top fifth declined 2 percent.

13. For example, state taxes in Massachusetts are 15 percent of personal income for individuals in the $8,000–$10,000 range; 10 percent for those in the $20,000–$25,000 range; and 7 percent for those in the range $30,000–$50,000. See Federal Reserve Bank of Boston, *Options for Fiscal Structure Reform in Massachusetts*, Report 57 (Boston: FRBB, 1973), p. 152.

14. See Melville Ulmer, "How Unfair Are Our Taxes?" *New Republic*, 7 November 1970, pp. 17–19. Ulmer cites a study by Glenn D. Morrow, appearing in the *National Tax Journal*, September 1963, based on a comparison of tax returns with confidential census questionnaires. This presumably still underestimates the true extent of nonreporting, however.

15. Kolko, *Wealth and Power in America*, pp. 43–44. The 1976 tax reform, however, closed some estate tax loopholes and made the system somewhat more progressive. At the time of writing the real effect of the 1976 reforms has not yet been determined.

16. The 1969 Tax Reform Act created some changes which marginally improved the progressivity of the tax system. Notably, it established a "minimum tax" of 10 percent, designed to prevent wealthy taxpayers from avoiding all federal taxes through use of tax-free bonds and other loopholes. The act itself contained loopholes, however, allowing over a hundred individuals in 1973 to escape federal taxes altogether. Moreover, the act left unchanged the tax-free status of state and local bonds, the tax preference for capital gains income, and other loopholes. As one writer has noted: "The highly preferential treatment of long-term capital gains has led to an increasing search by tax lawyers and their wealthy clients for devices that convert ordinary income into capital gains. These devices encompass everything from cows to office buildings to oil wells and apartment houses. Tax shelters today are advertised like aspirin. The National Association of Securities Dealers reports that in 1971, 405 syndicated tax shelters were offered representing a gross investment of [$]4.2 billion." (See "Tax Shelters," *New Republic*, 24 February 1973, p. 7.) The 1976 tax revision, however, increased the minimum tax on the wealthy and curbed certain other abuses. See "Tax Bill Cleared," *Congressional Quarterly*, 18 September 1976, p. 2499. Note that during the 1970s the net effect of inaction on reform was regressive. This was because, as inflation drove dollar (but not real) incomes upward, many Americans found themselves in unduly high tax brackets. See "Inflationary Effect: Tax Burden Heavier Despite Reductions," *Congressional Quarterly*, 12 April 1975, pp. 743–44.

17. Morgan Reynolds and Eugene Smolensky, "The Post-Fisc Distribution: 1961 and 1970 Compared," *National Tax Journal* 27 (December 1974): 515.

18. See, for example, Richard Pelton, "Who Rules America?" *Progressive Labor* 7 (February 1970): 16–36.

19. U.S. Federal Trade Commission, *Economic Report on Corporate Mergers* (Washington, D.C.: USGPO, 1969), p. 3.

20. Senator Lee Metcalf, *Congressional Record*, vol. 121, no. 34 (4 March

1975): S3007. On concentration among multinationals, see Richard Barnet and Ronald Muller, *Global Reach* (New York: Simon and Schuster, 1974).

21. U.S. Federal Trade Commission, *Economic Report on Corporate Mergers*, p. 242.

22. Ibid., p. 251. Comparing 1966 with 1954, the FTC group found concentration had increased in the following industries: furniture, transportation equipment, food, electrical machinery, instruments, stone and clay, textiles and apparel, lumber, paper, and other machinery. However, although the general tendency is toward monopolization, the concentration ratio of several industries was actually reduced in the same period: rubber, primary metals, fabricated metals, and chemicals. To the extent a trend exists, moreover, it is not one which is strong or rapid.

23. Bureau of Economics, Federal Trade Commission, *FTC: Statistical Report on Mergers and Acquisitions* (Washington: USGPO, 1973), p. ix.

24. "The New Monopolies," *Consumer Reports* 40 (June 1975): 378, citing studies by William G. Shepard of the University of Michigan.

25. Senate Committee on the Judiciary, Subcommittee on Antitrust and Monopoly, *Hearings on the Industrial Reorganization Act* (Washington, D.C.: USGPO, 1973), Part 1, p. 305.

26. See also John Kenneth Galbraith, *The New Industrial State* (Boston: Houghton Mifflin, 1967), ch. 18.

27. Walter Adams, *The Structure of American Industry* (3rd ed.; New York: Macmillan, 1951).

28. *Hearings on the Industrial Reorganization Act*, p. 46.

29. Ibid., p. 36.

30. Ibid., p. 46. Arthur Burns, chairman of the Federal Reserve Board under Nixon, had gone along with the idea of giving the market a chance to prove itself in 1969. After its failure, Burns changed his views. "Structural reforms are also needed," he said. "Not a few of our corporations and trade unions now have the power to exact rewards that exceed what could be achieved under conditions of active competition." This causes an inflationary pressure which would not exist in a predominantly competitive economy. (Ibid., p. 47.)

31. Cited in *"The New Monopolies,"* p. 379.

32. Current corporate tax laws allow tax exemptions for gains associated with corporate reorganization. In particular, the accumulated holdings in a company can be sold without paying any capital gains tax. (U.S. Federal Trade Commission, *Economic Report on Corporate Mergers*, p. 142.) This enables the acquiring company to offer the stockholders of the acquired company an untaxed premium over the premerger market value of stock held. Moreover, the acquiring company can offer to trade, say, $10 of its stock for each $8 of the acquired company's stock, then subtract interest payments on this stock from its taxable income. This has the effect of substituting deductible interest for the taxable dividends of the acquired firm. This tax gain may then be reflected in a higher earnings per share ratio for the acquiring company. Although need for investment, tax gains, and growth itself are all motivations for merger, the major source of financing of merger expansion is stock and debenture flotations underwritten by commercial banks. Reversing previous practice, banks have also become increasingly involved directly in merger activities. (Robert Dietsch, "The

Merger Boom: Who Owns What?" *New Republic,* 1 February 1969,
p. 14.) Use of corporate credit underwritten by financial institutions
through stock and debenture flotations, not simple loans, has played
a far more important role in capital concentration than has government tax policy. On the other hand, 1976 reforms have tightened
antitrust enforcement. See "House Vote Clears Antitrust Bill," *Congressional Quarterly,* 18 September 1976, p. 2578.

33. Pelton, "Who Rules America?" p. 19.
34. House Committee on Banking and Currency, Subcommittee on Domestic Finance, *Commercial Banks and their Trust Activities: Emerging
Influence on the American Economy,* vol. 1 (Washington, D.C.:
USGPO, 1968), p. 13. This is often called the Patman Report.
35. Ibid., p. 29. An interlock is a member of a board of directors who
also serves on the board of another organization.
36. Robert J. Larner, "Ownership and Control in the 200 Largest Nonfinancial Corporations, 1929 and 1963," *American Economic Review*
56 (September 1966).
37. House Committee on Banking and Currency, *Commercial Banks and
their Trust Activities,* pp. 13–15. Patman's study of the 5 or 6 largest
banks in ten cities (including New York, Chicago, Boston, and Philadelphia, but excluding San Francisco) showed these 49 banks controlled 5 percent or more of the common stock in 147 of the 500 largest
industrial corporations, 17 of the 500 largest merchandising firms, 17
of the 50 largest transportation companies, and had 768 interlocking
directorships with 286 of the 500 largest industrial corporations, 73
interlocks with 27 of the 50 top transportation companies, 86 interlocks with 22 of the 50 top utilities, 146 interlocks with 29 of the 50
largest life insurance companies, and 64 interlocks with 26 of the 50
largest merchandising firms (p. 91).
38. Lee Metcalf, "Special Report from Washington, D.C.," p. 1 (mimeo,
n.d.). See Senate Government Operations Committee, Subcommittee
on Budgeting, Management and Expenditures and Subcommittee
on Intergovernmental Relations, *Disclosure of Corporate Ownership*
(Washington, D.C.: USGPO, 1974). The "cover-up" refers to use of
nominees and street names for masking the identities of large stockholders. See also Vic Beinmer, "Power of the Big Banks," *New Republic,* 23–30 December 1972, pp. 23–25.
39. Wright Patman, "Other People's Money," *New Republic,* 17 February
1973, p. 16.
40. Robert A. Wilson, "The High Price of Corporate Inflation," *Wage-
Price Law and Economics Review* 1 (1975): 75.
41. W. Lloyd Warner, Darab B. Unwalla, and John H. Trimm, *The Emergent American Society* (New Haven: Yale University Press, 1967).
Warner and his associates studied the managers and directors of the
500 top corporations and found that these 3,150 individuals held a
total of 6,280 directorships in their firms. The majority of these interlocks tie together large enterprises located in the same metropolitan
areas, but about one-third of the interlocks tie together corporations
in the same industry, and a substantial minority link the corporations
to the banks.
42. As a case in point, Harold Geneen, head of ITT, is one of those holding such elite economic positions. ITT came under intense—and un-
favorable—public scrutiny in 1973, partly as a result of the publication

of Anthony Sampson's muckraking work, *The Sovereign State of ITT*
(Briarcliff Manor, N.Y.: Stein and Day, 1973), and partly due to its
CIA-connected attempts to interfere in Chilean politics. As the ninth
largest American corporation, ITT employs 400,000 persons in 70 countries. Its long history includes controversial international involvements
going back to its subsidiaries supplying the Luftwaffe with planes used
to bomb American allies during World War II. Due to government
involvements, the ITT image had sunk to such a low in 1973 that the
ordinarily staid *Newsweek* was moved to comment, "What an over-
weening, arrogant, dissembling group these ITT managers are!" ("The
Geneen Machine," *Newsweek*, 23 July 1973, p. 71.) In mid-January
1974, ITT began a $6.4 million campaign to improve their public
image. Commented the *New York Times'* columnist on advertising,
"Within six months there was a definite improvement in public attitudes toward ITT, and within a year, a profound improvement." He
concluded, "Despite torrents of negative news stories, a corporation
can quickly rebuild its image if it is willing to spend the money for
good deeds and advertising to let the world know about them." Phillip
H. Dougherty, "How ITT Improved Its Image," *New York Times,* 18
April 1975, p. 51.

43. Thurow and Lucas, *The American Distribution of Income*, p. 15.
44. U.S. HEW, *Toward a Social Report* (Washington, D.C.: USGPO,
1969): 20 and 21. For the next-to-the-top ability quintile, 84 percent
go to college from the top economic class and only 36 percent from
the poorest quarter of the population. For students of only average
ability, fully 69 percent of students in the highest economic group go
on to college anyway, whereas only 25 percent of students in this
ability category from the poorest quarter do so.
45. Jerome Karabel, "Community Colleges and Social Stratification," *Harvard Educational Review* 42 (November 1972): 521–62. See also
Samuel Bowles and Herbert Gintis, *Schooling in Capitalist America*
(New York: Basic Books, 1976), pp. 203–12.
46. "Closing College Doors" (editorial), *New York Times,* 21 April 1976,
p. 34.
47. Kolko, *Wealth and Power in America*, pp. 118–120; U.S. HEW, *Toward
a Social Report,* pp. 8–9. See also Bradley R. Schiller, "Stratified Opportunities: The Essence of the 'Vicious Circle,'" *American Journal of
Sociology* 76 (November 1970): 426–42. Schiller concludes that class
inequality of opportunity (not family background or ability) is responsible for socioeconomic achievement lag in poor children.
48. Louis Kriesberg, "The Relationship between Socioeconomic Rank and
Behavior," in G. W. Thielbar and S. D. Feldman, eds., *Issues in Social
Inequality* (Boston: Little, Brown, 1972), p. 472–73. However, note
that the distribution of health benefits as measured by inequalities of
health rather than of health *service* reveals rather striking class differentials. See E. S. Greenberg, *Serving the Few* (New York: Wiley,
1974), p. 157.
49. Herbert E. Alexander, *Money in Politics* (Washington, D.C.: Public
Affairs Press, 1972), p. 79. Campaign spending in 1976 again reached
record levels. See "Reagan and Ford Lead in Primary Spending," *Congressional Quarterly,* 25 September 1976, p. 2606.
50. Herbert E. Alexander, *Political Financing* (Minneapolis: Burges, 1973),
p. 33.

51. Louis S. Loeb and Daniel M. Berman, *American Politics: Crisis and Challenge* (New York: Macmillan, 1975), p. 146.
52. David Nichols, *Financing Elections: The Politics of an American Ruling Class* (New York: New Viewpoints, 1974).
53. See Jeffrey M. Berry and Jerry Goldman, "Congress and Public Policy: A Study of the Federal Election Campaign Act of 1971," *Harvard Journal on Legislation* 10 (February 1973): 331-65.
54. "The New Money Rules," *Newsweek*, 16 June 1975, p. 27. However, the wealthy can still funnel additional contributions through relatives and, more important, spend funds to hold fund-raising parties for candidates, using social pressure to encourage their managerial employees to contribute.
55. Ibid., p. 26. The Supreme Court has overruled the protests of third-party candidates. See "Congress Finance, Congress Weighing New Law," *Congressional Quarterly*, 7 February 1976, pp. 267–68.
56. Since World War II there have been four major spending programs: military, highways, welfare, and urban renewal. Regarding the other three areas not discussed in this section, the following books are recommended: Richard J. Barnet, *The Economy of Death* (New York: Atheneum, 1970); James L. Clayton, ed., *The Economic Impact of the Cold War* (New York: Harcourt, Brace & World, 1970); Seymour Melman, ed., *The War Economy of the United States* (New York: St. Martin's, 1971); Ben Kelley, *The Pavers and the Paved* (New York: Donald Brown, 1971); A. Q. Mowbray, *Road to Ruin* (Philadelphia: Lippincott, 1969); John L. Donovan, *The Politics of Poverty* (2nd ed.; Indianapolis: Bobbs-Merrill, 1973); Joe R. Feagin, *Subordinating the Poor* (Englewood Cliffs, N.J.: Prentice-Hall, 1975); Frances Fox Piven and Richard A. Cloward, *Regulating the Poor* (New York: Pantheon, 1971).
57. Among the twenty-five organizations testifying against renewal legislation were five bankers' associations, eight construction firms and organizations, three owners' and realtors' associations, two conservative political groups, and several general business organizations, including the Chamber of Commerce.
58. House Committee on Banking and Currency, *Hearings on HR 7839* (Washington, D.C.: USGPO, 1954), p. 33.
59. Ibid., p. 735.
60. William R. Riordon, *Plunkitt of Tammany Hall* (New York: Knopf, 1948), p. 22.

Part III

Class Analysis and Business Power

8. Is Class Consciousness Important in American Politics?

Many factors affect our political consciousness: class, ethnicity, race, religion, education, childhood experiences, and parental attitudes. Even if we *wanted* to think in "class terms" it would often be impossible since many political matters are multi-faceted in their effects. That is, it is frequently difficult to predict what the net effect on social classes a bill to reform the congressional committee structure will have, for example. What is the "working-class interest" in school integration? In congressional budget reform? Not only are such class effects difficult to discern, but much of politics is directed at blurring class consciousness and achieving consensus. Political issues are routinely presented in terms of nationalistic, patriotic, and other unifying symbols which channel opinion away from class consciousness. (Recall Edelman's work on politics as symbolic action, discussed in Chapter 1.)

Nonetheless, class consciousness *is* important in America. It forms a potential and often actual basis for political action. Class consciousness is most important among groups of high status. While great diversity exists, at elite levels there *does* exist a distinctive, subjective set of political attitudes which contrast with working- and lower-class beliefs and values. So there *is* reason for thinking that the inequalities in the social backgrounds of top leaders (discussed in Chapter 6) may be translated into political action. This in turn may well include actions that sustain the maldistribution of economic benefits outlined in the previous chapter.

The Question of Social Mobility

Does mobility into elite positions involve too much turnover for one to assume stable political attitudes? Pluralists often suggest that upward mobility is so open and top positions so merit-oriented that family dynasties, social connections, and "old boy" politics are gone forever. In their place, they suggest, has arisen a post-industrial meritocracy with no stable class attributes. Therefore there is said to be no basis for political class consciousness in America.

This image of America is inaccurate. Mobility in the United States has been no greater than in various European societies, such as France, which are often considered societies in which class is critically important to politics.[1] Most social mobility in America is due to changing occupational structure, not "opportunity" in the abstract. Mobility is created by decreasing the number of farm and manual jobs and increasing the number of service-sector jobs.[2] But most Americans have the same general status as their fathers.[3] They *want* to associate with those of higher status, but they actually associate with people in their own class.[4] This pattern has been true since the early part of this century, if not longer.[5]

The Horatio Alger rags-to-riches myth has little basis today. In a recent study of the several dozen wealthiest men in America, for example, only one was found to come from lower-class origins.[6] The percentage of richest Americans coming from lower-class backgrounds has declined markedly since 1900.[7]

In politics the United States *does* have more mobility into top civil service positions compared to Europe. This is because, except for the diplomatic service, civil servants in America have lower status. As Chapter 6 demonstrated, however, most top civil service jobs are still filled by members of the upper and upper-middle class in the United States. Moreover, American *elected* officials show much *less* mobility than their European counterparts. This is due to the absence of labor parties in America. There is no institutionalized ladder from the workplace through unionism to high political position.[8]

Surveying mobility into top positions, two conservative political scientists concluded that "in the United States, political and nonpolitical leaders come from essentially similar upper-middle-class environments.... The American pattern promotes harmony and understanding between the leaders of society and those of the polity."[9] That is, because social and political leaders come from the same upper levels of the class system, they are able to cooperate and collaborate.

Actually, when one considers the numerous *behavioral* differences between upper and working classes, the existence of *attitudinal* differences seems hardly surprising. Some of the behavioral differences have been discussed by George Kirstein in *The Rich: Are They Different?* (1968). These include education at preparatory rather than public schools, residence in elite rather than working-class neighborhoods, recreation at clubs and resorts rather than in the streets. Even some of our words indicate the difference: philanthropy in the upper class (mostly to education) versus charity in the working class (mostly to religion). Domhoff emphasized other behavioral differences: intermarriage patterns are distinctly class-oriented, as are acquaintance patterns, occupations, and even child-rearing practices. Berelson and Steiner, surveying many social science studies, found class differentials in life chances, family relations patterns, life styles, and personality traits.[10] Given dramatic differences in the behavior of individuals of different social classes, would one not expect differences in political consciousness as well?

Social Class as a Factor in Attitudes

Most studies show that the higher the social class, the more conservative the individual. Similarly, the higher the social class, the more emphasis on education, the higher the aspirations, and—as people move up the economic ladder—the more they become co-opted into the norms and attitudes of their new status levels. Thus, Berelson and Steiner's survey concluded: "The more the upward mobility, the greater the conservative political preferences." This is not to say that upper-status groups are reactionary. In fact, higher status is associated with greater liberalness on matters other than class and economic issues. For example, upper-status individuals are often more liberal on civil liberties.

Class issues have not been decisive in recent election campaigns. Instead noneconomic issues have come to the fore (such as race), along with issues of morality (such as law-and-order issues and post-Watergate emphasis on political integrity) and foreign policy (such as Vietnam, or more recently Reagan's 1976 criticism of President Ford's Panama Canal policy). Consequently, class has declined as a factor in voting behavior.[11] This is especially so among the young, but even working-class voters have been more prone to desert their traditional parties. Perhaps the return of difficult economic times and more political attention to economic issues would reverse this trend, but at present class politics is on the decline. Even so, it is still among the best predictors of voting preferences in America and other countries.[12]

But what of the elite level? Certainly American leaders differ sharply on foreign-policy, economic, and social issues.[13] Berelson and Steiner have noted that "although concern is often voiced about 'the labor vote' there is probably a more solidary 'business vote' in the sense that there is less deviation from the class vote among upper status groups—who, being better educated and better informed as well as more homogenously supported in personal contacts, are more likely to recognize and express their class interest."[14]

In *The Rich: Are They Different?*, Kirstein, himself well-to-do, agrees that the wealthy *are* different in their political attitudes. They stand well to the right. Unlike the common man, Kirstein quips, the rich really do have "a friend at Chase Manhattan," as the advertising of that banking institution has it. He then buttresses his point with anecdotes about the favors done by bankers for their wealthiest clients. These favors are in stark contrast to the treatment of working-class depositors.[15] But is this serious evidence? Is there really a "business viewpoint" or is pluralistic fragmentation the rule, even within the elite?

Francis X. Sutton was among the first to study this question systematically. This work, *The American Business Creed* (1956), analyzed the content of speeches by business leaders, advertisements, and other business documents. Sutton and his associates demonstrated the following definable common business viewpoints:

1. Glorification of the "free enterprise system."
2. Rejection of unionism in favor of settling labor problems through human-relations techniques.
3. Viewing business as a service to customers.
4. Believing competition assures the lowest prices.
5. Holding that free competition requires absence of government regulation.
6. Believing social legislation to be largely unnecessary since capitalism can solve most problems independently of government.

This business view is quite different from public opinion in general. The average American is a believer in "free enterprise," but he or she is a Democrat, believes in unionism, thinks business has too much power, wants expanded government programs, and is skeptical that business serves the consumer well or provides the lowest possible prices.

A more recent study than Sutton's sought to demonstrate the change in business viewpoints over time. Thomas Christ also analyzed the content of American businessmen's speeches to compare the 1900–1929 period with that of 1950–1967. In particular, Christ studied changes in "traditionalism" and "anti-statism":

Traditionalism: *Statements reflecting a past orientation using capitalist symbols and a positive direction. Such as: "Our system of free enterprise has given us the world's highest standard of living." This statement, incidentally, is illustrative of actual speeches but is false in content.*

Anti-statism: *Statements reflecting a negative evaluation of government. ("Unjust taxation is sapping the lifeblood of the nation," for example.)*

Pluralist theory predicted that corporate management would come to represent more popular beliefs as it was freed from traditional family-firm control. But Christ found that corporate managers were actually becoming *more* traditionalist and *more* anti-statist. He attributed this conservative shift to an attempt by business to regain legitimacy after a "fall from grace" during the Depression. That is, as business became more regulated, business attitudes became more deviant from popular beliefs. Not only did Christ find a distinctive business point of view, but it seemed to be more deviant as time went on.[16]

Thus it is perhaps not surprising that a classic study by Richard Centers found 87 percent of large business owners to be conservative or ultra-conservative. Centers also found that three-fourths of the unskilled, semi-skilled, and skilled workers considered themselves "working class." In all, some 51 percent of the American people described themselves as "working class" in Centers's post–World War II study.[17] A more recent survey found no decline in working-class consciousness (as measured by self-labeling) in the postwar period.[18]

While self-labeling is a highly subjective method for gauging class consciousness, classes do make a considerable difference in political attitudes. Robert Erikson and Norman Luttberg summarized some of these differences:[19]

1. Poorer people are more likely than the well-to-do to favor government social welfare programs.

2. Since FDR, preference for the Democratic party has decreased as status increased.

3. The lower the status, the more conservative on noneconomic issues like racial integration (whites only) and tolerance toward civil liberties and dissent (this is tied to lower education).

4. The lower the status, the less internationalist and (slightly) the more dovish on war issues.

As noted earlier, class consciousness remains of critical importance so long as politics is dominated by domestic economic issues. The well-to-do are more liberal on such questions as school integration, abortion, use of marijuana, and approval of women's liberation. There are a number of reasons for this. The more affluent are more educated, and education generally (but not always) breeds tolerance. The less affluent perceive issues in a different context. For them, integration is not an abstract ideal but has immediate impact on job competition, crime, community control, and other aspects of daily life. Finally, the less affluent are more traditionalist in religion, and this, too, tends toward conservatism. This is especially true of issues like abortion, drug use, and toughness of punishment of criminals.

Because of this importance of religion, ethnicity, and other nonclass factors in American life, Richard Hamilton has suggested that class politics in America be discussed in terms of six distinct groups:

1. *Non-Southern, white Protestant working class:* solidly Democratic, with better-paid workers being as Democratic as poorer workers.

2. *White Protestant nonmanual class:* increasingly Republican as level of income increases.

3. *Catholic working class:* even more Democratic than Protestants as a group, but among whom increased income is associated with lower Democratic affiliation.

4. *Catholic nonmanual class:* also more Democratic than Protestant counterparts, Republican only in the top strata.

5. *Jewish nonmanual class:* heavily Democratic even at top strata.

6. *Blacks:* heavily manual in occupation and heavily Democratic.

Thus the upper class is not uniform in outlook. Upper-class Catholics and Jews are very important to the Democratic party. It is the upper-middle-class white Protestants who stand out as being "more conservative than any other group in society." [20]

It is, of course, this class which was shown in Chapter 6 to dominate leadership positions in America. Hamilton's conclusions about class and politics in America clearly undermine the pluralist way of interpreting power in the United States. [21]

Hamilton's findings are corroborated by those of Joan Huber and William Form in *Income and Ideology* (1973), who discovered clear differences in political attitude by class. And the more concrete the subject, the greater the differences:

The most advantaged stratum, rich whites, felt the greatest confidence that the tenets of equal opportunity and equal political influence were operative, while the least advantaged strata, the blacks and the poor, tended to deny that these tenets operated for them.

Consensus on the tenets of the ideology was greatest when they were put in general terms, rather than as situations specifically comparing the opportunities available to the rich or poor. . . . This finding is of fundamental importance because it demonstrates that ideologies legitimize a system most effectively when stated in global terms rather than in specific economic terms that can be tested against everyday experience. This observation points to one function of a dominant ideology: to gloss over differences in rank and thereby legitimize a given distribution of goods and services. Thus, ideology becomes the political formula of the dominant stratum, whose rule is more easily justified when advantages in the market and the polity are concealed in a shower of glittering generalities.[22]

That is, Huber and Form not only show that the dominant stratum holds a distinctive point of view, they have also shown how this viewpoint has become a generalized ideology. That is, their study spells out Marx's dictum that "in every age, the ideas of the ruling class become the ruling ideas." (Recall the discussion of symbolic politics and political hegemony in Chapter 1.)

Pluralist theory portrays beliefs existing in a marketplace of ideas, competing freely with one another in terms of merit and intrinsic appeal. As Edgar Litt has pointed out, this is erroneous. Dominant belief systems have a competitive advantage in the "marketplace." Litt criticized pluralism on much the same basis as Form and Huber, holding that "to try to understand power, then, by discovering who prevails in a specific decision contest (the pluralist approach), is to overlook an important dimension of power, specifically the dominant myths, symbols, and belief orientations which envelop the minds of men and set limits to their struggles, their perceptions, and their wills."[23]

Dominant belief systems are self-validating. Those who believe in equality, opportunity, and in hard work bringing success—those who believe class to be unimportant—will not act in class terms. Much of American politics is directed toward sustaining this sort of belief. The means used vary: emphasis on regional, religious, ethnic, racial, and national differences; the privatization of social problems ("Poverty is my own fault," for example); encouragement of aspirations toward higher class status (anticipatory socialization); and the diffusion of class conflict into intraclass struggles for jobs and benefits. Through such processes the working class becomes divided into the categories discussed by Hamilton and, indeed, into finer distinctions that undercut working-class consciousness in America. (The second half of this chapter will discuss this process in historical terms.)

Those who belittle the importance of class consciousness in American politics are thinking of these processes which fragment the working class. But the process is very different for the highest strata of society. This difference is due to a powerful psychological tendency, the definition of the self so as to improve self-image. As Elizabeth Bott has described, social class functions as a reference group. People tend to perceive themselves equal to those at their own objective (that is, income) class level and the next level toward which they aspire. But they also tend to draw sharp distinctions beneath them, contrasting lower status levels. The working class and those at the bottom of the stratification system have the most psychological incentive to emphasize equality. Their self-image is improved by avoiding class imagery. Their self-concept needs make them especially vulnerable to the pluralistic ideology-of-opportunity discussed by Huber and Form.[24]

In contrast, those at the top of the class system have the greatest psychological incentive to draw class distinctions. An emphasis on class enhances their self-image. Thus, as a leading American political scientist has observed of the upper strata, "as a class they are more highly organized, more easily mobilized, have more facilities for communication, are more like-minded, and are more accustomed to stand together in defense of their privileges than any other group." [25] Class consciousness *is* important in America, and it is most important at the highest levels of the class system.

The Forging of a Dominant Ideology: An Historical Inquiry

The belief systems of the upper strata do not become dominant simply through diffuse filtering-down of elite culture. In addition, elites devote prodigious efforts to make their beliefs dominant. The implicit power which accrues to them in this way, through manipulative socialization of lower strata, is far more important than the influence which the maldistribution of economic benefits can secure directly. Explicit socialization of the working and lower classes is only the more readily observable tip of the overall process of asserting political hegemony. But since it is observable, we may treat it here as an illustration of how class consciousness affects the American political environment.

The Americanization of the immigrants was the single most important example of the process of asserting political hegemony. The "ideology of citizenship" which was its focus is still a basic feature of American political culture. Nearly all contemporary organized efforts at political socialization in schools, churches, and other institutions grew out of this historic process. What was it, and how does it show class consciousness underpinning American politics?

Marx long ago saw how civil religion stabilizes the state. In "On the Jewish Question," he emphasized the religious-like attraction the state in normal times holds for the individual. In citizenship we can regard ourselves as communal beings. As an individual under capitalism, in contrast, the worker is "the plaything of alien powers." He treats others and is himself treated as a means. Citizenship in the state is thus an attractive fiction. The social relations of production, on the other hand, are real but unattractive. In both situations men are alienated and unfulfilled. In citizenship, however, the worker may pretend to be fulfilled as "an imaginary member of an imagined sovereignty." Thus, Marx wrote: "The political state is as spiritual in relation to civil society as heaven is in relation to earth. . . . The democratic state, the real state, needs no religion for its political fulfillment. It can, rather, do without religion because it fulfills the human basis of religion in a secular way." [26] To fulfill the human basis of religion in a secular way is the purpose of citizenship as ideology.

Patriotism and New Wealth in the 1880s and 1890s

Citizenship does not have an eternal, unchangeable nature. On the contrary, it is an historic phenomenon like all others. It has a past and future. It is difficult to keep in mind that present social forms had an historic origin. But at one time they did not exist, and had to be created to serve emergent needs. And more than created, they had to be legitimated. Like many of the modern social forms we now take for granted, citizenship acquired its modern form in a particular period in American history. It grew to its modern form in the late nineteenth and early twentieth centuries when the consolidation of corporate capital was giving rise to the trusts and to new men of wealth.

E. Digby Baltzell, in his social history of the upper class, cited "the new wave of ancestral associations" formed at the end of the nineteenth century.[27] The president-general of the Sons of the American Revolution noted the connection of the ancestral associations to reaction against the tide of immigration. "Not until the state of civilization reached the point where we had a great many foreigners in our land," he wrote, "were our patriotic societies successful." [28] In all, thirty-five patriotic, hereditary, and historical associations were formed around the 1890s, on the heels of the establishment of the elite *Social Register* in 1887. These included the Colonial Dames (1890), the Daughters of the American Revolution (DAR) (1890), and the Society of Mayflower Descendents (1894). These were primarily associations of the upper class.

Baltzell viewed the formation of such associations as part of a "quest for old-stock roots" among the newly wealthy of the late nineteenth century. During this period the upper class was consolidating around new social institutions such as summer resorts. Northeast Harbor, Maine, became the first elite resort, during the 1880s. This social trend included the formation of elite suburbs such as Tuxedo Park, N.Y. (1886); the first country club (Brookline, Mass., 1882); and the founding or restructuring of metropolitan men's clubs, elite preparatory schools, and college fraternal societies.[29]

In this rush of institution-founding it is impossible to separate patriotic from merely social elements. Illustrative is the sports movement of this period. The new resorts and country clubs were centers of new sports, like golf [30] and bicycling.[31] Earlier and more striking was the resurgence of college sports and amateur athletics. The National Association of Amateur Athletes was founded in 1879, merging a decade later with the American Athletic Union.[32]

Edward Chase Kirkland, in *Dream and Thought in the Business Community* (1956), noted that athletics became an enduring part of college life in the 1890s. Its "adventitious appearance on campus might make college education more acceptable to the business community," he wrote.[33] The spirit described by Kirkland was one of intense activity and an overriding concern for "making the team" as part of the struggle for success in life. One finds a striking parallel to the English concept of "the playing fields of Eton" being the training grounds for the rulers of empire. Not only in this diffuse way, but also in the form of martial and patriotic band music and flags, the sports movement acquired a mood which strangely if not untypically blended patriotism, nationalism, masculinity, competition, and personal success as values for the rising elite who took part in college and amateur athletics.

The athletic clubs themselves tended to give way to explicitly elite institutions. "The highboard fence athletic field has been supplanted by the country house," one magazine wrote, "designed not for its athletic facilities alone but for the pleasures of country life." [34] Though the rigors of athleticism did not carry the day among the social elite, "the athletic fury" continued apace at Princeton, Yale, Harvard, and similar colleges. The wedding of the sports movement and patriotism reached a peak at the Chicago World's Fair and in the revival of the Olympics, heavily influenced by the American movement.

Patriotism and Play for the Masses

An 1896 issue of *Scribner's Magazine* observed: "There has always been an aristocracy of 'sport' and it has existed until very recently. It has been so necessarily for the successful prosecution of sport has required the possession of time and means...."[35] But between 1880 and 1920 the sports movement was brought to the masses by more privileged groups. The blending of mass athletics and patriotism was illustrated in a speech by Colonel Charles Larned, head of the U.S. Military Academy. Speaking before the third annual convention of the Intercollegiate Athletics Association, Larned cited the example of the Public School Athletic League of New York City. "For 1905," Larned stated, "the League motto was DUTY; for 1906, THOROUGHNESS; for 1907, PATRIOTISM; for 1908, HONOR; for 1909 it is OBEDIENCE. Three, I may add, constitute the motto of the Military Academy; and all, its basic principles."[36]

The use of the schools to inculcate patriotism and, more broadly, assimilation into "the American way of life," was a pattern which evolved over a long period of time in the nineteenth century.[37] The institutionalization of patriotism became greatly accelerated during the 1890s, however, in reaction to "the menace of unchecked immigration." Foremost in this respect was the American Protective Association (APA, founded 1886).

The turning point in the APA's growth came in 1893. Between 1893 and 1896 it claimed a membership rise from 70,000 to 2.5 million members.[38] W. J. H. Traynor, president of the APA, claimed that "the American Protective Association is the strongest and purest political force that the world ever knew. It grew from the parent stem of pure motives and patriotism."[39] The APA, along with the Immigration Restriction League (IRL), fought a long and successful campaign culminating in the passage of the literacy test for immigration in 1917.[40]

In addition to the "patriotic" efforts of the APA and IRL and of the traditional patriotic societies like the Colonial Dames,[41] liberal reform efforts displayed similar tendencies if not rhetoric. These liberal efforts were illustrated, for example, by the YMCA government courses for immigrants and the founding of American International College. At AIC's School of Citizenship, American history and ideals were taught in the form of talks based on the lives of eminent Americans. Other subjects included American government, patriotism, sanitation, and personal hygiene.[42]

Patriotic exercises in the school were viewed as an exciting experiment in reform. It was a means to fight antisocial "Bohemianism" and to instill a "wholesome spirit." In 1892, Jacob Riis described how the public schools sought to transform surly Bohemians "into that which his father would have long since become, had he not gotten a wrong start—a loyal American, proud of his country, and a useful citizen." Riis pointed to the New York City schools as a model:

Very lately a unique exercise has been added to these schools that lays hold of the very marrow of the problem with which they deal. It is called "saluting the flag," and originated with George T. Balch of the Board of Education, who conceived the idea of instilling patriotism into the little future citizens of the Republic in doses to suit their childish minds. To talk about the Union, which most of them had but the vaguest notion, or of the duty of the citizen, of which they had no notion at all, was nonsense.

In the flag it was all found embodied in a central idea which they could grasp. In the morning the star-spangled banner was brought into the school and the children were taught to salute it with patriotic words. Then the best scholar of the day before was called out of the ranks and it was given to him or her to keep for the day. The thing took on at once and was a tremendous success. . . .

Every morning sees the flag carried to the principal's desk and all the little ones, rising at the stroke of the bell, say with one voice, "We turn to our flag as the sunflower turns to the sun!" One bell, and every brown fist is raised to the brow, as in a military salute: "We give our hands!" Another stroke, and the grimy little hands are laid on as many hearts: "And our hearts!" Then with a shout that can be heard around the corner: "To our country! One country, one language, one flag!" [43]

In 1898 an act was passed in the state of New York to "provide for the display of the United States flag on the schoolhouses of the State," in connection with the public schools, and to encourage patriotic exercises in such schools. In 1900 the legislature authorized preparation of a *Manual of Patriotism* for school use.[44] This specifically welcomed and endorsed the work of the Colonial Dames, the DAR, the GAR, and other patriotic societies of the upper class. After its success in New York, this pattern spread to other states.

Social Work and the Institutionalization of Citizenship

As in the public schools, the social-work movement of the 1890s and 1900s paralleled the political thrusts of other elite efforts to Americanize the immigrant. At Chicago's Hull House, Jane Addams's Working People's Social Science Club heard "addresses and discussions by judges, lawyers, and businessmen." [45] The Boys Clubs, E. J. Wendell wrote, "will do more than anything else ever can do to counteract the dangerous influences of the street and make them honest, true, and law-abiding citizens." [46] The first club was founded in 1878, the second in 1884, and about a dozen more between 1889 and 1891. Working-Girls Clubs featured "practical talks" on such topics as "When women take men's places and cut down wages, what is the effect on the home?" [47] In all these activities the uniting political theme was the virtue of "good citizenship."

Much of the social-work thrust had a missionary aspect in a religious sense. The Salvation Army began its Slum Brigade in New York City in 1890.[48] Even earlier, the Fresh-Air Fund, started by Pastor Willard Parsons in 1877, had given rise to predominantly church-related "vacation societies for about every class of the poor." [49] In the year of the great railroad riots, 1877, the first Associated Charities settlement house was formed at Buffalo, N.Y. Andover House was formed in Boston in 1891, drawing support from the Andover Theological Seminary. One supporter wrote that "there is a fervor about this consecration to the work of social Christianity." [50]

In 1907 the YMCA sponsored a conference for social workers, philanthropists, businessmen, and other leaders "for the specific purpose of forming an organization to accomplish the civic betterment of the immigrant." [51] The result was the North American Civic League. It was based on "representatives of the more conservative economic interests" and was devoted to educating the immigrant in close cooperation with the public schools. By the 1910s the movement to Americanize the immigrant had cloaked itself with the sanction of law, allying industrial, state, and federal agencies.[52] These efforts in the name of "good citizenship" were consciously and specifically directed toward "lessening the danger of industrial disorder" and "that type of socialism which is synonymous with treason."

World War I and the Consolidation of the Citizenship Ideal

With World War I the close connection between social work and the more conservative uses of "citizenship" as ideology was revealed. In the field of recreation, for example, the "play movement," which had started in Boston's sand gardens (1885–1895), gradually evolved through emphasis on model playgrounds and small parks to institutionalization first as recreation centers and later as organizations for civic welfare and community service.[53] The tone of this movement may be inferred from a 1914 letter to the directors of small parks: "Three fundamental and generic purposes to be secured are (1) the preservation of health, (2) raising civic and industrial standards, and (3) increasing industrial efficiency." [54]

The emphasis on industrial efficiency is not obscure. In the 1910s social work had a significant impact on industry. Recreational programs were introduced in factories to promote a more wholesome work force and to diminish disruption.[55]

The Playground Association of America was formed in 1906. Its first president, Luther Gulick, came out of YMCA work. Even before the war, the links between the recreation movement and more general public concerns were clear. Between May 1916 and November 1918, seven states (N.Y., N.J., Nev., R.I., Cal., Md., Del.) adopted laws requiring physical training in school. Eventually most states followed suit. In New York this law was associated with the state's Military Training Commission. The California law linked physical education to promoting "such desirable moral and social qualities as appreciation of the value of cooperation, self-subordination, and obedience to authority." [56]

Secretary of War Newton Baker wrote in 1917 that he had at first been skeptical of the "emphasis on the body" rather than straight indoctrination of the mind. But he said his attitude changed as he began to see the effect on Army recruits. "There has grown up in America this new attitude," he wrote, "which finds its expression in public playgrounds, in the organization of community amusements, in the inculcation throughout the entire body of young people in the community of substantially the same form of social inducement which the American college in modern times has substituted for the earlier system of social restraints." [57]

Recreational social work was a new and more effective form of social restraint. It found its fruition in World War I. In 1917 the War Department's Commission on Training Camp Activities called on the Playground and Recreation Association (PRAA) to aid in war mobilization. The joint War Department/PRAA effort led to the establishment of over a hundred war recreation secretariats serving 170 cities by the beginning of 1918.

In each area commanding officers took a census of each recruit stationed in the district. This information was funneled to the war recreation secretaries. "The [census] cards," it was reported, "make it possible to know a man's church, fraternity, college, professional, and trade affiliations and put him in touch with the groups in the cities with which his former interests and relationships would naturally tie him up. The cards also disclose a man's favorite form of recreation and hobby and with this knowledge the local committees are better able to plan their programs. The information on the cards makes it possible for the churches to extend personal invitations to their members, for lodges, clubs, and fraternal organizations to entertain their brothers in camp, and is giving a personal touch to all the work." [58] Separate parallel activities were undertaken for blacks. In this effort there was close cooperation with the Rotarians, Masons, Elks, Knights of Columbus, churches, and other "nonpolitical" organizations.

Other activities were directed toward the public, such as "Patriotic Play Week" [59] and May Day celebrations.[60] Through the National Americanization Committee and other organizations, many reform efforts aimed at the immigrant became blended in the movement for the war effort.[61] George Creel's Committee on Public Information became the first national-level propaganda agency in America, mobilizing 15,000 publicists, scholars, and civic leaders behind a campaign against criticism of the war. The schools were also mobilized behind patriotic slogans. As the author of *Teaching the Child Patriotism* put it, "War is often a purifying fire. It has its noble and uplifting side. This is the side which is emphasized in the heroic tales which have been mentioned, and which makes for the development of patriotism in the child and in the man." [62]

Patriotism was also used as a theme to promote industrial peace. For this purpose a critical organization was the Alliance for Labor and Democracy, a front group for the Creel Committee. As Creel wrote: "The loyalty of 'our aliens,' however splendid it was, had in it nothing of the spontaneous or accidental. Results were obtained only by hard, driving work. The bitterness bred by years of neglect and injustice were not to be dissipated by any mere war-call, but had to be burned away by a continuous educational campaign." [63]

The wartime propaganda campaign for patriotic Americanism formed the backdrop to the mass repression of the Palmer Raids of 1919–1920. It also lay behind the anti-union drives of the 1920s and the rise of a new generation of middle-class patriotic groups such as the American Legion, which became a political force during the 1920s and 1930s. Under such organizations as the American Legion, the American Security League, the League for Constitutional Government, and the Daughters of the American Revolution, the danger of "Bolshevism" was used to fuel a drive to destroy the inroads radicals had made among immigrants and laborers prior to the war.[64]

Civic Education After World War I

With the general disillusionment that followed the war came a pessimism about the civic potential of the common man. In-

fluential works such as Walter Lippmann's *The Phantom Public*
(1925) attacked the notions of "the public interest," arguing
that on nearly all issues the average person lacked an informed
opinion. As this viewpoint became common among intellectuals,[65] the basis was laid for a belief in insulating the highest
echelons of government from the influence of the ignorant many.
Thus, ironically but not accidentally, a tendency to curtail the
substance of citizenship appeared at the very time patriotism
and citizenship were being instilled vigorously as suitable ideals
for the new immigrants.

Ideas such as Lippmann's were unsettling for postwar intellectuals and reformers. During the war, reformers and industrialists, liberals and conservatives, were united in a patriotic
effort to "make the world safe for democracy." But after the war
new concerns and new divisions arose over the nature of democracy at home. Many accepted Lippmann's criticism of the public and turned to civic education as a remedy.

In the late 1920s and early 1930s Charles Merriam led a
number of social scientists in a comparative study of civic education. They documented the many sources of socialization:
schools, political groups, religious organizations, economic interests. What these studies tended to show was the pervasive
effect on civic education by private, often conservative groups,
quite apart from the schools.[66]

With the coming of the Depression, more urgent, visionary
appeals were made to recapture citizenship training. Reformers
again sought to use civic education as an instrument of democratic response to crisis. George Counts, a leader in education,
reflected this tone in the title of his *Dare the Schools Build a
New Social Order?* (1932). In *Education and the Social Crisis*
(1932), William Kilpatrick, a spokesman of the Progressive
Education Movement, called on the education profession to be
"critical of social life around us." He sought education such that
"life will have less power to miseducate the young." [67]

In spite of the social milieu of the Depression, such progressive ideas failed to displace traditional, more conservative
notions of civic education.[68] The institutions of patriotic (as opposed to critical) citizenship had already become firmly established. More important, the rising Fascist threat favored the more

solidaristic, patriotic versions of citizenship. Even the reformers' own emphasis on the need for educating an "ill-prepared" electorate contained profound conservative implications. This was especially so as the limited capacity of civic education to transform the citizenry became clear.

In his presidential address to the American Political Science Association in 1934, Walter Shepard urged that the task of the electorate be "simplified" greatly. "The dogma of universal suffrage," he wrote, "must find a way to a system of educational and other tests which will exclude the ignorant, the uninformed, and the antisocial elements which have hitherto so frequently controlled elections. . . . There is a large element of fascist doctrine and practice that we must appropriate." [69] Though Shepard went on to urge civil liberties and education "untrammeled by propaganda," the general thrust of his thought was toward social control, not building a new social order.

The transformation of civic education from a policy to renew democracy to one of inculcation of patriotism began long before World War II. Though some retained progressive views, they were overshadowed by the perspective represented in Elmer Ellis's *Education Against Propaganda* (1937). Sponsored by the National Council for Social Studies, this work's negative concept of "education against" was conservative in concept.

In part education against propaganda had origins in concern for the importance of nongovernmental groups in the socialization process. Far more important was the increasing emphasis on value consensus as war drew closer. By 1940 the question had changed from building a new social order to guarding democracy against fascism. As Francis Wilson noted of FDR, "Roosevelt's doctrine is, withal, a doctrine of conservative nationalism. There is authority, legitimate authority, in the nation because of the moral contribution it makes to the life of each citizen. . . . The morality of a national society expresses itself in a unified will." [70]

With the outbreak of World War II, civic education became a matter of information management. Harwood Childs wrote that "the public opinion problem which the United States faces is something more than a problem of good journalism. It is a problem of rallying the American people, and the people of the world for that matter, behind the philosophy of life, a democratic way, which gives sense and meaning to rapidly shifting international events." [71] Civic education had become a vehicle for national mobilization again. It was a channel whereby the nation might make its "moral contribution to the life of each citizen."

Even after the war, with the advent of the cold war, this orientation continued. It was illustrated in the series of conferences on citizenship sponsored by the Citizenship Committee, the Commission for the Defense of Democracy through Education (an organ of the National Education Association) in cooperation with the Department of Justice. President Truman wrote to the 1947 meeting of this group: "With the serious problems of this postwar period confronting us daily, our country needs the strongest and most unified citizenship that it is possible to attain." [72] The tone of this continuing organization was suggested by slogans such as "responsible citizenship" or the quotation heading its report, "The peril of this nation is not in any foreign foe! We, the people, are its power, its peril, and its hope!"

The internal peril, and education to overcome it by training responsible citizens, was a continuing theme of the cold war period. Through organizations such as the CIA-funded Congress for Cultural Freedom, the postwar period saw an infusion of anticommunism as the central theme of the ideology of citizenship, descending at times even to a defense of McCarthyism.[73]

Conclusion

The period after World War II was marked by an academic "celebration of America." [74] The "pluralists" in political science, the "consensus school" in history, and the "functionalists" in sociology all viewed the American system in very favorable terms. Characteristic was the concept of "the end of ideology," by which was meant the end of class-based politics. Seymour Martin Lipset wrote, for example, that "the pattern of stable Western democracies in the mid-twentieth century is that they are in a 'post-politics' phase. . . . In large measure this situation reflects the fact that in these countries the workers have won their fight for full citizenship." [75]

The history of citizenship suggests, however, that political moderation and quietism are more associated with a successful fight to foist the ideology of citizenship *onto* the working class. Certainly the image of citizenship as something gained by immigrant workers against the will of resisting upper social groups is a misleading myth. In fact, that myth is itself part of the "ideology of citizenship."

Political scientists today are increasingly aware of the largely symbolic nature of voting and of the norms of civic duty and citizenship.[76] Nonetheless there is no strong value consensus binding the working class to liberal democracy through citizenship.[77] On the contrary, low commitment to democratic norms is an established feature of American politics. This has to do with "multiple consciousness." [78] That is, under the surface ideology of satisfaction one finds far-ranging discontents and alienation. The same individual is apt to believe simultaneously in the value of voting *and* in the corruption of politics and the primacy of money.

The contradictory nature of this multiple belief system cannot be understood adequately as "value consensus." On the basis of a study of national opinion surveys, Michael Mann concluded:

Thus there are strong suggestions that the necessary mixed model of social cohesion in liberal democracy should be based more on Marxist conflict theory than sociologists have usually thought. A significant measure of consensus and normative harmony may be necessary among ruling groups, but it is the absence of consensus among lower classes which keeps them compliant. And if we wish to explain this lack of consensus, we must rely to some extent on the Marxist theories of pragmatic role acceptance and manipulative socialization.[79]

Mann thus supports those who have noted more cohesion of elite ideology than of working-class beliefs.

In this chapter we have argued that there *is* a distinctive business elite point of view which contrasts with public opinion in general. While working-class beliefs are divided rather than united in opposition to elite beliefs, we may still find reason to believe it *does* make a difference what the social background of our leaders is. Moreover, the evidence cited in this chapter supports the inference that the elite draws tremendous implicit power from the socialization process in general and from the "ideology of citizenship" in particular. Of such ideology Thorstein Veblen once wrote that "no other consideration is allowed in the abatement of the claims of patriotic loyalty and . . . such loyalty will be allowed to cover a multitude of sins." [80] The religious-like attraction the ideology of citizenship holds for the individual preserves social cohesion by obscuring class inequities.[81]

Notes

1. Seymour Martin Lipset and Reinhard Bendix, *Social Mobility in Industrial Society* (Berkeley: University of California Press, 1959), p. 72.
2. T. B. Bottomore, *Classes in Modern Society* (New York: Vintage, 1968; orig. 1965), p. 43–44.
3. Richard Centers, "Occupational Mobility of Urban Occupational Strata," *American Sociological Review* 13 (April 1948): 197–203.
4. Edward O. Laumann and Richard Centers, "Subjective Social Distance, Occupational Structure, and Forms of Status and Class Consciousness," *American Journal of Sociology* 81 (May 1976): 1304–38.
5. See Peter Blau and O. D. Duncan, *The American Occupational Structure* (New York: Wiley, 1967).
6. Vance Packard, *The Status Seekers* (New York: McKay, 1959), p. 289.
7. C. Wright Mills, *The Power Elite* (New York: Oxford, 1956), p. 105.
8. Lipset and Bendix, *Social Mobility in Industrial Society*, p. 73.
9. Z. Brzezinski and S. Huntington, *Political Power: USA/USSR* (New York: Viking, 1964), p. 138.
10. Bernard Berelson and Gary Steiner, *Human Behavior* (New York: Harcourt, Brace and World, 1964), ch. 11. See also Lucile Duberman, *Social Inequalities: Class and Caste in America* (Philadelphia: J. B. Lippincott, 1976), chs. 5–9.
11. John W. Books and JoAnn B. Reynolds, "A Note on Class Voting in Great Britain and the United States," *Comparative Political Studies* 8 (October 1975): 360–75. However, class continues to be strongly related to nonvoting. See Sidney Verba and Norman H. Nie, *Participation in America* (New York: Harper & Row, 1972), 339–40; see also Robert Weissberg, *Political Learning, Political Choice, and Democratic Citizenship* (Englewood Cliffs, N.J.: Prentice-Hall, 1974), ch. 5. Weissberg reviews numerous class-related studies and concludes that "it is nevertheless clear that lower-class children, black children, and young females are socialized to be handicapped in the political struggle" (p. 120).
12. S. Verba and N. Nie, *Political Participation* (New York: Harper & Row, 1972), p. 336.

226   Class Analysis and Business Power

13. Allen H. Bourton, "Consensus and Conflict among American Leaders," *Public Opinion Quarterly* (Winter 1974–75): 507–30.
14. Berelson and Steiner, *Human Behavior,* pp. 427–28. More recent data by Books and Reynolds support this contention (see note 11, Table 3), though data are for "nonmanual" rather than "business" specifically.
15. George G. Kirstein, *The Rich: Are They Different?* (Boston: Houghton Mifflin, 1968), pp. 228–29.
16. See Thomas Christ, "A Thematic Analysis of the American Business Creed," *Social Forces* 49 (December 1970), 239–45. Entrepreneurs who were not corporate managers continued to be traditionalistic and, like managers, were becoming more anti-statist.
17. See Richard Centers, "The Psychology of Social Class" (1949), excerpted in P. Blumberg, ed., *The Impact of Social Class* (New York: Crowell, 1972), pp. 246–54.
18. E. M. Schreiber and G. T. Nygreem, "Subjective Social Class in America," *Social Forces* 48 (March 1970): 348.
19. See Robert S. Erikson and Norman R. Luttberg, *American Public Opinion: Its Origins, Content and Impact* (New York: Wiley, 1973), ch. 6.
20. Richard Hamilton, *Class and Politics in the United States* (New York: Wiley, 1972), p. 518.
21. Ibid., pp. 519–20. Hamilton writes, "The key factual assumptions of the revised pluralist theory, thus, prove to be largely unsupported. The established, secure, educated upper-middle class, in particular the more influential white Protestants, do not appear to be especially responsible, either in matters concerning immediate economic welfare or in matters at some remove such as support for more adequate education; nor are they especially supportive of civil rights initiatives.... The findings of this work indicate that many of the dangers and threats to the democratic regime issue instead from the ranks of those who have been portrayed as the guarantors of the democratic arrangement." Hamilton concludes with a discussion of the misrepresentation of public opinion by more conservative elite groups, accomplished in the interest of legitimating conservative policies not consonant with majority public opinion.
22. Joan Huber and William H. Form, *Income and Ideology: An Analysis of the American Political Formula* (New York: Free Press, 1973), pp. 153–54.
23. Edgar Litt, *Democracy's Ordeal in America* (Hinsdale, Ill.: Dryden, 1973), pp. 58–59.
24. Elizabeth Bott, "The Concept of Class as a Reference Group" (1954), reprinted in G. Thielbar and S. Feldman, eds., *Issues in Social Inequality* (Boston: Little, Brown, 1972), pp. 47–69.
25. E. E. Schattschneider, quoted in Litt, *Democracy's Ordeal in America,* p. 63. As mentioned in Chapter 1, Schattschneider emphasized the capacity of this elite group to influence general opinion through "the mobilization of bias": the creation of what Marx called "false consciousness," and Gramsci terms "class hegemony."
26. Karl Marx, "On the Jewish Question" (1843), in L. Easton and K. Guddat, eds., *Writings of the Young Marx on Philosophy and Society* (New York: Doubleday, 1967), pp. 225, 228–29.
27. E. Digby Baltzell, *The Protestant Establishment: Aristocracy and Caste in America* (New York: Vintage, 1964), pp. 114–16.

28. Quoted in ibid., p. 115.
29. See ibid., ch. 5. See also Robert Grant, "The North Shore of Massachusetts," *Scribner's Magazine* 16 (July 1894): 3–20; W. C. Brownell, "Newport," *Scribner's Magazine* 16 (August 1894): 135–56; F. M. Crawford, "Bar Harbor," *Scribner's Magazine* 16 (September 1894): 268–84; George A. Hubbard, "Lenox," *Scribner's Magazine* 16 (October 1894): 420–37.
30. Henry E. Howland, "Golf," *Scribner's Magazine* 17 (May 1895): 531–47.
31. James Townsend, "The Social Side of Bicycling," *Scribner's Magazine* 17 (June 1895): 304–308.
32. Charles H. Sawyer, "Amateur Track and Field Athletics," *Scribner's Magazine* 7 (June 1890): 775–82.
33. Edward Chase Kirkland, *Dream and Thought in the Business Community, 1860–1900* (Chicago: Quadrangle, 1956), p. 110.
34. Duncan Edwards, "Life at the Athletic Clubs," *Scribner's Magazine,* 18 (July 1895): 8.
35. "Aristocracy and Sport," *Scribner's Magazine* 19 (February 1896): 255–56.
36. Charles W. Larned, "Athletics from a Historical and Educational Standpoint," *Proceedings of the Third Annual Convention of the Intercollegiate Athletics Association of the United States* (IAA, 1909), p. 32.
37. See Michael B. Katz, *Bureaucracy and the Schools: The Illusion of Educational Change in America* (New York: Praeger, 1971; rev. ed. 1975); *The Irony of Early School Reform* (Boston: Beacon Press, 1968). See also Joel H. Spring, *Education and the Rise of the Corporate State* (Boston: Beacon Press, 1972).
38. W. J. H. Traynor, "Policy and Power of the APA," *North American Review* 162 (June 1896): 662, 666.
39. Ibid., p. 666.
40. See Edward George Hartmann, *The Movement to Americanize the Immigrant* (New York: Columbia University Press, 1948), p. 31.
41. Ibid., pp. 33 ff.
42. Ibid., p. 31.
43. Jacob Riis, "The Children of the Poor," *Scribner's Magazine* 11 (May 1892): 548–49.
44. Charles R. Skinner, *Manual of Patriotism* (Albany, N.Y.: Brandow Printing Co., 1900).
45. Joseph Kirkland, "Among the Poor of Chicago," *Scribner's Magazine* 9 (June 1891): 952. See also Spring, *Education and the Rise of the Corporate State,* pp. 71–72.
46. E. Wendell, "Boys' Clubs," *Scribner's Magazine* 9 (June 1891): 952.
47. Clara S. Davidge, "Working-Girls Clubs," *Scribner's Magazine* 15 (May 1894): 620.
48. Maud Ballington Booth, "Salvation Army Work in the Slums," *Scribner's Magazine* 17 (January 1895): 105.
49. Willard Parsons, "The Story of the Fresh-Air Fund," *Scribner's Magazine* 9 (April 1891): 523.
50. William Jewett Tucker, "The Work of the Andover House in Boston," *Scribner's Magazine* 13 (March 1893): 372.
51. Hartmann, *Movement to Americanize the Immigrant,* p. 38.
52. Ibid., chs. 3 and 4.

53. Clarence Rainwater, *The Play Movement in the United States* (Chicago: University of Chicago Press, 1922), p. 46.
54. Ibid., p. 148.
55. On the industrial recreation movement, see "Measurable Effects of Welfare Work in Industry," *The Playground* 12 (January 1919): 428–36; "Federating Industrial Athletics," *The Playground* 13 (March 1920): 584–85; John Glenn, "Industrial Recreation," *The Playground* 18 (September 1924): 337–39.
56. Thomas A. Storey, "State Legislation for Physical Training," *The Playground* 12 (November 1918): 352.
57. Newton Baker, in *The Playground* 11 (January 1918): 477.
58. "War Camp Community Service: A Nation-Wide Experiment in Friendliness," *The Playground* 11 (January 1918): 484.
59. C. H. Gifford, "Suggested Procession and Pageant for the Patriotic Play Week," *The Playground* 12 (September 1918): 225–27.
60. Constance D'Arcy McKay, "May Day Programs," *The Playground* 12 (January 1919): 436–40.
61. See Hartmann, *Movement to Americanize the Immigrant*, ch. 8.
62. Kate Upson Clarke, *Teaching the Child Patriotism* (Boston: Page, 1918), pp. 20–21.
63. Quoted in Alan Wolfe, *The Seamy Side of Democracy: Repression in America* (New York: McKay, 1973), p. 157.
64. See Hartmann, *Movement to Americanize the Immigrant*, ch. 9; and William Gellerman, *The American Legion as Educator* (New York: Teacher's College, Columbia University, 1938). After World War I, "Americanism" was transformed from the wartime idea that common interest overrode class and sectional interests to the more conservative notion of "100 percent Americanism," by which was meant "one hundred percent agreement with the American Legion point of view on many matters of public policy which in ordinary circles are considered to have several sides, any one of which may be taken without arousing any question as to one's patriotism or intelligence" (Gellerman, p. 85).
65. See G. David Garson, "On the Origins of Interest Group Theory: A Critique of a Process," *American Political Science Review* 68 (December 1974): 1505–19.
66. These studies included Charles E. Merriam, *The Making of Citizens* (Chicago: University of Chicago Press, 1931), and *Civic Education in the United States* (New York: Scribner's, 1934); Bessie Louis Pierce, *Citizens Organizations in the Civic Training of Youth* (New York: Scribner's, 1933); and A. C. Krey, *Conclusions and Recommendations: Report of the Commission of the Social Sciences* (New York: Scribner's, 1934).
67. William H. Kilpatrick, *Education and the Social Crisis: A Proposed Program* (New York: Liveright, 1932), p. 80.
68. R. Alan Lawson, *The Failure of Independent Liberalism, 1930–1941* (New York: Capricorn, 1971), esp. Part II.
69. Walter Shepard, "Democracy in Transition," *American Political Science Review* 29 (February 1935): 18–19.
70. Francis G. Wilson, "The Revival of Organic Theory," *American Political Science Review* 36 (June 1942): 459.
71. Harwood Childs, "Public Information and Opinion," *American Political Science Review* 37 (February 1943): 67.

72. National Education Association, *Report of the Second Annual Conference on Citizenship* (Washington, D.C.: NEA, 1947), p. 5.
73. Christopher Lasch, "The Cultural Cold War: A Short History of the Congress for Cultural Freedom," in B. Bernstein, ed., *Towards a New Past: Dissenting Essays in American History* (New York: Random House, 1967), p. 338. Joseph McCarthy was a senator who came to symbolize persecution of radicals during the early 1950s.
74. C. Wright Mills, "On Knowledge and Power" (1955), in I. L. Horowitz, ed., *Power, Politics and People: The Collected Essays of C. Wright Mills* (New York: Ballantine, 1963), pp. 602–603.
75. Seymour Martin Lipset, *Political Man: The Social Basis of Politics* (Garden City, N.Y.: Doubleday, 1960), p. 82.
76. See, for example, Edgar Litt, "Civic Education, Community Norms, and Political Indoctrination," *American Sociological Review* 28 (February 1963): 69–75; Murray Edelman, *The Symbolic Uses of Politics* (Urbana: University of Illinois Press, 1964); Louis Lipsitz, "On Political Belief: The Grievances of the Poor," in P. Green and S. Levinson, eds., *Power and Community: Dissenting Essays in Political Science* (New York: Random House, 1969); and Jack Dennis, "Support for the Institution of Elections by the Mass Public," *American Political Science Review* 64 (September 1970): 819–35.
77. See Michael C. Thomas and Charles C. Flippen, "American Civil Religion: An Empirical Study," *Social Forces* 51 (December 1972): 218–25.
78. See G. David Garson, "Radical Issues in the History of the American Working Class," *Politics and Society* 3 (Fall 1972): 25–32; and "Automobile Workers and the Radical Dream," *Politics and Society* 3 (Winter 1973): 163–77.
79. Michael Mann, "The Social Cohesion of Liberal Democracy," *American Sociological Review* 35 (June 1970): 437. Pragmatic role acceptance refers to being "satisfied" with one's lot because no realistic alternatives are perceived. Manipulative socialization refers to inculcation of elite beliefs through the schools, churches, media, and other socializing institutions.
80. Thorstein Veblen, "The Nature of Peace" (1917), excerpted in Max Lerner, ed., *The Portable Veblen* (New York: Viking Press, 1948), p. 588.
81. For an excellent discussion of these issues, see Frank Parkin, *Class Inequality and Political Order* (New York: Praeger, 1971), ch. 3.

9. An Historical Case: The Politics of Oil

The ideology of citizenship may be contrasted with the world of elite politics. By selecting the politics of oil for an historical case study, we can investigate the claims of the pluralist and elite theorists. That is, we can investigate the argument that business is merely one among many opposing interests (the pluralist view), or that business is a preeminent interest often acting outside the public interest (the elite-theory view). This approach will complement the historical treatment of citizenship in the previous chapter and will introduce the history of government-economic relations to be treated in Chapters 10 and 11. As in earlier chapters we will find *neither* pluralist *nor* elite theory is sufficient. Instead there is a need for a new framework transcending both.

The Exxon Corporation, formerly known as Standard Oil, is one of a small handful of companies that dominate the politics of oil in America. Until recently they did so in the world as well. Though the rise of the Organization of Petroleum-Exporting Countries (OPEC) has fundamentally restructured international oil, Exxon remains an obvious example of economic concentration. It employs three times as many people overseas as the U.S. State Department. It operates a tanker fleet twice as large as that of the USSR. Its interlocking directorships tie it closely with many banks, insurance firms, utilities, universities, transport companies, and other manufacturing and distributing enterprises. Exxon operates over 250 suborganizations in more than fifty nations. Its own intelligence and paramilitary networks protect its functions.

As David Horowitz has written, Exxon "is not a secret organization but it is run by a self-perpetuating oligarchy whose decisions and operations are secret. And these affect directly and significantly the level of activity of the whole U.S. economy." [1] Because of the size of organizations such as Exxon, broadly influencing political affairs, the term "private government" has been coined. This indicates the similarity to political institutions. And as with political institutions, one of the best ways to understand a private government like Exxon is to ask how it came to have the size and power it does.

Standard Oil (EXXON): An Historical Perspective

In the first half of the nineteenth century, oil was merely a curiosity. Its use was largely confined to popular medicine. By 1850, however, the supply of whale oil for lighting was becoming short. At first, kerosene, coal oil distilled from coal and oil-shale, seemed to provide the best alternative. Then, in 1859, oil was discovered at Drake's Well in Titusville, Pennsylvania.

Drake's well precipitated an oil rush. This was part of the movement to exploit natural resources in the mid-nineteenth century. The American movement included the famous gold rush in California in 1849. It also included a silver rush in Colorado and Nevada, a copper rush in Michigan, and an iron rush in New York. As elsewhere, the oil rush created a boom-town atmosphere. Many new enterprises were created, prices fluctuated wildly, investors rapidly accumulated or lost wealth. An intense and unregulated market in oil was created. The historic role of Standard Oil and the Rockefeller family was to bring order to this free and unruly competition.

The history of oil and of the Rockefeller family is intertwined. It began, as democratic ideology suggests it should, with a personal success story. John D. Rockefeller, son of a stern itinerant peddlar, learned bookkeeping at Cleveland Central High School and started work at $15 a month. Three years later his pay was $50 a month. Out of this he was able to save $800, enough to start a small produce business. Securing bank loans, Rockefeller gradually expanded into grains and other foodstuffs. He became a prosperous local merchant as the Civil War brought a sharp rise in profits.

In 1860 Rockefeller was sent by a group of Cleveland investors to scout out the potential of the Pennsylvania oil rush. Ironically, after noting the wildly shifting market and the fact that big investors like Andrew Carnegie quickly left after making a killing, Rockefeller returned to recommend against investment in oil.[2]

Three years later Rockefeller was approached by Samuel Andrews, owner of a still and inventor. Andrews sought funding for a new, more efficient oil-refining process. Rockefeller invested $5,000. In 1865 he was able to leave the produce business to become Andrews' partner. The Rockefeller-Andrews refineries benefitted from a superior product and less waste of byproducts. The traditional stories portray Rockefeller driving hard bargains, saving on everything, building contacts with Southern markets (in spite of the war!), and getting into the export market with his brother, William.

Even with these advantages, however, Rockefeller-Andrews oil was only one of thirty refiners in Cleveland alone. In order to expand further, Rockefeller needed capital. This he found in whiskey-fortune heir Henry Flagler. With this aid Rockefeller opened a second refinery, becoming Cleveland's largest. He undersold his competitors by a small margin. But since he was less favorably located than refiners in Pittsburgh, Rockefeller still faced formidable problems.

In order to solve the problems of supply costs, Rockefeller (on his own later admission) approached Vanderbilt's New York Central Railroad, which carried his oil. In secret negotiations Rockefeller demanded and received secret rebates to make his oil competitive with that refined in Pennsylvania and New York.

These rebates were made in secret because common law viewed such special dealings as criminal conspiracies in restraint of trade. Rockefeller expanded rapidly after this. Increased volume brought even more rebates. Between 1867 and 1870

Rockefeller-Andrews-Flagler Oil increased from 1,500 to 3,000 barrels a day. They incorporated in 1870 as the Standard Oil Company of Ohio. Standard had become the largest single refining company in the world, worth over a million dollars. Rockefeller was thirty years old. He and his brother owned half of Standard Oil, and no income tax yet exists to diminish his rapid accumulation of profits.

From the Founding of Standard Oil to the Acquisition of the Last Independent Pipeline (1870–1883)

In *Evolution of Modern Capitalism*, the English economist J. A. Hobson wrote:

> *Each kind of commodity, as it passes through the many processes from the earth to the consumer, may be looked upon as a stream whose channel is broader at some points than at others. Just as a number of German barons planted castles along the banks of the Rhine, in order to tax the commerce between East and West which was obliged to make use of this highway, so it is with these economic 'narrows.' Wherever they are found, monopolies plant themselves in the shape of rings, corners, pools, syndicates, or trusts.*[3]

In the case of oil, the "narrows" were the refineries. They mediated between the unruly competition of the drillers and the mass of consumers. Rockefeller's plan for consolidation went under the mantle of the Southern Improvement Company. He later recalled, "I had our plan clearly in mind. It was right. I knew it as a matter of conscience. It was right between me and my God. If I had to do it tomorrow I would do it again in the same way—do it a hundred times." [4]

In 1871 Rockefeller and Flagler took over a defunct Pennsylvania corporation whose charter authorized it in vague terms to do virtually anything. Together they drew up a list of principal refiners. Each was approached with a secret agreement to enter into a price-fixing consortium. Once the consortium was established, Rockefeller again approached the railways. He went as representative of men in secret control of the bulk of American refining interests. Rockefeller obtained a 40–50 percent rebate on crude oil shipped to the consortium and a 25–50 percent rebate on oil shipped by them. Other refiners found themselves paying up to twice the shipping costs of the Southern Improvement Company conspirators. Because of secrecy, however, they were unaware of their competitive disadvantage.

The price-fixing conspiracy went even further. A portion of his competitors' transportation fees were secretly channeled back to the Rockefeller group. This illegal "drawback" enabled them to receive up to 50 percent of the shipping costs paid by their competition. The railroads even agreed to supply the Southern Improvement Company with waybills and other documents enabling Southern to check the enforcement of these illegal arrangements.

By 1872 the new conspiracy had decimated the outsiders. Rockefeller would inform other Cleveland refiners, for example, that only insiders would survive. They could become insiders only by selling out to Standard at a value set by Rockefeller's appraisers. This was usually only half or a third of the actual value.[5] So solidly were the Rockefeller interests entrenched with the railroads that when Alexander Scofield and Son, a large competitor, resisted and protested to the railroad, the railroad itself told Scofield to sell out. In three months all twenty-five Cleveland competitors had surrendered. All this was done in secret.

It was perhaps inevitable that the main opposition to the conspiracy came from oil-drillers and consumers rather than other refiners. The Oil War of 1872 was initiated when the Titusville *Oil City Derrick* published the names of the conspiracy members. The Rockefeller group was blacklisted by a newly formed association of fifty oil drillers who refused to sell to Southern Improvement members at any price. A national scandal ensued. Though Rockefeller planned a bitter struggle, Vanderbilt gave in because his railroads were losing money in the contest—no oil was being transported. Vanderbilt reduced freight rates for the outside refiners. Moreover popular agitation led the Pennsylvania legislature to revoke the charter of the Southern Improvement Company, scattering its members in retreat.

After the furor died down, however, Rockefeller was again able to arrange new rebate deals with the railroads. These gave him a 25 percent advantage over his Cleveland competitors. Again, this was done in secret. Rockefeller then undertook another national effort to amalgamate with other oil refiners. Between 1875 and 1878, fifteen of the largest were brought into the Standard Oil fold. These represented some 80 percent of U.S. oil refining. Smaller firms were simply driven out of the field or bought at lower prices. Thus, initial reforms proved illusory in the long term. (Recall the discussion of business reformism in Chapter 8.)

Josephson, an historian of the era, provides a case in point:

A manufacturer of improved lubricating oils set himself up innocently in Cleveland and became a client of Standard Oil for his supply of residuum oil. The Rockefeller Company encouraged him at first, selling him 85 barrels a day on contract. He prospered for three years, then suddenly when the monopoly was well-launched in 1874, his supply was cut down to 12 barrels per day, the price was increased on some pretense, and shipping costs over the railroad also increased. It became impossible to supply his trade. He offered to buy from Rockefeller 5,000 barrels to stock a supply of oil, but Rockefeller refused. 'I saw readily what that meant,' Morehouse related. 'That meant squeeze you out—buy out your works. . . . They paid me $15,000 for what cost me $41,000.' [6]

After this Rockefeller launched a program of establishing a national marketing system. He cut out wholesalers and middlemen. He supplied oil to each town by his own tank wagons. Retailers were forced out partly by manipulating railroad rates. Also, direct threats were made to enter competition with grocery stores and other retailers. (In the pre-auto age, grocery stores were the main oil outlets.) This was done to force them to stock only the Standard Oil line of products. In another affair, a Standard subsidiary (Vacuum Oil) hired an employee of a competing refinery to blow it up. He did and was tried for it, exposing Standard's nefarious side to public view.

Through these methods Rockefeller interests controlled half of all oil pipelines by 1876. Its largest remaining competitor was

Colonel Joseph Potts of the Empire Transportation Company. Potts was then expanding his operations, buying New York refineries. Rockefeller first tried to get the railroads to put the squeeze on Potts. For a time a price war raged during which the railroad lost revenues. They were forced to cut back on wages and lengthen the workloads of railroad workers. (This in turn was a major contributing factor to the Railroad Riots of 1877, the worst labor disturbances in American history.) The railroads, in their weakened condition, finally gave in to Rockefeller. With these advantageous concessions to his competitor, Potts was forced to capitulate. He sold out in 1878.

By the end of 1878, Rockefeller owned or controlled all existing oil pipelines, but this monopoly was ended rapidly with the discovery of new oilfields in Bradford, Pennsylvania. These were outside Standard's control. A new oil rush started. This provided the opportunity for the Tidewater Company to undertake an independent pipeline to these fields. This line threatened to break Rockefeller's strategy of forcing down the price of Bradford oil through his control over its transportation. But in spite of Rockefeller's lobbying efforts, the new pipeline was built in 1879.

Worse, the independent oil interests launched a successful public-relations drive to brand Rockefeller as a monopolist. The state of Pennsylvania was induced to indict Rockefeller, Flagler, and others for criminal conspiracy in constraint of trade. Similarly, the Hepburn Committee in New York exposed the railroad's involvement in the conspiracy. It became a national scandal. The conspirators took the Fifth Amendment, refusing to testify against themselves. Without adequate proof, the trials came to nothing.

Turning to deal with the new Tidewater pipeline, Rockefeller first offered to buy all the oil it piped. In this way he hoped to reestablish his monopoly. When this was refused, he built a competing, parallel pipeline from the new Bradford oil fields direct to Standard's refineries in Bayonne, New Jersey. Meanwhile he also harried Tidewater by suing it for receivership, bringing various injunctions, trying to undermine its credit, hiring away its officials, and secretly buying up its stock. In 1882 Rockefeller was finally able to induce Tidewater to sell. With this new power he once again approached the railroads. This time he secured an agreement under which they stopped transporting all oil in return for an annual payment from Standard. The demise of Tidewater was the key to consolidation of the Standard Oil monopoly.

From the Consolidation of the Trust to the Dissolution of Standard Oil (1883–1911)

Now came the golden age of the oil trust. When Tidewater was absorbed, the Rockefeller interests included 37 stockholders of over 40 companies. Rockefeller consolidated this by having the 37 turn their stock over "in trust" to nine trustees. These included Rockefeller himself and his brother, John. In return the 37 received "trust certificates." The result was that the nine trustees held two-thirds of the stock and controlled the Standard empire.

In this period Standard controlled some 90 percent of the domestic oil market. Though costs decreased due to bigger volume and improved technology, these benefits were not passed on to consumers. By maintaining the price of oil for twenty years, Rockefeller and his associates accumulated unprecedented wealth.

In 1888 Rockefeller met a young minister named Frederick Gates. Gates became his financial agent. He secured, for example, purchase of the Merritt iron fields in Minnesota. It was Gates who directed Rockefeller into philanthropy. The then-parochial University of Chicago received $600,000. Almost overnight the Rockefeller image changed in the public mind. Rockefeller was portrayed as a devout Christian and a noble altruist who gave to the poor.

The monopolistic and, indeed, criminal manner in which Rockefeller had accumulated his wealth was generally soon forgotten. But among those who did not forget was the state of Ohio. There legislative action resulted in the dissolution of Standard operations in its home state. Nonetheless, this was of little moment. After a delaying action of several years, the company simply reemerged as Standard Oil of New Jersey, outside Ohio's jurisdiction.

Meanwhile, Standard's profits mounted. Profits of $15 million in 1886 became $45 million in 1899. This was a fabulous amount of wealth for the time. Rockefeller and his associates used their wealth to become some of the nation's largest financiers as well as oil monopolists. After the Panic of 1893 (which Standard bore without difficulty), Rockefeller began to gain control over many nonoil-related concerns. These included banks, insurance companies, utilities, and railroads. And through his banks, yet more corporations came under the sway of Rockefeller interests.

Rockefeller's Standard Oil dominated the American market at the turn of the century. But as powerful as he was, Rockefeller could hardly control the encroachments of other great capitalists. In 1893, for example, Standard was forced to buy up a pipeline and half-completed refinery started by Andrew Mellon. Mellon had built these expressly to sell out to Rockefeller at a large profit. Later, in 1901, Mellon was sought out by speculators controlling the new Spindletop Gusher, a gigantic oil discovery in Beaumont, Texas. Mellon invested heavily, squeezed out the original partners, and emerged as the dominant interest in what was to be Gulf Oil. Like Rockefeller, Mellon was in a position to back his challenge through control over a host of interrelated banks, transportation companies, and other corporations.[7] Gulf became Standard's chief domestic competitor.

International competition developed as well. At the turn of the century, Standard had dominated the export trade. Russia at first seemed to pose serious competition and actually surpassed American production briefly. But even before the Russian Revolution, this threat subsided substantially. Nonetheless, to meet Russian oil Standard organized importing companies in Great Britain (Anglo-American Oil), the Netherlands, and in Belgium, Scandinavia, and Italy. In France an agreement was reached with the *Cartel des Dix* (Cartel of Ten) for 80 percent of French imports to be Standard. By 1900 Russian oil had some one-third of the British and one-fifth of the continental market. But Standard had virtually all the rest. In Latin America and the Far East there was no competition at all. And in 1898 Standard bought out Imperial Oil, thereby gaining 60 percent of the Canadian market.

But as the Russian threat eclipsed, a new international challenger emerged. These new interests eventually became known as Royal Dutch Shell. It was based on Dutch and English firms which had merged in 1907 to meet Standard's dominance of the European market. In addition, they sought to compete with Standard in the Far East, using a subsidiary, the Asiatic Petroleum Company.

Between 1900 and 1914 an international oil price war broke out between Standard and Shell. Earlier, Standard had offered to buy Shell out for $1.25 million. By 1911 it had upped its offer by nearly one hundred times! Shell refused to sell. It proposed instead a cartel-like division of world markets into separate spheres of influence. This proposal eventually prevailed, but only after a fight. Shell used Russian oil to invade American markets. Standard retaliated by organizing Koloniale Petroleum to compete with Shell in its home base, the Sumatra oil fields of Indonesia.

At the same time new domestic oil discoveries added to Standard's competition. As with Mellon's Gulf Oil, new, smaller, troublesome oil firms arose in the United States: Texaco, Phillips, Union, Sunoco. Between 1880 and 1910, Standard's share of the American market shrunk from 90 percent to 60 percent.[8] In spite of this, however, Standard profits remained enormous. It averaged $79 million per year in earnings and gave dividends of $40 million annually. The Rockefellers personally owned 25 percent of Standard stock and were enriched accordingly.

In the years prior to World War I, Standard and Rockefeller interests still controlled three-fifths of both the domestic and international oil markets. But underneath there were signs of deteriorating position. Numerous lawsuits were launched against Standard in the Progressive years before World War I, 13 in 1906 alone. But these were overshadowed by the action of the Supreme Court in 1911. Though Theodore Roosevelt's "trust-busting" activities were minimal in practice, the one great accomplishment came at Rockefeller's expense. On the basis of the 1890 Sherman Anti-Trust Act, the Supreme Court ordered the dissolution of Standard Oil. Standard of New York, Standard of California, and other parts of the empire were separated from the main body.

Standard of New Jersey remained the world's largest oil firm even after 1911. It was an economic giant second only to U.S. Steel. But its power was diminished from the grand position it had once held. Even the old Standard companies began to present some competition over time. In the years before World War I Rockefeller could look with satisfaction on the unprecedented power of Standard Oil. But decline was certain.

Oil Politics between World Wars

As a result of the war, Standard's profits had reached $165 million by 1920. This height was not attained again until after World War II. But these achievements paled in comparison to the growth of Royal Dutch Shell. Shell soon outproduced Standard by a 3-to-1 margin worldwide. And at home, the Oklahoma oil boom led to even more domestic competitors for Standard.

Gabriel Kolko wrote that "the American oil industry passed through a revolution from 1900 to 1920, and Standard failed to participate fully in it." [9] Oil production shifted westward, outside the control of Standard. Standard, seemingly preoccupied with the administration of its own vast operations, was slow to invest in Texas, the Gulf, and other new areas. In contrast, between 1911 and 1926 the investments of the Texas Company (Texaco) grew 572 percent. Gulf Oil investments grew 1,022 percent.[10] Likewise, Standard's management seemed unprepared to exploit the possibilities of automobile gas stations and other new markets.

Ironically, the Supreme Court's 1911 dissolution order jolted Standard out of its lethargy. Standard's component companies merged with many of the aggressive, new, independent oil firms.[11] World War I provided the occasion for the reassertion of old, monopolistic patterns. Under Woodrow Wilson, representatives of the largest oil giants were brought together in the National Petroleum War Service Committee. Though including some small oil-producer representatives, the committee's members were dominated by the majors. The "members were simply seeking preference for their own companies. Under the mantle of patriotism the petroleum barons had forged a cartel greater than the old Standard Oil Company." [12]

The establishment of the U.S. Fuel Administration in 1917 seemed to threaten government regulation of oil. But in fact it merely served to reinforce the overall policies of rationalization the largest oil firms already desired. This involved pooling production, conserving oil to restrict production and maintain prices, and planned allocation of supplies.

After the war the Petroleum War Service Committee was disbanded. Its general functions continued privately under the newly organized American Petroleum Institute (API), founded in 1919. The API became the chief lobbying arm of the oil industry. It pressed for numerous bills to curb competition and promote "coordination" in the absence of the old Standard Oil monopoly.

Similar pressures were building for international coordination. The 1920s were marked at first by an international oil war, primarily between Standard and Shell (but also involving British Petroleum—BP—important after 1908 and based on Persian oil). Much of the "war" centered on attempts to gain influence over Russian oil after the Bolshevik Revolution of 1917. In larger measure it was an extension of the long-standing competition discussed earlier. The oil war culminated in a series of worldwide anticompetitive agreements.

One such agreement followed the lines proposed by Shell years earlier. Meeting at Achnacarry, Scotland, in 1928, Walter Teagle (Standard), Sir Henri Deterding (Shell), and Sir John Cadman (BP's Anglo-Persian Oil) and others established what was in essence a world cartel in oil. The Achnacarry agreement was designed to limit world production and keep prices high. The cartel also agreed to charge all consumers the expensive Texas production prices, even though the actual oil supplied came from the nearest source. All new markets after 1928 would be split among the cartel members in proportion to their 1928 shares.

This anticompetitive agreement complemented a similar agreement reached the same year in Ostend, Belgium. The Ostend agreement (the so-called Red Line agreement) provided for a cartel to exploit Arabian oil. This cartel was composed of Shell, BP, the Compagnie Française des Petroles, Standard, Mobil, and Gulf (Gulf later sold its interest to Standard and

Mobil). Later, Justice Department prosecutor David Haberman said of this agreement, "Prevention of competition was the sole purpose of many of the principal provisions" it contained.[13]

Though the world hegemony of Standard Oil had been dismantled, by 1928 a broader cartel had risen to perform similar monopolistic functions. The question remained, however, whether the same cartelization would occur domestically. In the United States, however, the oil industry was operating under the pall of the infamous Teapot Dome scandal of 1922.

This flagrant example of political corruption occurred after authority over naval oil reserves was transferred from the Navy to the Interior Department. In signing the transfer order, President Harding stated with unknowing foresight, "I guess there will be hell to pay." [14] Secretary of the Interior Albert Fall leased the oil reserves to H. F. Sinclair and E. L. Doheny, both large financial contributors to the Republican party in 1920. In return Fall received a little black bag containing $100,000 in cash, later described as a loan. He used this in part to restore his deteriorating New Mexico ranch. Fall's new-found prosperity aroused the suspicion of progressive senators, notably LaFollette. They demanded a full investigation. The investigation in turn led to Fall's resignation, a fine of $100,000, and imprisonment. Doheny and Sinclair—the oil company's representatives—nevertheless escaped conviction for fraud and corruption. Sinclair alone served briefly in jail for contempt of the Senate and contempt of court.

Partly in response to Teapot Dome, President Coolidge created the Oil Conservation Board (OCB). The OCB was initially supported by the API and oil interests. They endorsed its goal of restricting supply, which kept prices up. Later, when they wanted to increase production, the oil firms found the OCB an obstruction and opposed it. They preferred instead "conservation" laws at the state level, where their political influence was greater.

After acrimonious legislative battles in Texas and Oklahoma, these conservation laws were passed. Later, other states followed suit. These laws came just in time to curb the price-reducing effects of the new East Texas oil discoveries. Eventually the oil companies were able to secure federal enforcement of these state conservation laws. The Interstate Transportation of Petroleum Act (1935, known as the Connolly "Hot Oil" Act, named after its sponsor, Senator Tom Connolly of Texas) brought this about. This act made it a federal crime to ship oil interstate if it was produced in violation of state conservation laws. In addition, through the Interstate Compact to Conserve Oil and Gas, the Bureau of Mines cooperated with state conservation commissions to estimate prorations. Production in excess of official rates could be confiscated under state law. In this way the oil industry was able to use government police powers to enforce a price-fixing system which, if done privately as Standard Oil had in its heyday, would have been illegal.

The second major use of governmental power for the private ends of the oil industry was the oil depletion allowance of 1926. Ostensibly this tax concession was simply the oil industry's counterpart to the depreciation of equipment allowed manufacturing industries. The previous system of estimating the declining value of oil and gas fields as the resources were extracted had proved arbitrary and cumbersome. In 1926 Congress set a standard depletion rate of 27.5 percent as a simpler rule-of-thumb estimate. That is, the oil companies were allowed to deduct 27.5 percent of their gross *income* (which might be as much as 50 percent of *net* income) before paying corporate income taxes.

As the *Congressional Quarterly* has noted, "Percentage depletion, by setting the deduction at an arbitrary percentage of production, bears no relation to costs and permits tax-free recovery that in some cases vastly exceeds the amount invested in the property." [15] For example, between 1964 and 1967, the Atlantic-Richfield Oil Company earned profits of $465 million but also accrued federal tax credits of $629 million. Hence it not only paid no taxes, but actually was owed tax credits by the government!

The oil depletion allowance represents more than a vast subsidy of the oil industry. It also allowed tax credits for the production of crude oil rather than for refining. This gave the oil companies an incentive to set artificially high crude-oil prices. Because the large companies as producers sold this oil to themselves as refiners, this was a matter of internal accounting with two major consequences. First, high crude prices further inflated the depletion allowance subsidy received by all oil companies. Second, because high crude prices meant high costs for small independent refiners, the possibilities for increased competition of oil refiners was diminished.[16]

In addition, the oil industry received other advantages from government. They were allowed to deduct from taxes the costs of exploration, drilling, and development, including the whole cost of unsuccessful dry wells. The largest companies also dominated the "code authority" established during the Depression under the National Industrial Recovery Act. By securing Congress's approval of the Interstate Compact to Conserve Oil and Gas, the oil industry turned aside the then-mounting pressure to place oil in utility status (which would increase government regulation). And at the state level, commissions such as the Texas Railroad Commission proved amenable vehicles for limiting production and increasing prices. More blatant, in 1931, Texas Governor Ross Sterling (a former president of what is now part of Exxon) ordered state troops to close new wells in order to maintain prices. Moreover, the tremendous economic advantages of the oil industry enabled them to pay their workers high wages and benefits, undermining the development of internal union opposition that had so disrupted the coal industry.

World War II and Eisenhower's "New Partnership"

World War II further centralized the American oil industry. But the war's end also marked the decline of the international cartel which had existed since the Achnacarry agreement. Citing wartime necessity, Britain had been able to get the cartel to abandon the practice of assessing fictional transportation costs from Texas. Under the postwar Marshall Plan, the Texas pricing system was gradually phased out. By 1957 it was dead. American crude oil was dramatically undercut in price and disappeared from world markets. Between 1945 and 1960, moreover, American oil reserves were eclipsed by the discovery of vastly greater reserves elsewhere in the world, notably in the Middle East. In this period, American reserves dropped from 40 percent to only 11 percent of the known world total.

American oil companies also faced the rise of socialist and nationalized oil companies outside the cartel. In addition to the increasingly important Communist-bloc oil industry, these included the Organization of Petroleum Exporting Countries (OPEC, which includes the Middle East plus Venezuela), ENI (the Italian nationalized industry), and nationalized firms in Sri Lanka, Egypt, Indonesia, India, Iran, Kuwait, and Latin America.

At the same time, American oil firms continued their price-fixing "conservation" policies at home. This restricted American output while production expanded abroad. In Texas, production was held to eight days per month. Standard Oil had acquired the I. G. Farben process of making gasoline from coal, a process used to power Hitler's war effort. But it then used these patents to foreclose development by others, not to pursue investment in the process.[17] By 1948 the United States had become a net crude oil importer.

During the war antitrust activities had been suspended. Through the secretary of the interior, transportation and supplies had been pooled. After World War II the National Petroleum Council was created as an advisory body composed of representatives of the oil industry, especially the large producers. It secured for the oil industry a quasi-official status in the Interior Department.

Recent testimony before the Senate Foreign Relations Subcommittee on Multinational Corporations threw light on industry-government collaboration during this period. In 1974 the subcommittee heard three Justice Department antitrust lawyers testify "how a series of secret oil agreements, made frequently with the blessing of high U.S. officials, led to a cartel-like domination of world oil supplies by a handful of companies." Truman and Eisenhower, "acting in the name of national security, successfully thwarted antitrust proceedings begun by the Justice Department in the 1950s against five major U.S. oil companies." [18]

The *Congressional Quarterly* summarized this testimony by noting that the action of Truman and Eisenhower in effect gave

approval to the continuation of illegal price-fixing begun decades earlier by the major oil companies. (Government documents clarifying the actions of Truman and Eisenhower remained classified until 1974, hidden from public view.)

Internationally as well the government was active in col-
laborating with the oil industry. In a secret ruling in 1950, the
Treasury Department, at State Department insistence, allowed
the oil companies to avoid paying U.S. income tax on profits
earned abroad. This was accomplished through the device of
allowing tax credits for royalty payments to foreign governments. This in turn enabled the Arabian-American Oil Company
(ARAMCO, then controlled by the government of Saudi Arabia
plus the four largest American firms) to increase its royalty
payments to Saudi Arabia as part of a policy aimed at subsidizing Arab states. The goal was to prevent their falling under
Communist influence. Wall Street lawyers were even sent to the
Middle East to help the Arab states rewrite their tax laws to
complement American internal revenue codes. While not strictly
illegal, these activities allowed the oil companies to amass further huge and untaxable profits on the basis of a secret agreement with the U.S. government.[19]

In order to retain control over oil, and due to military interests in the Middle East, the United States went much further.
The Central Intelligence Agency helped overthrow Iranian
Prime Minister Mosadeq in 1953. Mosadeq had nationalized
British Petroleum facilities in Iran. He was then unable to sell
Iranian oil, however, because of a boycott by international oil
firms which controlled oil tanker transport. A settlement of the
dispute allotted 50 percent of oil profits to the Iranian government, deductible from oil company taxes. After the coup a
billion-dollar aid program was initiated to bolster "anti-Communist" forces in the Iranian leadership.[20]

Iraq was the scene of similar events in 1958. In that year
the pro-Communist leader of Iran, General Abdul Karim el-
Kassem, was overthrown.[21] Also in 1958 Eisenhower landed
Marines in Lebanon under the Eisenhower Doctrine. This sanctioned the use of troops anywhere in the world whenever communism seemed to threaten, provided troops were "invited." As
late as 1970 the United States was pressuring Britain not to

withdraw its remaining troops from the Middle East. Failing that, the United States undertook construction of a multimillion dollar joint Anglo-American military base in the Indian Ocean.

These military and paramilitary maneuvers were overshadowed by an event which marked a turning point in the Arab world: the nationalization of the Suez Canal in 1956. Following a brief war in which Great Britain, France, and Israel attacked Egypt, American oil interests used the crisis atmosphere to justify a 35¢-a-barrel increase in the price of crude oil. During the emergency the American government revived the Oil Industry Advisory Board (now the Middle East Emergency Committee). This board was encouraged to develop a plan for diverting Arab oil from North America to Europe to defeat the Arab oil boycott. The planning was free from any threat of antitrust action.

The 1956 crisis had many ramifications. First, it led to an increased amount of imported oil entering America. This angered smaller domestic companies. They lobbied to establish mandatory licensing controls over imported oil, and secured this goal in 1959. This served to insulate the American market from a world drop in oil prices. Price and profit levels were kept high. While the international oil cartel did not suffer immediately from this shift, it marked the opening of a rift between the interests of the international cartel members and the smaller domestic firms.

More important, the nationalization of the Suez Canal meant that the political influence of the cartel members had been undercut. Independent oil companies outside the cartel—Occidental and Getty in the United States, ENI in Italy, Japan's state oil company—could not be prevented from expanding their operations into the lucrative Middle East oil market. This in turn meant that the Arab oil-producing states were able to gain noncartel outlets for their oil. They began to slip from under cartel control. In effect, the central cartel weapon—its monopolistic control of transport—began to crumble after 1956.

This caused an Arab revolution in the control of oil. The political revolution was aided by a technological revolution in the 1960s, the advent of gigantic oil supertankers. These also enabled independent, noncartel transport of oil. Soon new companies were coming to noncartel agreements with Middle Eastern countries. For example, Occidental came to such agreements in the large, rich Libyan oil fields, as did Phillips in the Trucial States, Standard of Indiana in the Persian Gulf, and Standard of Indiana in the Neutral Zone separating Kuwait and Saudi Arabia.

The Rise of OPEC

The international oil cartel, though seriously weakened, has remained of utmost importance in the two decades since Eisenhower dropped antitrust activities against the monopolists. Recently, for example, the Federal Trade Commission charged Exxon, Shell, Gulf, Mobil, Texaco, Standard of California, and Standard of Indiana with price conspiracy. For the entire period since 1950, the FTC said, these firms had monopolized oil refining.[22]

While maintaining monopolistic pricing, the cartel became deeply involved in domestic politics. The connection of oil, Texas, and President Lyndon Johnson was much-noted, for example. But this was somewhat beside the point. In fact the oil industry has had substantial direct and indirect representation in all recent administrations. Nixon, Johnson's successor, was a major recipient of oil money as far back as his 1952 campaign for the vice-presidency. He consistently supported pro-industry measures such as the tidelands oil bill. Critics charged this "gave away" offshore oil preserves to the industry. In 1956 Nixon had cooperated with Lyndon Johnson to block a Senate move to investigate the oil industry on charges of attempting to bribe Senator Francis Case (S.D.). Atlantic-Richfield was among the largest clients of Nixon's law firm, and its president was among the largest contributors to Nixon's 1968 presidential campaign.

Proposals were made within the Department of Justice to prohibit certain oil industry practices, but the efforts were stalled by what officials called "a political climate favorable to big oil."[23] Similarly, later, under Nixon, "... 'when John Mitchell was Attorney General, it was well understood that oil was not a highly favored subject for litigation,' said one former lawyer at the Justice Department." [24]

In these years the oil industry became the largest single group in terms of contributions to presidential and other political campaigns. Washington journalist Erwin Knoll, for example, reported an investigation by former Majority Secretary Robert Baker, finding that "money is easily—and bipartisanly—available to legislators who can be counted on to vote the industry's way." Knoll went on to detail the following account, which presents some of the flavor of oil politics in this period:

On Thursday evening, November 6, 1969, the governors of three states met over a quiet dinner at the Tavern Club in Washington with Frank N. Ikard, a former Texas congressman who is now president of the American Petroleum Institute, the trade association of the nation's largest oil companies. There is no public record of what the four men discussed, although—by coincidence or otherwise—the same three governors and a fourth were at the White House early the next morning to urge the Nixon administration to retain the 11-year-old system of oil-import quotas, which costs consumers more than $5 billion a year in higher prices for petroleum products.[25]

Nixon retained the system for another four years, until a worldwide crisis in oil forced its demise.

The image of the oil industry as a freewheeling, big-spending, politically invulnerable giant on the American scene was being eroded from many sides. Of these none was more important than the rise of the Third-World oil-producing nations themselves. The American grip on the politics of the Arab states had never been strong, sufficient though it had been in the past. Secretary of State Dulles's Central Treaty Organization (CENTO), for example, had failed to attract Arab support in the 1950s. Only Iran joined permanently, after a CIA-connected coup.

In 1959 and 1960, in what even the American press called "an arrogant move," the international oil cartel arbitrarily cut the posted price for oil. These formed the basis for royalty and tax payments to Arab countries.[26] Iran, Iraq, Kuwait, Saudi Arabia, and Venezuela formed the Organization of Petroleum

Exporting Countries (OPEC) in response. OPEC was at first merely a vehicle for coordination of production schedules. But after the 1967 Six-Day War with Israel and the ensuing unsuccessful Arab oil boycott, OPEC came to be seen as a device for uniting Arab and non-Arab oil-producing interests for purposes of countering the power of the international cartel.

By 1970, American oil companies produced 25 percent of Iraq's oil, 40 percent of Iran's, 75 percent of Libyan oil, and 100 percent of Saudi Arabian oil. However, not only were independent oil companies beginning to gain footholds in the Middle East, but in 1969 the Soviet Union finally broke the Western monopoly on Arab oil exploitation by securing management of the new, huge North Rumaila oil fields in Iraq. Then, in 1970, the cartel's fears were realized. In that year the new revolutionary government of Kaddafi in Libya withheld production in order, successfully, to force a price increase on Occidental, an independent whose operations relied on Libyan oil. Because of the better terms offered Arab states by the independents, the Arab "take" had been edging up. But Occidental's capitulation threatened to open the gate to soaring profits for OPEC in the 1970s.

In February 1971, the Teheran Conference was called to deal with the rapidly shifting situation. Here the large oil companies tried to press for a united front vis-à-vis OPEC. They sought to avoid the sort of disunity marked by Occidental's caving in to Libyan demands. The oil companies were undercut, however, not only by the independents but also by the U.S. State Department itself. The department, seeking better Arab-American relations, let it be known that the United States was not committed to the single-agreement approach.[27] Failing to reach accord, the oil companies agreed to concessions to the Arab governments.

A report of the Teheran Conference noted that "with the closing of the Suez Canal, the shutting of a major pipline, and a shortage of tankers to carry oil around Africa, OPEC apparently held the high cards."[28] The concessions to OPEC amounted to some $1.2 billion, plus an increase in the tax rate from 50 percent to 55 percent on profits. Supposedly the oil firms received in return an assurance of five years of price stability.

For the American oil firms, the outcome of Teheran was not so bad. The extra 5 percent could be deducted from American taxes and the extra costs passed on to the consumer. Since only 3 percent of domestically used oil came from the Middle East at that time, moreover, the consumers to bear the extra costs were primarily America's industrial competitors, Europe and Japan.

Occidental's capitulation and the Teheran Conference gave way to a spiral of oil price increases. The international oil cartel found itself unable to control the independents or to monopolize the transport of oil. In 1972 the six Persian Gulf states collectively demanded the United States pay some $400 million immediately plus $75 million monthly to make up for losses due to the devaluation of the dollar. Negotiations settled at a cost of $700 million for 1972 alone. Shortly afterward, the Persian Gulf states demanded 20 percent ownership of oil-company subsidiaries operating within their borders. This was to increase to 51 percent by 1985.

ARAMCO (30 percent owned by Exxon) agreed to sell 20 percent as demanded. In October 1972 the oil companies agreed to the 20 percent demand in general and to 51 percent Arab ownership by 1980. OPEC organized a multimillion-dollar fund to insulate any Arab nation that might have its oil boycotted by the international cartel. And in Iraq, the Iraq Petroleum Company (owned by U.S. and European interests) was nationalized as part of an "offensive against the oil companies." In June 1973, Libya nationalized a small American oil company. And after the Arab-Israeli Yom Kippur War of 1973, the Arab OPEC states reduced production 25 percent, boycotted the U.S., and sent oil prices skyrocketing amid this nation's first major energy crisis.

The Energy Crisis of 1973–1974

Ironically, the oil companies in the 1960s were worried that a world glut of oil production would send prices and profits plummeting. In fact, since the end of World War II inexpensive foreign oil had threatened to undercut more expensive American oil even within American markets. This pressure had contributed to the fall of the Texas pricing system in the 1950s.

The oil industry brought its complaints to Washington. Eisenhower initially responded with a weak, voluntary plan whereby oil importers would promise to limit foreign oil to 12 percent of domestic consumption (the level it had reached by 1954, up from only 0.3 percent in 1947). After voluntary curbs proved unsuccessful, mandatory import quotas were established in 1959. Their establishment was aided by oil interests seeking to preserve the supply-limiting system of state "conservation" laws by limiting access to foreign oil as well. The import quotas also appealed to nationalistic concerns for self-sufficiency in energy for reasons of national defense.

Eisenhower's adviser, Sherman Adams, noted that in spite of Cold War rhetoric surrounding passage of the import quotas, the central motivation was economic protection of the large American oil producers. Producers were then being hurt by the refusal of large independent oil producers to obey the voluntary quota system. The economic effect of the quotas was to hold the prices of American crude oil at approximately double the free-market price. The costs, moreover, were borne inequitably. New England, for example, paid disproportionately. Nonetheless, the import-quota system seemed adequate for preventing a price-dropping oversupply of oil until well into the 1960s.

The import quota issue emerged in the 1960s when Occidental, having secured an independent base in Libya, sought to undercut the major companies by selling its oil through a proposed new refinery in New England. Though having the support of New England politicians like Kennedy, Brooke, and Muskie, President Johnson was able to stall the proposal until the end of his term. At the suggestion of the American Petroleum Institute (which is dominated by the majors), Nixon created a special task force which endorsed a compromise. The compromise plan provided for restriction of foreign oil as under the quota system, but proposed an alternative device: a tariff on imported oil.

The tariff proposal was attacked by spokespersons of the smaller oil companies because they believed "over the long run it would mean that control of crude production would wind up in the hands of a very few big oil companies" [29]—the majors which held foreign oil investments. On the other hand, the major companies were not enthusiastic about the tariff proposal either, since it did contain the possibility of opening the American market to foreign competition. The result was the rejection of the proposal and the retention of import quotas. In July 1970 the House followed industry wishes and made the quota system law (hitherto it had been based on presidential order). This had the effect of killing Occidental's bid for a free trade zone for imported oil in New England.

Not only did the oil companies seek to restrict the amount of oil supplied to the United States, but they also fought the spectre of "oversupply" in other ways. Since 1956, exploratory drilling had been cut back some 60 percent. After 1970, domestic production actually declined. Moreover, in the decade prior to the energy crisis of 1973–1974, no new refineries were built in the United States. Partly these restrictive policies reflected a desire to avoid oversupply. They also were part of a drive to invest where it was most profitable—namely, abroad.[30]

Between 1970 and 1973 the Nixon White House was under increasing pressure from New England leaders and others to drop the import quotas. This would have brought an inflow of foreign oil to assure supply and perhaps lower prices. Independent domestic producers in 1970 began to predict shortages, as well. This showed again the inability of the majors to cement a united oil front. In spite of Exxon assertions of "no need for additional imports," [31] in 1972 Nixon began a series of small increases in the quota allotments.

In spite of these, the overall constriction of supply precipitated an unprecedented national energy crisis. The Senate Banking Subcommittee held hearings on the quotas. Its chairman asserted that "meeting immediate crises by allocating a few more barrels of oil a day is a patchwork remedy." Rather, he said, the quota system itself was "the root of the problem." [32]

At the same time the upward price spiral of Middle East oil was beginning to eliminate the oil companies' need for import quotas. If foreign oil was to be no longer cheaper than that produced in America, domestic producers need not fear being under-cut. On April 18, 1973, the same day President Nixon announced he was ending the import-quota system, the president of the American Petroleum Institute, Frank Ikard, stated that "all the elements of the petroleum industry agree that there is a definite need to increase imports substantially over the next decade if we are to meet the energy requirements of the American people." [33] In place of the quota system, Nixon substituted a new system of license fees which, in effect, constituted a sort of tariff on imported oil as had been proposed—and rejected—just three years earlier.

The mere repeal of import quotas was not enough to remedy immediately the shortages that had been emerging for several years. In consequence the winter of 1973–1974 saw gasoline shortages marked by long lines at filling stations and no gas on Sunday. Shortages also occurred in home heating oil, requiring 68-degree thermostats and 10 percent delivery cutbacks. This created a crisis atmosphere in which the oil industry found new support for its plans to go ahead with a number of projects, stalled by its environmentalist critics, notably the Transcontinental Alaskan Pipeline.

During the energy crisis fuel prices soared. Oil companies reaped unparalleled profits. Bitterness was added to the controversy when it became commonly charged that the oil companies were holding oil in offshore tankers and in refineries, awaiting the benefits of further price increases.[34] In spite of growing criticism of the oil industry, the Arab oil boycott of the West during the 1973 Yom Kippur War provided a powerful scapegoat, deflecting criticism from the industry onto the Arabs.

Oil Politics in the 1970s

During the early 1970s, three issues dominated oil politics apart from the ones already mentioned. These were the proposal to build a pipeline from the new North Alaska oilfields, the antitrust issue, and reforms to remove longstanding tax favors from the industry. In addition, the mid-1970s brought a fourth issue, decontrol of oil prices.

The Alaska Pipeline

Of these four issues, perhaps the most intensely conflict-ridden was the Alaskan pipeline. In 1968 a major oil discovery was made on Alaska's North Slope. The state of Alaska sold leases for its development at a price totaling almost a billion dollars. However, the new environmental movement soon took note of the proposal to transport North Slope oil to the sea via an enormous pipeline across Alaska. The environmentalists sued the oil companies on the basis of the National Environmental Policy Act of 1969. The project became stalled in the courts.

The Alaskan pipeline project was also blocked because Nixon's secretary of the interior, Walter Hickel (an Alaskan), was not supportive of the oil industry position. When appointed, Hickel was thought to be a friend of the oil companies. Later, however, Hickel pursued progressive policies and incurred the criticism of oil industry leaders. Due to personal abrasiveness and policy differences, he was eventually fired by Nixon. Of his firing, Hickel said, "I obviously wasn't owned by the oil industry or by the conservationists. I probably wasn't owned by anybody and that's the problem."

Hickel's replacement was Congressman Rogers Morton (R, Md.), a vice-president of Pillsbury and director of Atlas Chemical Industries. Morton was a Yale graduate and a member of three elite men's clubs. He had had a strong pro-oil-industry record in Congress. In May 1972 Morton gave the go-ahead for the Alaskan pipeline, citing the energy crisis as justification.

During the energy crisis the oil industry advertised heavily. It felt the time was ripe to press for removal of environmental blocks to construction of the Alaskan pipeline. On July 17, 1973, the Senate overwhelmingly voted to license the 789-mile Alaskan pipeline. By a narrow vote (50 to 49, with Vice President Agnew breaking the tie) the Senate also voted to immunize the oil companies from court challenges to its construction.[35]

In endorsing the Alaskan pipeline the Congress was also ruling out the alternative favored by the environmentalists. This alternative, a trans-Canada route, would have lessened possible ecological damage. More important, it would have carried oil more inexpensively and have piped it to the Midwest, where need was greater. Instead, the Alaskan pipeline as planned by the oil industry and sanctioned by Congress delivered oil to the West Coast for shipment to Japan and other more profitable foreign outlets.[36]

Antitrust Action

The Alaskan pipeline issue also raised questions of antitrust. Exxon, BP, and Arco—the three major oil firms exploiting the North Slope—came to agreements to share leases and exploratory data, set production rates jointly, and cooperate in other areas. Critics anticipated "a potential antitrust violation in the oil industry unmatched since the 1930s."[37] These fears were compounded by permission, secured in 1971 by the industry from the Nixon administration, to take joint actions vis-à-vis OPEC without fear of antitrust activity. Moreover, during the energy crisis of 1973–1974, independents had difficulty securing crude oil from the majors. Some were forced out of business, again raising the antitrust issue in the national press.

In the 1970s antitrust issues relating to oil were arising on other fronts as well. For example, the large-scale purchase by oil companies of firms in coal, nuclear fuel, and alternative energy fields led to a 1970 Senate report, "Competition in the Energy Markets." This report concluded that the expansion of the oil industry was "comparable to the formation of trusts in the latter decade of the nineteenth century. In short, the oil companies, themselves portraying their activities as diversification, are in fact systematically acquiring their competition."[38]

In 1973 the Federal Trade Commission started price conspiracy proceedings against Exxon, Mobil, Gulf, and five other major firms. The FTC charged them with conspiring since at least 1950 to monopolize the refining of oil products. At the same time, the Justice Department sued Texaco and Coastal States Gas for refusing to sell to independents, a common monopolistic practice.[39]

Foreign governments launched antitrust actions of their own. In Japan, the Fair Trade Commission indicted twelve oil companies, including subsidiaries of Exxon, Mobil, and Shell, for agreeing to increase the price of oil by 93 percent. In West Germany the Cartel Office charged Exxon, Mobil, Shell, BP, and Chevron with manipulating prices to squeeze out independents, avoid German taxes, and create an artificial oil shortage in Europe. In France fifteen indictments were brought against prominent oil-company executives in a $200 million price-fixing scandal. Involved were officials of Exxon, Shell, and BP. In Italy a major scandal broke over revelations that the Italian Petroleum Union, representing all the important oil companies, had given $1.5 million to politicians for false bookkeeping to avoid taxes, apparently connected with government sanction of price increases.[40]

At this time the U.S. government proclaimed a policy of "energy independence." This was a reaction against the traumatic 1973–1974 energy crisis and the ensuing Arab oil boycott. Critics of the oil industry asserted the industry could expand domestic production by 7–10 percent annually, which would undermine the OPEC cartel by causing dwindling imports and excess OPEC capacity. Instead of mandating domestic expansion, however, the Ford administration endorsed a policy in which "energy independence" was to be achieved by embracing and guaranteeing *high* oil price levels.

The theory argued that high prices were essential to making nonoil energy sources profitable, decreasing our dependence on oil. As critics noted, however, "somehow, amidst the stirring calls for collective efforts and independence, [the oil companies] managed to contract domestic output steadily, by 3.4 percent from the second half of 1973 to the first half of 1974 and then by another 3.7 percent in the remainder of the year." [41] U.S. dependence on OPEC oil grew from 17 percent in 1973 to 22 percent in 1975. Dependence on foreign oil in general grew from 23 percent in 1970 to 41 percent in 1976. The record oil profits and reduced domestic production indicated that the private interest of the oil companies was well served by working within the new OPEC system, not by fighting it.

A number of alternative oil policies was proposed, contrasting with President Ford's. Liberals sought to place the oil industry in public-utility status under a new Federal Energy Commission. This FEC would set domestic production quotas (guaranteeing more rapid domestic expansion) and enforce this by tax penalties. The FEC would also regulate oil prices and set maximum quotas for imported oil. (Thus, ironically, by 1975 the industry and its critics had switched sides on the import quota issue.)

Senator Adlai Stevenson and others suggested establishment of a nationalized oil firm to be a "yardstick" against which to judge the performance of private oil firms. Senator Frank Church advocated establishment of two national oil purchasing boards, one for domestic and one for foreign oil. These would assure oil was sold on the open market, thereby preventing special trade agreements between the major oil corporations and OPEC and to prevent manipulation of the price of crude oil.

In 1976, a presidential election year, even more striking antitrust actions were put forward. A number of the Democratic candidates in the presidential primaries suggested the desirability of antitrust action against the oil industry. In spite of heavy industry lobby efforts, the Senate Judiciary Committee approved for floor action a bill requiring the major oil firms to divest themselves of vertically integrated holdings within five years. That is, companies like Exxon would have to sell off their holdings so that they would operate in only *one* of the following three fields: exploration and production, transportation, and refining and marketing. Though not expected to pass in 1976, the legislation was partly aimed at forcing the Ford administration to make its position on antitrust clear. Though avoiding clear public opposition to antitrust, the Ford administration soon issued reports condemning this Democratic legislation as unwise.

Thus the more radical and aggressive energy policies failed to attract the support of Congress, much less the Ford administration. Nonetheless, reform sentiment was clearly on the rise. Oil lobbyists found dramatically more opposition in Congress.[42]

Nonetheless, President Ford pressed for decontrol of oil prices and other measures to keep oil prices high. Ford policies, meshing neatly with those of the oil industry itself, were tantamount to America's joining the OPEC cartel. The main victims, it was anticipated, would be the European and Japanese economies, the main importers of Middle East oil. Meanwhile, U.S. energy policies under Ford exerted inflationary pressure on the economy, sustained high oil profits, and added to consumer burdens. Ford policies placed hopes for a solution in yet-to-be-developed alternative energy sources (such as solar energy and nuclear energy) which might arise in the next few decades. Critics charged that even these hopes would be illusory under the Ford plan, since it provided very limited support for solar energy, threatening "to slow and even abort promising solar technologies." [43]

Tax Reform

Oil industry priorities were well served on antitrust and the Alaskan pipeline, but it suffered a major defeat on tax reform. As mentioned earlier, the depletion allowance was a major subsidy for the oil industry and long the target of tax reform. It provided that 27.5 percent of gross income from oil and gas properties (up to 50 percent of net income) might be deducted for tax purposes. Though often defended in terms of providing compensation for the risk of exploration, the depletion allowance was actually an addition to other deductions allowing for the cost of drilling dry holes, royalty payments to foreign governments, and other costs. As a result, the tax rate on the oil industry had long been well below that on corporations generally. In 1969 a study of the depletion allowance by the Treasury Department showed it cost taxpayers some $1.5 billion annually. It generated only 10 percent that much in new oil reserves. Thus critics charged the depletion allowance had a "demonstrated 90 percent waste factor." [44]

Thus in 1968 American oil companies paid under 8 percent of their income in taxes, compared to over 40 percent for all corporations. The industry's net profit rate as a percentage of sales averaged around 9 percent, about double that of all manufacturing firms. Only the scandal-ridden drug industry averaged higher profits. Figures such as these served to rally reformers. The Tax Reform Act of 1969 cut back the depletion allowance to 22 percent. While this was not the 16 percent level sought by reformers, it was an historic defeat for the oil industry.

The Tax Reform Act of 1969 also did away with another tax subsidy to oil and to business generally. This was the investment tax credit, a device to encourage new investment. Critics charged this tax subsidy did not, in fact, increase productive investment. Instead the tax credits were used for speculative purposes, including financing the merger boom of the 1960s. Congress wavered, removing the tax credit in 1969 but reinstating it in 1971. The oil industry, however, was not particularly influential in its reinstatement.

Following the energy crisis of 1973–1974, a more liberal Congress was elected. The oil depletion allowance again came under sharp attack. With new support from Wilbur Mills, the powerful Ways and Means Committee chairman, the Oil and Gas Energy Tax Act of 1974 was reported. This provided for a three-year phasing out of the depletion allowance. Because of its various loopholes, however, liberal lobbyists and congressmen successfully pressed for more drastic action. On March 29, 1975, President Ford signed a tax-cut bill which also provided for abolition of the depletion allowance.

Abolition of the allowance cost the industry some $1.7 billion annually. On top of this, the act provided that payments to foreign governments in taxes would henceforth be treated as deductions from taxable income, not as credits against U.S. taxes. This cost the industry another estimated $1.5 billion annually. Taking the period from 1969 through 1976 as a whole, then, the capacity of the oil industry to defend its privileges vis-à-vis Congress declined markedly.[45] Even so, Congress overruled environmentalists on the Alaskan pipeline and has, as yet, been unable to agree on any far-reaching antitrust and national energy management policy. This continuing influence was underlined in 1975 by the inability of reformers to override President Ford's veto of continuing oil price controls.[46] High oil prices were assured by controls being scheduled to be phased out by 1979.

Summary

The politics of oil illustrates the complexity of the elitist–pluralist debate. There are many instances of undue corporate elite power: century-old monopolistic pricing practices, long-standing tax favors, governmental support for coups, U.S. acquiescence in the present policy of collaboration with OPEC, and acceptance of the high price levels this involves. (About half the benefit of the 400 percent increase in crude oil prices had gone to the oil companies and half to OPEC.) On the other hand, pluralists can point to many instances of corporate weakness: the dissolution of Standard Oil in 1911, the abolition of the depletion allowance in 1975, and the inability to control OPEC itself.

Complexity is further aggravated because many events suggest *both* power and weakness. Does the ability of the environmental lobby to delay the Alaskan pipeline for years say more about oil industry weakness than the securing of an ultimate go-ahead from Congress says about its strengths? For that matter, is the abolition of the depletion allowance clear proof that business often loses to countervailing forces, as the pluralists say, or should we instead emphasize the wonder that the gigantic subsidy lasted so long in the first place? Is the 1911 trust-busting of Standard what is significant, or should we emphasize the fact that today, over half a century later, the major oil firms are still being charged with monopolistic pricing?

On national television in 1974 the president of the American Petroleum Institute said: "I don't think the oil companies ... have much influence." Commonly those whom others perceive to be at the very pinnacle of power themselves feel constrained on every hand. Their options seem severely limited by their organizational environment. But when such leaders are viewed from below, the average observer is awed by his or her own relative powerlessness compared to these leaders.

C. Wright Mills, in *The Power Elite*, began with this point:

The powers of ordinary men are circumscribed by the everyday worlds in which they live, yet even in these rounds of job, family, and neighborhood they often seem driven by forces they can neither understand nor govern. . . . But not all men are in this sense ordinary. As the means of information and power are centralized, some men come to occupy positions in American society from which they can look down upon, so to speak, and by their actions mightily affect, the everyday worlds of ordinary men and women. [Ordinary people] feel that they live in a time of big decisions; they know they are not making any [and therefore they] assume that there is an elite and that its power is great.[47]

On the other hand, those who occupy elite positions emphasize the awareness of the *system* within which they operate and the degree to which they, as leaders, are compelled by the inertia of institutional arrangements and the pace of world events.

Where the view from below is conducive to elitist theories, the view from above supports pluralist interpretations of American politics. As Mills observed, "many who believe that there is no elite, or at any rate none of any consequence, rest their argument upon what men of affairs believe about themselves, or at least assert in public." [48]

Is there a third way of looking at this issue? In a political economic approach emphasis is placed on *system* functions rather than *elite will*. In this respect it is similar to pluralist theory. That is, it recognizes, for example, that oil industry leaders are not free agents who can prevail over all rivals. Rather, they must use their corporate resources and limit their options so as to present their decisions as being in the public interest. For example, the Alaskan pipeline could not be built simply by a decision of oil executives. It had to await circumstances (the "energy crisis") that made its construction appear to be essential to national well-being.

On the other hand, the political-economic approach also emphasizes class interests and the far-reaching effects of socialization to dominant beliefs. These rationalize the political system. In this respect it is similar to elitist theory. One may emphasize, for instance, the ability of the oil industry to sustain a system of private taxation of consumers (through artificially high prices), which maldistributed major economic benefits. And, as in the self-created energy crisis of 1973–1974, it showed the oil industry's implicit power based on sustaining a favorable public-opinion climate.

The political-economic approach emphasizes the *development* of a political system over time, just as we have treated the oil industry. Before generalizing about historical change, however, we will spend Chapters 10 and 11 looking at the broad political-economic history of the United States. This provides the general backdrop for the earlier histories we presented on the oil industry, on citizenship training, and on the military. And it will lead to the last chapter, which presents political economy as an alternative to elitism or pluralism as ways of looking at American politics.

Notes

1. David Horowitz, "Social Science or Ideology?," *Social Policy* 1 (September–October 1970): 30.
2. Matthew Josephson, *The Robber Barons* (New York: Harcourt, 1962; orig. 1934), pp. 47–48. The following account draws in part on this work.
3. J. A. Hobson, *The Evolution of Modern Capitalism* (rev. ed.; New York: Scribner's, 1926), p. 142, as quoted in Josephson, *The Robber Barons*, p. 115n.
4. Cited in John T. Flynn, *God's Gold: John D. Rockefeller and His Times* (New York: Harcourt, 1932), as quoted in Josephson, *The Robber Barons*, p. 116.
5. Josephson, *The Robber Barons*, pp. 119–20.
6. Ibid., pp. 267–68.
7. See William S. Hoffman, *Paul Mellon: Portrait of an Oil Baron* (Chicago: Follett, 1974).
8. David Howard Davis, *Energy Politics* (New York: St. Martin's, 1974), p. 44. The following account draws in part on this work.
9. Gabriel Kolko, *The Triumph of Conservatism* (Chicago: Quadrangle, 1967; orig. 1963), p. 41.
10. Ibid.
11. Ibid., p. 42.
12. Davis, *Energy Politics*, pp. 46–47.
13. Quoted in Edward Jay Epstein, "The Secret Deals of the Oil Cartel," *New York*, 23 June 1975, p. 47. For further discussion of oil company pressure on the U.S. State Department to help secure anticompetitive oil agreements during the 1920s through the 1950s, see testimony by David Haberman in *Congressional Quarterly*, 2 March 1974, p. 571.
14. Quoted in J. Dunner, *Dictionary of Political Science* (Totowa, N.J.: Littlefield, Adams, 1970), pp. 517–18.
15. "Tax Breaks for the Oil Industry," *Congressional Quarterly*, 26 January 1974, p. 171.
16. See Melville Ilmer, "The Oil Masters," *New Republic*, 5–12 January 1974, p. 14.
17. See *UAW Journal*, 15–31 July 1973, p. 5.
18. *Congressional Quarterly*, 2 March 1974, p. 571.
19. Ibid., 2 February 1974, pp. 191–92.
20. See Andrew Tully, *CIA: The Inside Story* (New York: Morrow, 1962), pp. 76 ff. Note that Mosadeq is sometimes spelled Mossadegh.
21. Ibid., pp. 64–75.
22. *New York Times*, 18 July 1973, pp. 1–3.
23. Ibid., 12 March 1974, p. 26.
24. Ibid.
25. Erwin Knoll, "The Oil Lobby Is Not Depleted," *New York Times Magazine*, 8 March 1970, pp. 26 ff.
26. "Over the Mideast Oil Barrel," *Newsweek*, 23 July 1973, pp. 59–62.
27. *Congressional Quarterly*, 2 February 1974, p. 191.
28. *Newsweek*, 8 February 1971. For a business commentary, see Committee for Economic Development, *International Economic Consequences of High-Priced Energy* (New York: CED, 1975).

29. *Congressional Quarterly,* 8 May 1970, p. 1225. *Newsweek* (27 October 1975, p. 82) attributes the defeat of the New England project, mentioned in this paragraph, to Exxon influence.
30. Lawrence Lockwood, letter to the editor, in *Monthly Review* 25 (April 1974): 57. See also Don Stillman, "The Energy Crisis—Part 2," *UMW Journal,* 1–15 April 1974, p. 9.
31. *Congressional Quarterly,* 15 December 1973, p. 3279.
32. Senator McIntyre in "Nixon Administration and Support for Import Quotas," *Congressional Quarterly,* 15 December 1973, p. 3279.
33. Frank Ikard in "Nixon Administration and Support for Import Quotas," *Congressional Quarterly,* 15 December 1973, p. 3279.
34. See Christopher T. Rand, "After the Oil Embargo," *New York Times,* 27 March 1974. Rand reported domestic oil stocks were higher during the embargo than a year previous to the "shortage."
35. *New York Times,* 18 July 1973, p. 1. Prior to the Senate's vote, the State Department had reported that there "was no alternative" to the Alaskan route. But in fact Canada had dropped its insistence on 51 percent ownership and our embassy was optimistic about the trans-Canada alternative. Senator Mondale called this a "misrepresentation" by the State Department, geared to manipulate a pro-oil-industry vote. See "Oil Slip-Up," *New Republic,* 11 August 1973, pp. 11–12.
36. Davis, *Energy Politics,* pp. 70–71.
37. Muriel Allen and Richard Levy, "Whose Alaskan Oil?" *New Republic,* 28 July–August 4, 1973, pp. 14–16.
38. Quoted in Phil Primack, "Many Believe Oil Firms Are Moving for Control of Entire Energy Market," *Mountain Eagle,* 17 December 1970, p. 2. Alan Miller, "Oil Groups Absorbing Nuclear Fuels Industry," *Mountain Eagle,* 23 September 1976, p. 11.
39. See *New York Times,* 18 July 1973, p. 1; and *U.S. News and World Report,* 30 July 1973, p. 28.
40. "The Oil Equation," *Politics and Money* 5 (January–March 1974): 15–16. For further reading on antitrust, see Stanley H. Ruttenberg and Associates, Inc., *The American Oil Industry: A Failure of Anti-Trust Policy* (New York: Marine Engineers Beneficial Association, 1973); Exxon Co., *Competition in the Petroleum Industry* (Houston: Exxon Public Affairs Dept., 1974).
41. Melville Ulmer, "Thwarting the Cartel," *New Republic,* 15 February 1975, pp. 9–10.
42. "Energy Lobby: New Voices and Ways and Means," *Congressional Quarterly,* 3 May 1975, pp. 939–46.
43. "Solar Energy: Funding Level Debated," *Congressional Quarterly,* 24 April 1976, p. 959.
44. Philip Stern, "Oil Profits," *New Republic,* 2 March 1974, pp. 19–20.
45. On continued tightening of oil tax loopholes in 1976, see *Congressional Quarterly,* 8 May 1976, p. 1110.
46. "Senate Sustains Oil Price Control Veto," *Congressional Quarterly,* 13 September 1975, p. 1939. See also *Congressional Quarterly,* 17 January 1976, p. 84.
47. C. Wright Mills, *The Power Elite* (New York: Oxford, 1956), pp. 3–5.
48. Ibid., p. 5.

Part IV

A Political-Economic Model

10. America's Political Economy: Revolution to the Civil War

When we examine power and politics in America, there are many ways to organize what we see. Pluralist and elite theories were two of these ways. Looking back over the broad sweep of American politics, a pluralist might see a nation born free from the European class system. With no traditional aristocracy and with the frontier continually generating new men of wealth, American politics could be expected to differ sharply. Pluralists often cite Tocqueville's observation that from the beginning, America was a nation of joiners. As nowhere else, groups became important in political life, their competition formed the stuff of politics. As America developed, waves of immigration added to the diversity. Government and labor groups arose to counterbalance the energetic thrusts of thriving free enterprise. Add to this a Constitution premised on checks-and-balances and a multilayered federal system of government, and the result is pluralism. Politics became the competition of many groups, no one of which could dominate, at least not for long or on many issues.

The pluralist idea of what American history is all about is a popular one. Contrasting with it is the increasingly held elite-theory view. Elite theorists often emphasize that the Founding Fathers were men of wealth and property and they wrote the Constitution to protect their interests. From Washington's treatment of the Whiskey Rebellion to FBI harassment of socialist parties in the 1970s, governing elites have strived to maintain their hegemony. The elite's manipulative control of the schools, churches, and other avenues of socialization has perpetuated an ideology of opportunity which legitimates the striking maldistribution of benefits in this country. Rather than act as counterbalancing forces, big labor and big government have been drawn into a marriage of convenience with the giant corporations. The result is regulatory agencies that do not regulate, antitrust laws that do not prevent monopolistic practices or increasing concentration in the economy, taxes that do not redistribute income, and a politics which denies the importance of class while generating leaders from the upper strata of society.

Each of these perspectives on American history has some plausibility. That is why so many believe in each of them. But in this chapter we would like to begin outlining a third way of looking at American politics. By emphasizing political economy we want to call attention to the systematic nature of the social system. That is, every system of organizing society is self-reinforcing. Socialism elicits socialist culture, education, laws, organizations, and governmental forms. Similarly, in America, capitalism has called forth capitalist culture, education, laws, organizations, and forms of government which protect and nurture capitalist production.

This tendency does not require a manipulative political elite. Rather, the normal function of government is to give primacy to the protection of property. Under capitalism, it is private property which is protected. Under socialism, state property is jealously guarded. The encouragement of economic production and productivity is also a normal system function of government. Under capitalism this takes the form of incentives and benefits bestowed on the private sector. Under socialism this function takes various other forms such as quotas and bonuses.

Some of the functions of government (such as its being a critical source of capital) affect different interests differently. The divergence of interests are broader than can be understood by focusing on the individual or even on the group. Such clusters of interests often assume class lines and form the basis for class conflict. To counter this, in order to maintain system stability, the government channels resources into activities which assert commitment to common, primarily noneconomic, cultural values. Symbolic action to maintain the state's legitimacy often takes the form of reform legislation which is greater in what it symbolizes than in actual effect.

System stability is also achieved by securing the joint interest of *both* capital and labor in the progressive expansion of the government sector. Ultimately, however, stability rests on system performance. When performance begins to break down, the bonds of socialization to common beliefs become eroded. Symbolic action has less effect on public attitudes. Elite power, whether based on unequal resources or the implicit power of socialized attitudes, may become insufficient to defend elite interests.

When we look back over American history from the perspective of political economy we are not asserting anything very complicated or new. But we are trying to avoid some of the pitfalls of pluralist and elite theory. For example, we do *not* assume that though resources may vary, all interest groups belong in the same category. Rather, we assume that the interests which implement the political-economic functions of the state are preeminent. Under the U.S. capitalist system, it is business interests which are most important. Labor and other interests do *not* belong in the same category of importance. On the other hand, we do *not* agree with some elite theorists' belief that elites dominate politics in the direct sense. True, because of the implicit power (as defined in Chapter 1) inherent in the culture and logic of production in a given political-economic system, certain interests tend to dominate. But they do not dominate because of direct power attributable to their unequal share in the distribution of national benefits. While the political-economic approach is simple in the way it looks at American politics, it is nonetheless a clear alternative to the pluralist and elite-theory views which most American political scientists now hold.

In Chapter 12 we will expand on what political economy *is*. Right now, however, we want to avoid a prolonged discussion of political economy as a *method* of studying American politics. Instead we will give an overview of how a political economist might look at the history of American politics. In so doing we recognize that political economic history is not *all* American history. We cannot pretend to explain the many cultural, ethnic, religious, and other forces that have shaped our nation. Nor can we even pretend that all political economists might agree with the brief analysis of political history presented in this chapter and the next. But the history presented below places in context the subjects treated in this book: the rise of military power, intervention in Vietnam, the elite social backgrounds of leaders, the maldistribution of benefits in America, the ideology of citizenship, the politics of oil, the relevance of social classes to political life. How are these related to the political-economic functions of government? Previous chapters have described what American politics is like in America today, but how has it come to be the way it is? To answer these questions we will attempt to give only a brief outline, but it is worth starting at the beginning of the story of our nation.

A Silent Democracy: Puritan Heritage in an Age of Mercantilism

The marriage of convenience between business and government is not new. It is not a peculiar characteristic of corporate capitalism. In colonial times, when American colonists' resistance to "unfair" laws was growing, this pattern also existed. Adam Smith, the famous eighteenth-century economist, noted:

Of the greater part of the regulations concerning the colony trade, the merchants who carry it on, it must be observed, have been the principle advisers. We must not wonder, therefore, if, in the greater part of them, their interest has been more considered than either that of the colonies or that of the mother country.[1]

From the English perspective, the American Revolution was part of the administrative breakdown of mercantilism as economic policy.[2] The inadequate performance of the centralized mercantile bureaucracy had been evident for decades.

Laws such as the Molasses Act (1733) proved to be administrative nightmares. Widespread smuggling easily avoided them. Attempts at enforcement through writs of assistance (general search warrants) simply aroused greater anger.[3] When French lands in America were added to the English mercantile empire, costs soared further. The Navigation Acts and direct taxation were created to cover these expenses.[4] These brought more resistance and more cost.

As the burden of mercantile administration intensified in its decline, royal administrators were increasingly viewed by the colonists as an oppressive ruling class. Benjamin Franklin was among those who cited the British theory of "virtual representation" as indicative.[5] This theory held that the colonists were represented in the English Parliament through the concern of English legislators, even though the colonies had no direct representation. This denial of the need for accountability in office, based on representative elections, clashed with Puritan beliefs. As early as the Great Awakening, Jonathon Edwards had preached forcefully about the proper "management of public affairs." [6]

Puritan ideals served as the cultural basis for the American reaction against mercantilism. These ideals were not democratic, but they contained the seeds of democracy. Perry Miller has warned against the tendency whereby "patriots, especially those of New England descent, are fond of celebrating the Puritans as the founders of the American tradition of rugged individualism, freedom of conscience, popular education and democracy." In fact, "The Puritans were not rugged individualists; they did indeed believe in education of a sort, but not in the 'progressive' sense; they abhorred freedom of conscience; and they did not believe at all in democracy." [7] For all this, the Puritan heritage gave way to revolutionary federalism. How did this happen?

"Covenant" was an early synonym for federalism. It was a Puritan concept which involved establishment of the church by agreement of its members. But this outwardly democratic idea was not originally democratic in substance.[8] In fact, the congregation was taught to remain silently subject to the instructions of the ordained minister. As the preacher Joseph Cotton said of this silent democracy, "the government is not a democracy if it be administered, not by the people, but by the governors." [9]

The undemocratic Puritan concept of the covenant was altered during the religious Great Awakening of the 1740s. Though not himself a democrat, Jonathan Edwards's powerful sermons taught that a congregation might legitimately judge the fitness of authorities.[10] It was only a short step from sermons against the worldliness of merchants and sinners to condemnation of the corruption and self-interest of English officials. Equally important, the Great Awakening "liberated liberalism." That is, it encouraged liberal ideas about the legitimacy of judgment by the private individual (as opposed to pastoral judgment).[11]

Edwards became the founder of a democratic Congregationalism.[12] The emerging advocates of liberal religion commonly believed in a radically decentralized form of government.[13] Their vision was one of a federation of autonomous congregations and free men. Government should, in their view, be limited to a few plain principles upon which all could agree. The congregational clergy "preached Federalism as well as Christianity, believing it was all the same battle." [14]

The congregational clergy became "the chief agitators for the Revolution, blessed it when it began, and supplied much of the morale which carried it through." [15] As another historian wrote:

The debates about ecclesiastical polity and the relative authority of congregations, elders, parsons, associations, and synods, which now seem so inconsequential, were far more than a dress rehearsal for the Declaration of Independence, the Revolutionary War, and the constitutional conventions. For these contestants fought their little battles with heavy guns. The principles they invoked were competent for deployment in the discussion of social and governmental policies.[16]

But just as the authoritarian principles of Puritanism were subverted by the liberal congregationalism it engendered, so liberal individualism was to come into stark contrast with the actual practice of the Federalist party it created.

Thus the American Revolution was preceded by a long period of interaction between state economic policy (mercantilism) and political culture (congregationalism). True, direct economic and class grievances played a role: the desire of bourgeois colonist manufacturers and tradesmen to be free from commercial restraints imposed on them by English mercantile interests, the desire of colonial investors and speculators to be free from the prerogatives of English financial policies, and the desire of farmers to settle in the trans-Allegheny lands. But direct economic grievances alone do not account for the Revolution. These had to be combined with the declining performance of British mercantilism and its attendant administrative crisis. As these latter factors eroded the legitimacy of the state, American political culture was transformed by a new, individualist, democratic set of beliefs which drew on a religious base to challenge a corrupt and aging system of political economy.

A Parish Federation: Democratic Republicanism in the Revolution

The end of the eighteenth century witnessed the fall not only of English mercantilism, but also of two other systems of political economy: confederalism and federalism. With this the foundation was laid for a political order disturbingly inconsistent with the congregational ideals just discussed. Confederalism came the closest to these values, but its rise and fall was rapid.

Confederation was the first model of the Continental Congress. Congress was to be supervised through a Grand Committee composed of one representative from each state. Though this vision proved impractical, it illustrated opposition to any powerful central authority.[17] This opposition was reinforced by the popular belief that the Revolution had placed sovereignty in the states.[18] Only a minority thought sovereignty had passed into Congress's hands. This minority was further undermined when, in reaction against its money policies, Congress was divested of authority to print money.[19] Madison wrote Jefferson predicting the total stop of central-government operations.[20]

Americans seemed determined not to allow the emergence of an economic elite such as had characterized mercantilism. In addition, congregational principles of local autonomy reinforced decentralization. The result was a weak Congress. Congress's Committee of Three, named to find a solution to the financial crisis, was unable to secure regular compliance from the states for support of Congress. At the same time the system of central purchasing broke down.[21] Inflation brought further chaos to the new postal service and other branches of government.[22] By 1781 Madison was worried that the financial crisis would bring general mutiny among the army.[23]

The fiscal crisis of confederalism (1779–1781) forced a centralization of government. Clinton Rossiter called this the "limited constitutional revolution" of 1781.[24] Nonetheless, the central government remained miniscule. By the middle of the 1780s the government was again in deep financial trouble. By 1786 its total income was less than a third of the interest on the national debt alone.[25] In part this resulted from the depression of 1785–1786. But to a larger extent it reflected continuing belief in weak central government.

Powerful economic forces were pulling the country toward centralism. Leading Americans had created the Bank of North America as a financial center. It was intended to attach "many powerful individuals to the cause of our country by the strong principle of self-love and the immediate sense of private interest." [26] In 1787 a coalition of merchants and speculators overthrew the Jeffersonian Ordinance of 1784 (which had envisioned political decentralization) and in its place established control over the West by the central government, as eastern investors favored.[27] The most important force for centralization, however, was the inability to pursue policies favored by those who were to form the Federalist party. These policies, frustrated by confederalism, included currency devaluation, national impost, central banking, and a strong federal government.[28]

Shays Rebellion in Massachusetts (1786) and the ability of debtor interests to gain power in seven states demonstrated to conservatives such as George Washington, Robert Morris, and

Alexander Hamilton that the radical decentralization of confederalism had to be overcome. In *Federalist*, No. 10, Madison argued that a strong central government was essential to prevent the capture of the state by "factions" (read "debtor interests"). As Merrill Jensen has observed: "The Constitution of 1787 was designed as a check upon the power of the states and the democracy that found expression within their bounds." [29]

The centralized political economy favored by the Federalists was starkly inconsistent with Revolutionary ideals. Clinton Rossiter wrote that "to the anti-Federalists the Constitution appeared as a betrayal rather than a fulfillment of the Revolution." [30] But though the mass of Americans seemed to favor decentralism in principle, practical considerations brought wide support to the Federalists. In particular, many working-class and poor Americans were persuaded by Federalist arguments that only through the abandonment of confederalism could economic chaos be ended. Only then could jobs, markets, and prosperity be assured. These arguments bore special weight after the depression of 1785–1786.[31]

Thus the ratification of the Constitution cannot be understood as a referendum on principles. Rather the ratification elections of 1788 reflected a short-lived political coalition. The bureaucracy which arose under the Federalist Constitution was born of partisan division rather than consensus. Federalist extension of the scope of government became the focus of bitter opposition.

The anti-Federalist opposition was epitomized by the democratic-republican societies which had grown up after the Revolution. For them, Godwin's concept of "a parish federation" was a serious ideal. Godwin, whose work influenced Thomas Paine and other Americans of the day,[32] envisioned a commonwealth of small states. "The popular societies followed this philosophy," one historian wrote, "fostering, wherever they could, the town meeting, the county association, and a state federation of these units." [33] Their "parish federation" never became the American system of government, but their work laid the basis for decentralized political parties, the Jeffersonian party in particular.

The anti-Federalists accused the Federalists of being aristocrats, and of making government costs excessive. They were said to be dominated by British interests.[34] The Republicans attacked the Bank Act of 1791 as corrupt, for example, noting that prized directorships in the bank went to leading congressional allies of the Federalists.[35] They also felt the military sector was far too large.[36] Washington's use of the military in suppressing the Whiskey Rebellion of 1794 undermined even *his* popularity. The increased Navy, the Jay mission of conciliation with the British, the excesses of the mint, and the creation of the city of Washington itself were all condemned as "bleeding arteries of waste." They were shocked that President Adams's four-year term in office would cost *eighty* times the amount of Washington's first fiscal year.[37] Charges of corruption often had a basis in reality.[38] The Republicans said Adams's powers of patronage exceeded those of the King of England himself.[39]

As criticism mounted, the Federalists abandoned their initial attempts to draw all factions into high cabinet posts. They became increasingly partisan. The Alien and Sedition Acts, attempts to squelch the Republican opposition press, brought outrage to the nation. As the Federalist party began to crumble, Hamilton sought to take over the reins. But the failure of Hamilton's "Cabinet Conspiracy" against Adams only exposed Federalist discord and deflated their legitimacy. "From that moment," one historian wrote, "the Federalists were a house divided against itself. . . . The Jeffersonians were jubilant." [40]

Ultimately the Federalist party failed because it came to be viewed as the ideology of an economic elite seeking to dominate American politics.[41] Ironically, federalism as a system of political economy continued on under the Jeffersonian Republicans. After the elections of 1800, the two parties switched positions. The Federalists, from their stronghold in New England, began to assert the doctrines of states' rights and decentralized power. And the new ruling party, the Republicans, became the staunchest defenders of the power of the central government.[42] Jefferson expanded the powers of the presidency and later Republicans continued basic Federalist economic policies. Of the more radical vision of a "parish federation," no trace remained at all.

An Accountable Administration: The Bureaucratic Ideal in an Age of Nationalism

From the start, Jefferson sought to compromise with the Federalists. "If we can hit on the true line of conduct which may conciliate the honest part of those who were called federalists," he wrote, "and do justice to those who have so long been excluded from it, I shall hope to obliterate, or rather unite the names of federalists and republicans." [43] That is, he hoped his administration would convert many federalists to the republican cause.

True, Jefferson conflicted with the Federalists in a number of areas. These included firing Federalist judges, less reliance on aristocratic class in high government appointments, repeal of the internal revenue system (with its vast patronage), and cutting expenditures for the army and navy by two-thirds.

But it was more significant that the Jeffersonians continued basic Federalist economic policies: domestic expansion, internal improvements, and even reliance on a national bank. As Leonard White concluded: "The Jeffersonians in fact carried the Federalist administrative machine forward without substantial alteration in form or in spirit for nearly three decades." [44]

Initially, Jeffersonian Republican policy seemed a radical break with federalism. The Republicans emphasized economy in government, drastic limitation on the armed forces, and protection of the rights of states against federal encroachment. But after the War of 1812, the economizing of the "Old Republicans" gave way to an expansive, nationalistic policy of rationalization under "New Republicans" like Calhoun, Clay, Crawford, and John Quincy Adams. The New Republicans were far closer to Federalist economics.

The War of 1812 led to extensive administrative changes under the New Republicans. In spite of Old Republican scruples, the dismal conduct of the war and the ensuing financial crisis seemed to mandate change. The national bank, much distrusted by early Republicans, was reestablished in 1816 with three and one-half times its former capital. Overruling the outcry from state banks, the Treasury Department was reorganized, centralizing economic control under its secretary, William Crawford. Secretary of War John Calhoun likewise centralized the military under a new general staff. Calhoun's bureaucratic principles of centralized authority, clear lines of accountability, and the merit principle became the model for other branches of government. Parrington wrote of Calhoun in this period, "There was little to distinguish him from a Hamiltonian Federalist. He was a thoroughgoing nationalist of the school of loose construction." [45]

In pursuing centralization of economic and government operation, the Republicans seemed to betray early, decentralist ideals. For men like Calhoun (before the slavery issue brought him back to a later defense of states' rights), democracy lay less in decentralism than in a clear line of administrative accountability. "If I understand correctly the structure of our Government," he stated, "the prevailing principle is not so much a balance of power as a well connected chain of responsibility." [46]

Later, of course, Calhoun held precisely opposite views.[47] Calhoun's later shift toward states' rights and decentralization was part of a social trend. The supporters of Jackson represented an emergent national mood of rebellion against the bureaucratic ideal in government. These forces tore down the political economy erected by the Federalists and New Republicans. The bank was destroyed. Professionalism in office was scorned as antidemocratic elitism. The principles of strong states and weak central authority were reasserted, harkening back to earlier ideals of congregationalism and confederalism. Though today conceived as a conservative philosophy, Jacksonian laissez-faire emerged as a radical alternative to Federalist–New Republican principles in politics and economics.

Laissez-Faire: The Rise and Fall of the Jacksonian Coalition

The War of 1812 led to a boom in American manufacture, followed by a disastrous collapse. The newly rechartered bank began to call in loans and mortgages. In the West, foreclosures made farmers bitter enemies of the bank and all it seemed to stand for. Nonetheless, Federalist-*cum*-New Republican economics lingered on for a decade. The New Republicans pressed on with their program of internal improvements, designed to encourage investment. Through the Missouri Compromise of 1820 they also sought to limit the slave economy to as small an area as possible. This policy looked to the West for expansion of Northern investment.

But the political economy of New Republicanism was being undermined in two ways. Just as the Federalists had come to be viewed as an undemocratic "power elite," now the Republicans themselves—having pursued similar programs—were attacked on the same grounds. Westerners increasingly perceived themselves as oppressed by banks of the Eastern Establishment. And in the South, the cotton gin and new economic conditions were revitalizing the southern slave economy. This, too, was eroding Republican control. The southerners were becoming aggressive in seeking expansion of the slave system into new territories. They were antagonistic to protective tariffs and uninterested in internal improvements. In both ways they opposed the northern merchants and investors who supported Republican programs.

As the political economy of the New Republicans fell into feuding factions, Jackson was the beneficiary. Those who elected Jackson in 1828 were a heterogenous amalgam of all those alienated from New Republicanism. These included southern plantation owners, western farmers, and small businessmen in the East seeking new opportunities. Jackson's election was a profound social upheaval. Its banner was laissez-faire. Jacksonianism was the second major system of political economy (Federalism–New Republicanism being first) in America, but its fall was to be as dramatic as its rise.

Laissez-faire meant leaving individuals and states as much as possible to themelves. As such it was a traditional vision of political order. In many ways it was a true heir to earlier, pre-Revolutionary Congregational and confederal ideals. More specifically, Jacksonian economic policy meant low tariffs, opposition to internal improvements, opposition to national banking, and acceptance of the slave economy in the South. The Maysville Road improvement project was vetoed. The U.S. Bank was disbanded. Credit was loosened and a brief era of easy money aided debtor interests and sparked a speculative boom.

Under these policies the state banks issued an avalanche of credit, fueling inflation. Jackson was forced to issue the Specie Circular of 1836 in an effort to reverse his currency policies. This deflationary measure combined with a drop in exports and a crop failure to produce the depression of 1837. This depression left deep wounds. Bread lines formed. Crowds mobbed grocery stores to obtain food. An Equal Rights party arose under the slogan, "Bread, Meat, Rent and Fuel! Their Prices Must Come Down!" Depression spread again among the western farmers. Small businessmen in the East, disillusioned, turned away from the Jacksonians. And in the South, plantation owners were having second thoughts as well.

Southern prosperity, based on King Cotton, led to an increasingly strong defense of slave economics. Between 1827 and 1837 cotton prices had tripled. Slaves were more valuable than ever. Acceding to Calhoun's wishes, Congress sought to reassure the South by passing six resolutions in early 1837. They promised autonomy to the states. They condemned the antislavery methods of abolitionist Lloyd Garrison. They promised no federal troops would ever be used to attack any region of the country. But these promises displeased the western farmers who had also supported Jackson. *They* wanted promises of open opportunity in the West, without slavery. Thus after 1837 the Jacksonian coalition began to disintegrate, in large measure due to the failure and inconsistency of its own political-economic policies.

But what system was to replace Jacksonian laissez-faire? It took the nation over two decades to find an answer. At first, men who in earlier times would have been New Republicans proposed the American Plan of Henry Clay. This had been offered in 1834, but it was pressed in Congress after the depression of 1837. The American Plan would have built a new coalition attracted by several policies. Westerners might support its internal improvements, which Jackson had vetoed. Northern workers and businessmen might like its protectionist tariffs, which Jackson had avoided in order to appease the South. And even in the South Clay hoped to attract men of commerce if not the plantation owners Jackson had often won. But this alternative remained a mere vision.

The Jacksonian Democrats were able to retain the reigns of power by appealing to noneconomic issues. Clay's opposition to the emerging expansionist war with Mexico cost him the presidency. The promise of internal improvements was no match for the Democrats' appeal to national expansion.[48] (Ironically, the war with Mexico forced acceleration of the railroads and internal improvements in the West.) But the lands gained in the aftermath of the Mexican War only fueled discord among the Democrats. Northerners felt the South had received Texas and other Mexican lands, but the North and West had had to settle for only part of Oregon—the result of a diplomatic agreement with Britain.[49]

Discontent again abounded. Van Buren split off from the Democrats to form the Free Soil party, calling for internal improvements, tariff protection, and denunciation of slavery. Because of the Free Soilers, the Democrats lost the elections of 1848. During the 1852 election, the Democrats managed to return to power under Franklin Pierce, a northerner sympathetic to the South. The last ante-bellum Democratic victory, in 1856, saw James Buchanan as a minority president elected by the slave states plus only four others. The Jacksonian party had finally fallen. The successors were the modern Republican party, following a tradition that incorporated elements of the Free Soilers and, before that, of the Whigs and the American Plan, going back to the tradition of the Federalists. The Republican party's policies were the third major American system of political economy, and in many ways the most critical to American political development.

An Industrial State: The Rise of the Republican Party

In 1860 the Jacksonian Democratic party lay in ruins. Clay and Van Buren had pointed the way for a new party, a party of business that could appeal to the common voter through the promise of growth and prosperity. The new Republican party held a clear vision of a new economic order in America. This vision was utterly inconsistent with southern interests in plantation economy or with the Jacksonian concept of laissez-faire.

Republican economic policies advanced America into the era of corporations. And by so doing, the basis was laid for the charge that America is dominated by a corporate elite.

When the Republicans were victorious in 1860, the worst fears of the South were realized. Even before Lincoln took office, congressional Republicans and their allies passed the Morrill Tariff Act, for example. This act was the first to systematically protect American industry from foreign competition. The result was to drive up the prices of manufactured goods. The South, as a net importer of such goods, had opposed protective tariffs for decades. Republicans passed further increases in later years, bringing the average tariff to 47 percent by 1864.

Though the tariff issue today seems obscure, it was the key issue of the last half of the nineteenth century. Tariffs raised prices. The difference between the tariff price and the free-market price represented a sort of private tax taken from the consumer to subsidize business prosperity. It also brought revenue to the government and helped avoid an income tax on the new corporate elite. Thus tariffs were the single greatest subsidy to business during the Republican period, and at the same time allowed accumulation of personal wealth free from direct taxation. This economic policy prevailed from the Civil War until World War I. During this half-century of Republican hegemony, the corporate giants which still dominate the American economy consolidated their power.

The Republicans also supported the internal improvements the Old Jacksonians had opposed. The Pacific Railway Act of 1862 used land grants and government loans to finance the greatest internal improvement up to that time. The transcontinental railway system was further subsidized by scandalous rates for transporting Union troops during the Civil War.[50]

Other Republican economic policies contrasted sharply with those of the Jacksonian era. The national banking and currency system was restored, for example. Though state bankers opposed the National Banking Act of 1862, the general investing community welcomed the stability and protection it brought. And the Homestead Act of 1862, bitterly opposed by the South, promoted colonization of the West by farmer-entrepreneurs. It foreclosed forever the use of the West by the plantation system.

And, of course, the Civil War itself brought many benefits to business. Wartime prices outstripped wages, giving business a profit advantage. Many of the early "robber barons" made their profits in this period. Illustrative was Jay Cooke, who organized the war-bonds drive and profited enormously from it.

A Reconstructed Nation: Conflict over Uneven Development

The new Republican party had found an effective strategy. It forged a new ruling political coalition on policies of high industrial tariffs, national banking and currency, and widespread business subsidies. Workers and farmers were appealed to on the issues of prosperity, land grants, and abolition of slavery. To accomplish these ends, the Republicans were entirely willing to use government power to build a new political economy. It was only later, after the crucial formative years of the corporate era, that Republicanism acquired a rhetorical overlay of laissez-faire and "free enterprise." But where Jacksonian laissez-faire had been directed against the *banks* and an economic elite, Republican laissez-faire was directed against *reformers* seeking to regulate the burgeoning corporate giants fostered by Republicanism and the growth of the American economy.

Republican rule can be treated in three segments: (1) a period of consolidation, expunging Republicanism's radical wing (1865–1880); (2) Republicanism's golden era, during which it brought to reality its image of a new political economy (1880–1900); and (3) a long period of division, decline, fluctuating fortunes, and, finally, collapse (1900–1930). In the section below we will discuss the first period, that of consolidation.

At the war's close, the Republican party contained a radical abolitionist wing. The radicals, while agreeing on the tariff and most of the economic program outlined above, differed on how the South ought to be treated. The radicals felt that stability required abolition not only of slavery but of the plantation system itself. They wanted the South to become like the North economically. The main requirement, they felt, was the establishment of a free labor market. Thaddeus Stevens argued that so long as an oppressed reserve of blacks existed in the South, southern politics would be inimical to the interests of other regions.

The moderate Republicans, in contrast, were content that the party had already enacted huge portions of their economic program. Industrialism was unstoppable, they saw. The plantation system was not a real hindrance. Why create antagonisms and disorder when the southern economy might simply be left in the industrial backwash of development? Under Lincoln and Johnson the moderates accordingly gave sweeping amnesty to southern leaders. They enfranchised the southern electorate of 1860, thereby excluding blacks. All they required was that the southern states renounce secession, abolish slavery, and repudiate the Confederate debt. Since the debt was held by wealthy southerners, repudiation wiped out the most significant block of capital formation that might otherwise have been used to finance economic development in the South. The plantation system reemerged in the South, based on wage slavery. It lingered on for decades, leaving the South a backward region.

The amnesty policy of the moderates led to old-guard governments in the southern states. "Black codes" were passed reinstating many aspects of the slave system, if not slavery itself. Leading Confederate politicians and officers were elected to Congress. The public was outraged at the sudden reassertion of rebel control of the South as the immediate outcome of the war. The beneficiaries of public opinion were the Radical Republicans. They found themselves in control of Congress and then, under Grant, of the presidency.

The Radical Republicans moved to place the South under military governorships rather than old-guard leaders. A black school system was started. Land redistribution was begun. The Thirteenth, Fourteenth, and Fifteenth Amendments to the Constitution and other laws were passed outlawing slavery, discrimination, and the activities of groups like the Ku Klux Klan. But these reforms were soon eliminated or ignored. The few industries established by the Radical Republicans had little impact. The last Radical Reconstruction government fell in 1876, only eight years after the first was created. At the same time the inflationary policies of the Republicans (both moderate and Radical), used to finance the Civil War, led eventually to the depression of 1873. In its aftermath the Radical faction of Republicanism was suppressed.[51] This laid the basis for the moderates consolidating their business principles as government policy.

The Triumph of Conservatism: The Golden Era of the Republicans

For the remaining quarter of the nineteenth century, moderate Republicanism was free to carry out its political economic program. Its slogans of prosperity won over large numbers of workers as well as businessmen. As the Democrats became, temporarily, a weak regional party, Republicanism enjoyed a golden era. Even during the period of Radical influence, the Republicans had legislated high tariffs, vast railroad subsidies, and had reestablished the national bank. Now, under Hayes, they moved to use federal troops on a mass scale to put down labor-movement demonstrations. And they reversed the cheap-money policies that had been the downfall of the Radical Republicans. The Republicans became identified with the movement to run government on "sound business principles," with civil-service reform. This in turn tended to attract middle-class support while erecting a barrier to immigrants seeking government jobs.

By the turn of the century the Republicans could look back with satisfaction on a new system of political economy which they had forged.

1. *Tariffs:* After the wartime Morrill Tariff, the Republicans increased tariffs regularly. The peak came with the Dingley Tariff of 1897, setting an average rate of 57 percent. This remained the law of the land for another twelve years. Tariffs represented a monumental private tax, subsidizing business more than any other government program. The tariff, by generating huge profits and frustrating competition, was called the "Mother of the Trusts."

2. *Trusts:* Republican appointees to the Supreme Court created a no-man's land effectively blocking economic regulation by either state or federal governments. The Sherman Anti-Trust Act (1890) was largely symbolic and was soon rendered impotent by the Court in the *E. C. Knight* case (1895). By 1902 the American economy

was dominated by the trusts: Standard Oil, U.S. Steel, American Sugar, Consolidated Tobacco, American Smelting, and many others.

3. *Tight Money:* The continual demands of debtor classes, farmers, and others for easier credit and even inflation were turned aside. Instead the national bank presided over a period of tight money. Under Republican deflation, debtors found themselves forced to repay loans in money worth more than when they had borrowed. With the defeat of Bryan in 1896, the monometallic gold standard was officially adopted. In this action cheap-money advocates seemed defeated for all time.

4. *Business Aristocracy:* By 1910 there were more millionaires in the U.S. Senate than there had been in the entire country before the Civil War. This was aided by the Supreme Court declaring even the very limited income tax of 1895 unconstitutional. The new men of wealth created a network of social institutions which to this day foster charges of elitism: the *Social Register*; ancestral associations like the DAR; elite suburbs like those on the Main Line in Philadelphia; elite resorts like Bar Harbor, Maine; elite preparatory schools like Groton; elite fraternities at the Ivy League colleges; and so on. The wave of elite institution-formation in the late nineteenth century was a direct outcome of the consolidation of corporate capital at this time. And the social institutions of the elite became subtly but pervasively associated with Republican politics.

Summary

Through the end of the nineteenth century America was dominated by three major systems of political economy. These were the Federalist–New Republican (centralization, national banking, internal improvements, hard money, expansion); Jacksonian (opposition to eastern economic elites, dismantling the U.S. Bank, opposition to internal improvements, easy money, acceptance of the slave system); and the modern Republican (high tariffs, large subsidies to business, internal improvements, hard money, autocratic labor relations, opposition to income taxation, encouragement of corporate consolidation, business principles in government, benign neglect of the plantation system).

Of these three systems, all of which contrast markedly with

the decentralist ideals of the pre-Revolutionary advocates of
Congregational democracy or the confederalists of the immediate post–Revolutionary War period, the first and last were
commonly viewed in their own day as elitist in nature. Much
of contemporary elite theory interprets America in terms of the
system of political economy erected by the third of our ruling
coalitions, the modern Republicans. And there is some plausibility to this since the institutions of that era—the trusts and
the elite social institutions, for example—are still very much a
part of American politics.

Were the golden era of Republicanism still the system of
political economy under which we live, the case for elite theory
would be very strong. But it is not. In the next chapter we will
consider the end of that era and what replaced it.

Notes

1. Adam Smith, *An Inquiry into the Nature and Causes of the Wealth of
   Nations,* excerpted in T. F. Marburg, ed., *Readings on the Develop-
   ment of the Modern Capitalistic Economy* (Princeton, N.J.: Princeton
   University Press, 1949), p. 72. See also E. L. Bogart and C. M.
   Thompson, eds., *Readings in the Economic History of the United
   States* (New York: Longmans, Green, 1921), pp. 155, 159–61.
2. See William Appleman Williams, *The Contours of American History*
   (Chicago: Quadrangle, 1966; orig. 1961), pp. 65–74. On the parallel
   breakdown of mercantilist labor organization, see Karl Polanyi, *The
   Great Transformation* (Boston: Beacon Press, 1957; orig. 1944), pp.
   86 ff.
3. Bogart and Thompson, *Readings in Economic History of U.S.,* pp. 136–
   38, 161.
4. Laurence A. Harper, "Mercantilism and the American Revolution,"
   Canadian Historical Review 23 (March 1942): 1–15. The Beards also
   emphasize the administrative unenforceability of the Navigation Acts
   compared to laws restricting manufacture. See Charles Beard and
   Mary R. Beard, *Basic History of the United States* (New York: Doubleday, 1944), p. 92.
5. Benjamin Franklin, in L. W. Larabee, ed., *The Papers of Benjamin
   Franklin,* Vol. 13 (New Haven: Yale University Press, 1969), p. 79.
6. Perry Miller, *Errand into the Wilderness* (New York: Harper, 1964;
   orig. 1956), pp. 164–66.
7. Ibid., p. 160.
8. The concept of the covenant was the heart of social thought within
   the Puritan tradition. Superficially, the Congregational covenant, with

its founding of the church through common agreement and its election of its minister by the congregation assembled, seemed to be firmly democratic in nature. Yet the covenant was part of a religious tradition entirely at variance with democratic precepts. For men such as John Cotton, the covenant was not a social compact but rather a solemn agreement by the saints of Jesus Christ to live by the teachings of His gospel. The act of the covenant by which the church was established was not a political plebiscite, but rather a confession before men by those present of their experience of baptism into faith by God's grace. The election of the minister was not what is meant today by an election, but was rather the public recognition by the congregation that a given individual, elect of God, had through his religious experience received the calling to the ministry. Because the election was by God and not by the congregation, which served only to confirm, the congregation remained silent before the instructions of the ordained minister.

9. Miller, *Errand into the Wilderness*, p. 161.

10. Where John Cotton and John Winthrop had equated the qualifications of sainthood with the qualifications for office as a matter of definition, in the 1740s Jonathan Edwards's powerful sermons taught that piety and good family were *instruments* to efficiency in government. The supreme qualification for office became possession of great natural "ability for the management of public affairs." As Miller (ibid.) has noted, this teaching was revolutionary, for it portrayed the ruler within a framework of utility and calculation rather than of divine ordination alone. By framing the attributes of rulers in this way, Edwards was presenting criteria by which believers themselves might judge officials.

11. The tests to be applied to authorities were external only in that they were no longer dependent upon the assertion by authority of an internal religious experience or divine ordination, passively to be accepted by a silent congregation. In another way the Great Awakening was supremely subjective—in its emphasis on the interior ecstasy of religious revival and a renewed sense of the importance of the individual's personal relationship with God. Both aspects tended toward the dissolution of silent democracy. As Donald Meyer has put it, "What was important was not a mediatorial system of covenants, but the direct confrontation of man and God." In this renewal of individualism, so long suppressed within the Puritan tradition, liberalism found its release. Meyer continued, "The Awakening, we have noted, liberated liberalism. The story can be seen in the case of the Massachusetts minister, Charles Chauncy, moving from anonymous dissent to proud advocacy of the new spirit of reason, free will, and practical progress. . . . These ideas, affirming the soundness of man's rational faculties, suggested that man might therefore be capable, in the light of that faculty, of advancing his own good. Was not this indeed the way God had arranged things, lawfully, so that man might take responsibility for himself?" Donald Meyer, "The Dissolution of Calvinism," in Arthur M. Schlesinger, Jr., and Morton White, eds., *Paths of American Thought* (Boston: Houghton Mifflin, 1970), pp. 75, 81.

12. Ironically, the right of private judgment was first dramatically expressed, revealing its revolutionary implications, in the unprecedented Congregational revolt that culminated in Edwards being dismissed

from his own parish. As Vernon Louis Parrington has written, "By a curious irony of fate, Jonathon Edwards, reactionary Calvinist, became the intellectual leader of the revolutionaries. . . . He became the creator of the new Congregationalism, which in accepting democratic principles elaborated by John Wise and establishing the local church as an autonomous unit, effectively nullified the Presbyterian tendencies of the old order." See Vernon Louis Parrington, *Main Currents in American Thought* (New York: Harcourt, Brace, 1930; orig. 1927), pp. 161–62.

13. The model of Congregational government was one embracing local autonomy with *very* little central oversight. This classic liberal politics was articulated by William Channing, the founder of Unitarianism, an influential tendency which emerged from Congregationalism in the Revolutionary period. "The crying sin of all governments is," Channing wrote, "that they intermeddle injuriously with human affairs and obstruct the processes of nature by excessive regulation." The natural order for human affairs dictated minimal government, one whose "measures should be intelligible, founded on plain principles, and such as common minds may comprehend . . . so that plain cases may in the main, if not always, be offered to popular decision. Measures which demand profound thought for their justification, about which intelligent and honest men differ, and the usefulness of which cannot be made out to the common mind, are unfit for a republic." See *The Works of William E. Channing*, Vol. 1 (Boston: James Munroe, 1841), p. 345. Channing inveighed against the formation of large associations of power, whether in government or in the private sphere. "We do fear," he wrote, "from not a few associations which exist, that power is to be accumulated in the hands of a few, and a servile, tame, dependent spirit to be generated in the many. Such is the danger of our times, and we are bound as Christians and freemen to withstand it." Ibid., p. 309. That Channing could say, after the Revolution, that individual action was the highest good, could seek to found government policy on popular decision, and could seek to limit government to a few plain principles which could be agreed upon by all—all this would have been unthinkable before the revolution in thought that marked the Great Awakening.

14. Conrad Wright, *The Beginnings of Unitarianism in America* (Boston: Starr King Press/Beacon Press, 1955), pp. 14–17.

15. Alice M. Baldwin, *The New England Clergy and the American Revolution*, cited in G. G. Atkins and F. L. Fagley, *History of American Congregationalism* (Boston: Pilgrim Press, 1942), p. 115.

16. Ibid.

17. Edward Cody Burnett, *The Continental Congress* (New York: Macmillan, 1941), p. 446.

18. Frederick Scott Oliver, *Alexander Hamilton: An Essay on American Union* (New York: G. P. Putnam's Sons, 1928), pp. 98–99.

19. Bogart and Thompson, *Readings in Economic History of U.S.*, pp. 175–81.

20. James Madison, *The Papers of James Madison*, Vol. 1 (Washington: Lantree and O'Sullivan, 1840), p. 46.

21. Burnett, *Continental Congress*, p. 516.

22. Melville C. Kelly, *United States Postal Policy* (New York: Appleton,

1932), p. 27. On top of this the postal charter of 1781, passed by the states, prohibited the use of the postal service to raise confederal revenues. (Ibid., pp. 78–79.)

23. *Papers of James Madison*, p. 61. In this crisis of confederalism, proposals circulated for radical changes—such as the plan for a "supreme dictator, with all the powers conferred by the Roman people"—put forward by General Schuyler, a leader of an important faction in New York state politics. See M. L. Paris, ed., *Memoirs of Aaron Burr*, Vol. 2 (New York: Harper, 1855), p. 41. In 1780 Madison wrote Edmund Pendleton that the lack of money "is the source of all our public difficulties and misfortunes," and that the obtaining of it "would reconcile the army and everybody else to our republican forms of government; the principal inconveniences which are imputed to their being really the fault of defective revenues." (*Papers of James Madison*, p. 59.)

24. Clinton Rossiter, *1787: The Grand Convention* (New York: Macmillan, 1966), p. 49. Single officers were placed in charge of diplomacy, war, and finance, and a national bank was established under Robert Morris. See *Papers of James Madison*, p. 104.

25. Rossiter, *1787*, pp. 48–49.

26. Williams, *Contours of American History*, p. 124.

27. Ibid., p. 130.

28. Staughton Lynd, *Class Conflict, Slavery, and the United States* (Indianapolis: Bobbs-Merrill, 1967), p. 118.

29. Merrill Jensen, *The Articles of Confederation* (Madison: University of Wisconsin Press, 1940), pp. 240, 243.

30. Rossiter, *1787*, p. 279.

31. Lynd, *Class Conflict, Slavery, and the U.S.*, pp. 118, 132.

32. Eugene Perry Link, *Democratic-Republican Societies, 1790–1800* (New York: Columbia University Press, 1942), p. 107.

33. Ibid.

34. Donald H. Stewart, *The Opposition Press of the Federalist Period* (Albany: State University of New York Press, 1969), p. 606.

35. Claude G. Bowers, *Jefferson and Hamilton: The Struggle for Democracy in the United States* (Boston: Houghton Mifflin, 1926), pp. 89–90.

36. Stewart, *Opposition Press of Federalist Period*, p. 74.

37. Ibid., pp. 77–78, 607.

38. Ibid., p. 114.

39. Louise Dunbar, *A Study of "Monarchical" Tendencies in the United States from 1776–1801* (Urbana: University of Illinois Press, 1923), p. 121.

40. Bowers, *Jefferson and Hamilton*, pp. 438–39.

41. For example, William Channing, a Federalist supporter, wrote: "Here was the rock on which Federalism split. Too many of its leading men wanted a just confidence in our free institutions and in the moral ability of the people to uphold them. Appalled by the excesses of the French Revolution, by the extinction of liberty in that republic, and by the fanaticism with which the cause of France was still espoused among ourselves, they began to despair of their own country. The sympathies of the majority of our people with the despotism of France, werein deed (*sic*) a fearful symptom.... That they had cause for

fear, we think. That they were criminal in the despondence to which they yielded, we also believe.... The Federalists as a body wanted a just confidence in our national institutions. They wanted that faith, which hopes against hope, and which freedom should inspire. Here was their sin, and it brought its penalty, through this more than any cause, they were driven from power. By not confiding in the community, they lost its confidence. By the depressed tone with which they spoke of liberty, their attachment to it became suspect. The taint of anti-republican tendencies was fastened on them by their opponents, and this reproach no party could survive." *The Works of William E. Channing,* Vol. 1 (Boston: James Monroe and Co., 1841), pp. 362–63.

42. William A. Robinson, *Jeffersonian Democracy in New England* (New Haven: Yale University Press, 1916), pp. 152–55.
43. Carl R. Fish, *The Civil Service and Patronage* (New York: Russell and Russell, 1904; orig. 1903), p. 31.
44. Leonard White, *The Jeffersonians: A Study in Administrative History* (New York: Macmillan, 1951), p. 558.
45. Parrington, *Main Currents in American Thought,* Vol. 2, p. 67.
46. Richard K. Cralle, ed., *The Works of John Calhoun,* Vol. 2 (New York: Appleton, 1856), p. 175. While Calhoun's nationalism never extended to viewing the states as hierarchically subordinate creatures of the national government, the thrust of his ideas lay in this general direction. "Were we a small republic," he observed in 1817, "the selfish instincts of our nature might, in most cases, be relied on in the management of public affairs." (Ibid., p. 191.) Speaking of the sections and states, Calhoun continued: "In a country so extensive, and so various in its interests, what is necessary for the common good may apparently be opposed to the interest of particular sections. It must be submitted to as the condition of our greatness." (Ibid.)

Similarly, some argued that the nation must be restricted to powers enumerated in the Constitution alone, but Calhoun and the "New Republicans" saw the Constitution as giving the broadest of mandates. His vision of government was inconsistent with the idea of "dual federalism"—the idea that the states and the federal government were to hold separate jurisdictions. Rather, Calhoun believed that the federal government had authority wherever not expressly forbidden. For example, in a speech to Congress in 1817, he asserted: "Suppose the Constitution to be silent, why should we be confined in the application of moneys to the enumerated powers? There is nothing in the reason of the thing, that I can perceive, why it should be so restricted; and the habitual and uniform practice of Government coincides with my opinion." (Ibid., p. 193.)

47. Wilfred Binkley, *President and Congress* (3rd. rev. ed.; New York: Vintage, 1962; orig. 1947), p. 125.
48. The Democrats believed that imperialism would reunite the Jacksonian coalition. Polk stated that "it is confidently believed that your system may be safely extended to the utmost bounds of our territorial limits, and that as it shall be extended the bonds of our union, so far from being weakened will become stronger." That is, as Wilfred Binkley has written, "The design of Democratic leaders was to satisfy the intense imperialistic urge of both southern and northern Democrats." (Ibid.)

49. A Chicago newspaper editorialized, "If no measures for protection and improvement of anything northern or western are to be suffered by our Southern masters . . . a signal revolution will inevitably ensue." (Quoted in Williams, *Contours of American History,* p. 277.) Some 20,000 people later attended a Chicago convention, joining in a denunciation of Polk's anti-improvement policies. Nonetheless, Polk's imperialism made necessary the policies he nominally opposed. As Eliot Janeway has written: "The new frontier of the Southwest, once annexed to the body of the Federal Republic, had to be connected with it. The age of capital investment in arterial expansion had been born, and the Mexican War was its midwife. If the causes of the Mexican War were precapitalist, its economic consequences were profound enough to unleash the revolutionary energies of America's emergent capitalism." Eliot Janeway, *Economics of Crisis* (New York: Weybright and Talley, 1968), p. 50.

50. The person in charge of making the contracts, Assistant Secretary of War Thomas Scott, was also head of the Pennsylvania Railroad. Scott's assistant was Andrew Carnegie.

51. Large costs had been incurred in the war which could not be paid for immediately from tariff revenues or land giveaways. In the short term the costs were financed by inflation, a policy the Radical Republicans inherited (and, it must be said, embraced) from the moderates. Some of the cost had been financed abroad, in the form of a half billion dollars in war bonds floated by the financier Jay Cooke. Though the Radicals were sympathetic to the popularity of inflationary policies with farmers and other debtors, the moderates after the war pressed for the Species Resumption Act to base the greenback on gold and assure hard-money practices. By 1873 inflation and railroad subsidies led to a wild speculative boom in heavy metals and agriculture, imports rose far faster than exports, dollars drained to Europe as interest on war bonds contributed to a decline of specie in circulation (per capita money supply decreased from $40.45 in 1865 to $17.51 in 1879).

In this worsening economic situation the government sought to lower its costs by introducing competition into government finance. Accordingly, it undermined Cooke's monopoly by splitting its patronage between his company and that of Morgan. Morgan capitalized on this by securing a similar action from the European financiers, the Rothschilds, who were induced to split their American business likewise. Combined with Cooke's overextended investments, these actions forced his bankruptcy. This precipitated a panic, the New York Stock Exchange closed, and paper values collapsed as a wave of loan and investment call-backs swept the nation. In that year there were 5,000 commercial failures, and many more in the next few years. The depression which swept the country was severe. Wages fell drastically and the labor unions of the time found their gains and even their existence swept under. Breadlines appeared in many cities and vagabonds scavenged the countryside. In these desperate conditions the Radical Republicans became the scapegoat, though their economic policies were shared with or necessitated by the moderate Republican regime which had preceded them.

The precipitant for the downfall of the radicals came in 1876.

In the election of that year, two competing slates of electors were put forward by Florida, Louisiana, and South Carolina, the last states to fall from Radical hands. Splitting on straight party lines, the Electoral Commission voted 8 to 7 for the Republican electors (Hayes) over the Democratic choice (Tilden). The Democratic party, which controlled the House, extorted certain concessions by threatening to refuse to go into joint session with the Senate to confirm the choice. The compromise provided that the remaining federal troops be withdrawn from the South and that internal improvements (such as railroads) be financed there as well. With the withdrawal of federal forces, the last Radical Reconstruction governments fell, in Louisiana and South Carolina. In a few years the crippled plantation system revived, though its anachronistic forms never revived the old prosperity and the South entered a long period as a backward region in a nation characterized by uneven economic development.

11. America's Political Economy: Reconstruction to the Present

The rise of corporate capitalism did not assure political power for a Republican elite. Though their political economic policies proved a powerful appeal, discontent emerged early in the history of Republicanism. We have already discussed the need to suppress the Radical faction of the party. Then there had been the morality issue. Reacting against the corruption of the Grant administration, many well-to-do citizens turned to Tilden, a Democrat of irreproachable principles. An even larger "patrician" segment left the Republican party in 1884 when the Republicans nominated Hayes—a man muddied with the scandals of the Grant administration. Third, agrarian discontent was severe. Farmers took the worst of the depression of 1873. Its aftermath left bitterness toward the banks, the railroads, and other monopolies associated with Republicanism.

The rise of corporations engendered not only Republicanism but also mass reform movements. The railroads, heavily subsidized by the Republicans, became the objects of popular hatred. In 1877 even middle-class Pennsylvanians and the state militia had sided in sympathy with rioters who burned the railroads. By the 1880s public opinion was solidly in favor of regulation, and the Republican party was prompted to establish the Interstate Commerce Commission. The ICC was the nation's first regulatory agency.

In the late 1880s an alliance was forged between farmers in the Grange, labor unions, and old supporters of the Greenback party. This Populist movement obtained state antitrust laws in the South and West. In 1890 Congress passed the Sherman Anti-Trust Act as a symbolic if ineffectual response. The Populists formed the People's party in 1892, but with limited success. Eventually they were absorbed by the Democratic party.

Though the Republicans were able to turn aside the Populist and other challenges to their power, their rule was being eroded. The labor movement was on the rise. The American Federation of Labor had been founded in 1893. Farmers were alienated. Even the middle class was increasingly worried about the trusts. The Democratic party was shedding its southern status to reemerge as a national force. Many younger Republicans saw the need to sharply reorient the party if it was to survive as the dominant party of the twentieth century. Among these was Theodore Roosevelt.

A Liberalized Republicanism? TR and the Square Deal

Theodore Roosevelt fit the role of a member of the Republican elite. Socially he was the son of an old wealthy family. He had been educated at Groton and Harvard. Politically he accepted the basic political-economic principles of Republicanism. He believed in hard money. While speaking of the need for reciprocal tariff treaties to improve trade, TR supported the existing high tariff arrangements. He condemned the trusts, but found their appearance natural to American growth. He won an anti-union reputation by bringing strike leaders to criminal court. In foreign policy he supported expanding capitalism into international markets. "On economic questions," one historian wrote, "he was as sound as McKinley." [1]

Why, then, is Roosevelt remembered as a "trust-busting" progressive? Just as New Republicanism had been consistent with the political-economic principles of Federalism, so a century later progressivism was consistent with economics of modern Republicanism. Progressives fought on the side of traditional forces, for example, when socialist and labor groups sought control of Los Angeles, Chicago, and San Francisco in the 1901–1911 period. Progressive organizations like the National Civic Federation, as another example, were "progressive" only in a capitalist, antisocialist sense.[2] The rhetorical battle over Republican progressivism tore the party apart. But the more important fact is that both factions of Republicanism supported the same basic principles of political economy.

Roosevelt sought to disassociate Republicanism from the scorned trusts. But he wanted to do this in a way which would leave intact Republicanism's role as a party of business. In office, initially he supported a few minor antitrust bills.[3] In 1902 he unprecedentedly used the Justice Department to seek dissolution of a major railroad holding company. After his reelection in 1904, Roosevelt became more aggressive. In all, he initiated forty-four antitrust suits against Standard Oil, Du Pont, American Tobacco, and other trusts. But Roosevelt distinguished between "good trusts" and "bad trusts," and he found most of them to be good.[4] Accordingly, trusts continued to prosper during his administration even if a few outrageous cases were brought to court. Between 1900 and 1904 the number of trusts had grown from 185 to 318, controlling 40 percent of manufacturing.[5] In spite of much-publicized cases, Roosevelt's second term did little to change this basic pattern.

Roosevelt also continued Republican high tariff policies. The tariffs were considered the "Mother of the Trusts." Many reformers, even Republicans (especially in the farming Midwest and West), wanted to see this form of business subsidy curtailed. But Roosevelt supported tariff reduction only for goods from the new American empire in Cuba and the Philippines. Since their goods were agricultural, *these* reductions were opposed by the farmer-reform element. The reformers said Roosevelt's policy would benefit only the sugar trust. High tariffs remained state policy.

Roosevelt's rhetoric suggested a change in Republican labor policy. He said that if he were a worker, he would join a union. But in practice Roosevelt continued repressive Republican policies going back to Hayes.[6] His use of troops in labor strikes in Arizona (1903), Colorado (1904), and Nevada (1908) all brought outcries from the labor movement. In 1906, as another example, Roosevelt went out of his way to support the reelection campaign of the governor of Idaho, then under strong labor attack for prosecuting unionists. And he refused to condemn the widespread, illegal use of ill-trained Pinkerton guards and other capitalist paramilitary groups then instrumental in fighting the growing labor movement.[7]

Finally, the Square Deal brought economic regulation as a supposedly new economic policy. The Republicans had reluctantly adopted regulation earlier, of course. But the ICC was mostly symbolic. By 1905 Supreme Court action had curtailed ICC powers severely; the remaining functions were mainly statistical. This gutting of reform led to renewed demands for railroad regulation. Roosevelt responded sympathetically, supporting the Hepburn Act. This gave the ICC strong rate-setting powers, subject to court review. This act, along with the Pure Food and Drug Act and the Meat Inspection Act, represented a change in Republican policy. Unlike imperialism, antitrust, tariff, and labor policies, regulation was a significant departure from Republican principles. While only a small innovation in some ways, this progressive reform became a bitter point at issue among Republicans.

Under Roosevelt's hand-picked successor—Taft—Republican economic policies returned to the traditional norm. Taft proved even more interventionist in foreign policy aimed at expanding markets, causing the term "dollar diplomacy" to be coined. Taft espoused tariff reform, but the Payne-Aldrich Tariff of 1909, which he supported, left the overall rate structure as high as ever. Taft issued a much-publicized call for antitrust action against U.S. Steel, but this ended in court defeat. More important, it aroused such strong business opposition that progressive Republicans subsequently backed away from antitrust. Taft also took the conservative position on labor relations, bank reform, and income taxation.[8]

Wilson's "New Freedom"

Roosevelt's progressivism, even though similar in economic principles to moderate Republicanism, was sufficiently potent that it split the Republican party in 1912. The beneficiary was the

Democratic candidate, Woodrow Wilson. Wilson's program, called the New Freedom, represented the beginning of a transition from Republican political-economic principles to those of the New Deal.

In many ways Wilson merely extended Republican economic policies into new situations. Much of this might well have been accomplished had Republicans been in office. Some of the measures were opposed by particular businessmen affected, but since they served to help the economic system as a whole they found widespread support even among businessmen. These areas included banking and currency reform (the Federal Reserve Act), for example. This was supported not only by Wilsonian Democrats but by progressive Republicans and even the Chamber of Commerce, as well. Similarly, in the antitrust area—in spite of reform rhetoric—Wilson accomplished little that was different from his Republican predecessors. In labor-relations policy, too, Wilson refused to support labor's main political objective, which was the exempting of unions from antitrust action under the Sherman Act. And Wilson continued the aggressive imperialist thrust of the Republicans in Asia and Latin America.

How then can the New Freedom be seen as something different from Republicanism in matters of political economy? First, Wilson attacked that mainstay of Republicanism, the high tariff. True, the link of tariffs to the scorned trusts made tariff reform acceptable even to progressive Republicans, but the Republican party had refused to take the step. Wilson became the first modern president to fight successfully for downward revision of the tariff. His victory in the Underwood Tariff greatly expanded the list of customs-free imported goods. On the remainder, rates were reduced. Second, Wilson introduced the nation's first successful progressive income tax. Needed to offset revenue losses from reduced tariffs, the income tax set very low rates. Nonetheless it was a first step toward an unprecedented principle: using taxes to redistribute income in a progressive way. (As shown in Chapter 7, however, little actual redistribution has occurred.) One of Wilson's cabinet members wrote, "Think of it—a tariff revision downwards. . . . A progressive income tax! I did not much think we should live to see these things." [9]

The Impact of World War I

World War I spelled the virtual end of New Freedom economic reforms. In its place came a period of business-government collaboration. Antitrust activities were suspended. The War Industries Board was established under industrialist and financier Bernard Baruch. Baruch was given wide economic powers over resource allocation and labor relations. When the eastern railway system fell into near collapse it was placed under de facto nationalization. And, as discussed in Chapter 8, the Committee on Public Information under George Creel flooded the country with patriotic propaganda.

Yet World War I also had a different sort of impact. It deepened the erosion of the system of political economy built by the Republicans in the half-century after the Civil War. To meet the high costs of war, it was necessary to increase the new income tax. Taxes on war profits and on luxury goods were added to gain additional revenue. As a result, after the war America found itself with a new tax structure, far more progressive than before. Also the need for labor-management cooperation for war production led to a spirit of national harmony. By 1919, hours had fallen, wages increased, and the American Federation of Labor had grown by 50 percent to reach 3.3 million members.

"Return to Normalcy"

As is often the case, conservatism followed the war. The 1920s provided a transient return to Republican political-economic principles. Warren G. Harding, the successful Republican candidate of 1920, drew his support from the conservative, business backbone of the party. He represented those policies which had forged the nation's longest-enduring governing elite. His slogan was "Back to Normalcy."

As president, Harding dismantled Wilson's wartime agencies for business-government collaboration. He stood by supportingly as employers mounted an intense, violent, and largely successful decade-long drive against the unions. He upheld the principles of high tariffs and low taxes. And if his presidency was marred by scandals (over the leasing of naval oil reserves, the sale of government positions, and over the Veterans' Bureau), this did not prevent his vice president, Coolidge, from succeeding him.

As governor of Massachusetts, Coolidge had gained his fame as a vigorous opponent of organized labor during the Boston Police Strike of 1919. Harding called him "a real conservative." Relying on powers of veto and appointment to fight a Democratic Congress, Coolidge continued the dismantling of government economic agencies. He returned the railways to private control. He sold off the government's freighters. And Coolidge continued support for high tariffs and tax reduction.

Coolidge's successor, Herbert Hoover, typified the strengths and weaknesses of the ruling Republican coalition. He faithfully continued half-century-old Republican principles of political economy, confident that these were the key to power. But these policies proved inadequate for the economic challenges of the twenties.

Hoover, as the last Republican president prior to the New Deal, carried government promotion of business development to new extremes. He promoted rationalization of industry, for example, by adopting standardization of business products (brick and screw sizes, for example). He pushed the growth of trade associations, encouraging businessmen to organize on an industrywide basis. These associations grew from about a dozen at the beginning of the 1920s to over two thousand by the end of Hoover's term of office. Antitrust activities were left aside. And in the Smoot–Hawley tariff Hoover could look with satisfaction on a 25 percent increase in duties. Together with the reduction of the income tax, these policies almost succeeded in reestablishing the golden era of the Republican elite.

The "return to normalcy" of the 1920s was not really a return to Republicanism's golden era. By 1929 the Republican party had only superficially healed from its split over Progressivism. More important, industrialization and immigration were changing the class structure of America. Nearly 13 million people immigrated to the United States between 1901 and 1920, and this eroded Republican strength. The lingering scandals of the Harding era and the Republicans' unpopular stance in favor

of Prohibition did not help, either. Were it not for his Cathol-
icism, the Democratic candidate of 1928, Al Smith, might well
have carried the Democrats to power even prior to the Depression. The Depression delivered the final blow. It exploded the
Republican campaign theme that as the party of business, the
Republicans would bring prosperity.[10]

Saddled with traditional Republican economic principles,
Hoover strove to create an economic plan to cope with the Depression. The Federal Reserve Board eased credit to encourage
investors. Since the 1920s had been marked by inadequate productive investment outlets in relation to investable capital, the
easing of credit had little effect. Hoover also tried to cope with
the depression in farming, the worst-hit sector. The Federal
Farm Board was created in 1929, but its activities were dwarfed
by the magnitude of the problem. By 1932 violent farmer demonstrations were the order of the day.

In other programs, Hoover increased public works. Tariffs
were raised to curb foreign competition. Individual welfare relief was held to a minimum in order to motivate people to work.
And eventually Hoover was forced to cooperate with the Democrats to establish the Reconstruction Finance Corporation
(RFC). The RFC provided subsidized loans to ailing giant corporations and, later, to middle-sized corporations. Some have
argued that these policies, particularly the Farm Board, public
works, and the RFC, were similar to those of the New Deal.
But their limited scale was qualitatively different from the New
Deal. The New Deal forged a system of political economy quite
different from that of Hoover. Hoover continued Republican
economic policies—high tariffs, subsidy of business, antagonism
to labor, resistance to the income tax, belief in the free-enter-
prise system, opposition to welfare—to the end.

The Welfare State: America's New Deal

Franklin Delano Roosevelt, though coming from a solid social
elite background, represented new forces in America. His willingness to use government intervention in the economy was opposed not only by the Republicans but also by the conservative
(Smith) wing of his own party. The early New Deal brought

various emergency measures, new regulations rationalizing capitalist institutions, sometimes intensifying economic concentration but also sometimes engaging in radical social experiments.

The bulk of the early New Deal was not so different from Republicanism. Many measures were simply emergency expedients supported by all but a few. For example, one of Congress' first acts was the Emergency Banking Relief Act, enabling banks to reopen. Coming at a time when many were pressing for bank nationalization, this measure seemed almost conservative. On the other hand, the Public Works Administration, the Federal Emergency Relief Association, and the Agricultural Adjustment Act brought welfare policies on a new scale. The use of massive welfare to stimulate consumer demand represented a clear break from Republican economics.

A more striking repudiation of Republicanism came with the turn away from hard-money principles. The Agricultural Adjustment Act of 1933 carried a rider enabling the president to print $3 billion in paper and to mint silver freely. It also reduced the gold content of the dollar to 50 percent. With the abandonment of the gold standard came an attack on that other bastion of the old order: the high tariff. The Reciprocal Trade Agreements Act of 1934 gave Roosevelt the power to reduce tariffs by 50 percent. Though tariff reduction was not implemented in a substantial way until years later, the New Deal set this forth early as one of its basic economic principles.

If massive welfare, easier money, and tariff reform distinguished the New Deal from Republicanism, other policies did not. Much of the early New Deal legislation rationalized capitalist institutions such as the Stock Exchange (compare the Federal Securities Act of 1933 and the Securities Exchange Act of 1934). Though often opposed initially by the business interests involved, these acts were aimed at questionable business practices long the object of reform efforts. In the main they came to enjoy wide business support after their passage. Some measures even intensified corporate power. This happened under the National Industrial Recovery Act (NIRA, 1933). Under NIRA, FDR's main program for economic planning, each industry was allowed to establish code authorities. The code authorities were exempted from antitrust action and given powers to set wages, prices, and other policies. This system allowed prices to increase faster than wages, and the larger firms in each industry tended to consolidate their power. Organized labor was initially alienated from Roosevelt, particularly when the NIRA clause pertaining to collective bargaining proved unenforceable.

The real claim of the New Deal to represent a distinctly different governing coalition in terms of economics does not rest on the "regulatory" agencies or the "economic planning" of NIRA. It rests on massive welfarism, cheaper money, tariff reform, and, more important, on its labor policy after 1934. In addition this claim rests on the exceptional case of the Tennessee Valley Authority (TVA), a power and development project of giant proportions which was (and is) vigorously opposed by the private power industry.

The New Deal did not distinguish itself in terms of labor policy until 1935, when the Wagner Act was passed. This act established the National Labor Relations Board (NLRB). Organized labor finally achieved a mechanism for forcing employers to recognize unions and to bargain collectively. After the Wagner Act, and particularly after the Supreme Court upheld its constitutionality in 1937, the labor movement made rapid gains. John L. Lewis, head of the mine workers and later the Congress of Industrial Organizations (CIO), organized workers under the slogan "The President Wants You to Join." Socialist labor leaders like Hillman and Dubinsky left the Socialist party to support the New Deal, saying the Wagner Act represented what they had sought from socialism. Labor support for the Democratic party was consolidated.

In addition, the more radical policies of 1935 extended welfarism further. The greatest achievement was the Social Security Act, which brought wide middle-class support to the party. Though not progressive in the way it distributes income, the Social Security Act did represent government competition with private industry. As with the TVA, this willingness to extend the governmental sector where appropriate represented a dramatic break with Republican political economy.

Finally, and reluctantly, Roosevelt led the Democratic party to support the new economic principles of Lord Maynard

Keynes. Keynesianism meant the belief that the economy could be controlled by fiscal and monetary manipulation—for example, running deficits in times of depression. Roosevelt preferred traditional balance-the-budget views. But after the attempt to balance the budget contributed to the further economic downturn of 1937, Roosevelt began to reassess his beliefs. Keynesianism began to appear an attractive alternative. Through it the government could take responsibility for the economy without engaging in direct economic planning. Wartime deficit spending forced a Keynesian policy, and its beneficial effects converted Democratic leaders to the Keynesian banner.

Elite theorists have often argued that the New Deal was just as elitist as the Republican governing coalition it replaced. Certainly one can rightly acknowledge the conservative and limited nature of the New Deal. Barton Bernstein wrote, for example:

The New Deal failed to solve the problem of the Depression, it failed to raise the impoverished, it failed to redistribute income, it failed to extend equality and generally countenanced racial discrimination and segregation. It failed generally to make business more responsible to the social welfare or to threaten business's preeminent political power. In this sense the New Deal, despite its shifts in tone and spirit from the earlier decade, was profoundly conservative and continuous with the 1920s.[11]

In contrast, pluralist theory emphasizes the New Deal as a period when "business lost." The New Deal is used to illustrate the argument that business is only one interest among many competing interests in the game of American politics. Arnold Rose, for example, makes much of the regulation of business introduced in this period. And one can cite the victory of the TVA over private power lobbies, the establishment of the Social Security Administration as a government agency (rather than funnel the program through the private insurance industry), and the fostering of unionism under the Wagner Act.

Both pluralist and elite theories contain truths. And both

308   A Political-Economic Model

contain flaws. Pluralist theory overrates the meaningfulness of the regulatory agencies, for example. It is highly misleading to view these agencies as defeats for business in any long-term sense. And pluralists fail to keep central the question of the distribution of benefits. On that score, in spite of the Wealth Tax Act of 1935, the New Deal *did* fail to move the society in an egalitarian direction. What equalization did occur was due to the wiping out of securities values (held primarily by the wealthy) during the Crash. Later, during the returned prosperity of the war, the distribution of economic benefits returned to its traditional, unequal form.

On the other hand, elite theory underrates the importance of the New Deal's contribution to the labor movement. Contrary to popular impression, the Depression per se did not lead to unionization. Unionization on a mass scale followed the collapse of employer resistance to collective bargaining, and this collapse was due to the Wagner Act. Unions, while not radical, have served to cancel (but not reverse) the inegalitarian income trends of the capitalist system. And unions have become the single most important interest group commonly opposed to business programs. As a mainstay of the Democratic party, unions have placed themselves in opposition to the politics of the great bulk of American business.

Both pluralist and elite theory reveal part of the New Deal. At the heart of the New Deal, as with other governing coalitions which have ruled America, was a belief in the primacy of the state's role in promoting economic prosperity and growth. Also prime was a belief in doing this within the context of protecting private property and accepting the prevailing (capitalist) economic order. Other questions, such as redistribution of income, were secondary to this. As a result the New Deal *did* have a quite conservative character, as the elite theorists emphasize. But within these political economic parameters, the New Deal *did* stake out a distinctly different program of political economy: massive welfarism, promotion of unionism, extension of the government sector, lower tariffs, repudiation of the gold standard, and eventual acceptance of Keynesian economic planning. In each area the New Deal was *not* "continuous with the 1920s."

The Economic Impact of World War II

Wartime mobilization brought a massive injection of Keynesian economics in the form of deficit spending. Its success in reviving prosperity brought great optimism about its methods and a corresponding loss of interest in the more radical alternative of direct economic planning. Even the weak National Resources Planning Board was allowed to lapse. After the war, the Council of Economic Advisers (CEA) was created as a new, indirect economic planning body. Liberal economists anticipated that the CEA's policy advice would follow Keynesian lines (such as deficit spending and tax cuts in recessionary times, and surpluses and increases in taxes in prosperous times). It was thought that with this new knowledge economic hard times would be ended forever.

Nonetheless, war required that coordination by private incentives (for example, government contracts and tax write-offs) be replaced by a more direct approach. The War Production Board was established in January 1942 to oversee labor relations, allocate materials, expand shipping, coordinate conversion from civilian to military production, and supervise rationing of civilian goods. Later its functions were taken over by the Office of War Mobilization (OWM). Under the OWM profits were guaranteed while wages were prevented from rising in equal fashion.

This retreat from policies favoring labor led to wide union discontent. CIO leader John L. Lewis led a massive strike against wartime wage restraints. Throughout the war years unauthorized wildcat strikes mounted to unprecedented proportions, even after the Smith-Connally Act (1943) made strikes interfering with military production illegal. But it should be noted that this act was passed over Roosevelt's veto. And though the War Labor Board sought to keep wages down to mere cost-of-living increases (thereby assuring wages would fall well behind profits), it did encourage the expansion of union membership. Between 1940 and 1945 union membership grew from 9 to 15 million.

To finance the war it was necessary to undertake a major revision of the tax system. The opportunity was created for a major redistribution of income. But though corporate and private tax rates were increased, the net effect was not very progressive. The main change was increasing the tax base from 13 to 50 million taxpayers. This placed the major weight of the income tax on lower and middle-income groups who had never before been subject to the income tax.

Wartime contracts favored the larger firms in each industry. Because of this the larger firms were less ready to reconvert to civilian production toward the end of the war. There was an unprecedented opportunity to reintroduce competition in the American economy. The issue was whether the smaller firms would be allowed to return to civilian production as soon as possible. This would give them as much as a year's edge on the civilian market. The War Production Board, however, refused to allow early reconversion. Its decision preserved markets for the oligopolistic pattern that was to prevail after the war.[12]

Wartime profits enabled the large corporations to enter reconversion backed by large capital accumulation. Moreover, rationing had delayed private consumption and increased savings. These factors fueled an economic boom after the war. Inflation became a central problem. Prices tended to rise faster than wages, benefiting business. President Truman fought vigorously for price controls but was defeated on this issue by the postwar Republican-controlled Congress. The wartime system of direct economic controls was dismantled virtually overnight.

In summary, World War II was a period of massive business-government collaboration. It was the basis for similar collaboration in the postwar period. The government guarantee of profits during the war had demonstrated the advantages of government involvement in the economy. The shift to a mass-based tax system seemed to remove the threat of "soaking the rich," a common Depression theme. At war's end, the business community had shifted toward acceptance of big government. It had begun to shed the ideology of the nineteenth century. In 1944, for example, the president of the U.S. Chamber of Commerce wrote a book (*America Unlimited*, by Eric Johnston) urging businessmen to make peace with the New Deal. This astounding friendliness said as much about the shift to the right of the New Deal as it did about the shift to the left of the business community. This rapprochement of business and government combined with the timely rise of Keynesian economics to make possible the contemporary political alignment in America.

The Eclipse of the New Deal

The progressive phase of the domestic New Deal had ended by 1938. The end of the war left a conservative coalition of Republicans and southern Democrats in control of Congress. By 1946 the weakness of the New Deal was apparent. Six years of prosperity afforded more room in politics for noneconomic issues like foreign policy and the race question. Better economic times also lessened the appeal of Social-Security-related issues. As those in need of government aid became a smaller, less middle-class group, the principles of the welfare state became less popular. Similarly, once the giant labor unions were established, the call for pro-union legislation seemed an issue of the past. At the same time the Republican party moved to the left, accepting Social Security and other major aspects of the New Deal. This made possible a rapproachement between the Republicans and the southern Democrats, alienated from the Democratic party because of civil rights legislation.

The new conservative coalition in Congress has been the governing coalition in postwar America, with little interruption. Only the Congresses of 1948–1949, 1964–1965, and 1974–1975 have been exceptions. The conservative coalition acted quickly to dismantle wartime economic controls, abolish price controls, and sell off government businesses to private industry. In 1947 the coalition, over Truman's veto, passed the Labor-Management Relations Act (the Taft-Hartley Act). This act was widely interpreted as a crucial defeat for organized labor and a sign of the eclipse of the New Deal even in the matter of labor relations.[13]

The "antilabor" Taft-Hartley Act was used by Truman as an example of the conservative actions of the "do-nothing" Congress during his 1948 election campaign. By raising the spectre that the conservative coalition was about to do a "hatchet job" on the New Deal, and by emphasizing economic issues, Truman won a surprising victory. After 1948 Truman's Fair Deal sought to extend the New Deal into national health insurance, aid to education, low-income housing, civil rights legislation, and repeal of the Taft-Hartley bill. On most points the Fair Deal was rejected by a conservative Congress. The major economic achievements were few. Chief was the urban renewal bill, which drew on strong veterans' support. But even this bill authorized far more public housing for the first six years than was actually built in the ensuing twenty. As urban renewal began to drive up rents and subsidize downtown businesses, liberals turned from support to opposition. And in the area of antitrust, Leon Keyserling, head of Truman's Council of Economic Advisers, argued persuasively for a sharply curtailed antitrust program. Rather than seek to redistribute income, Keyserling argued, liberals should join in a broad alliance to expand national production through Keynesian economic prescriptions. Thus the Fair Deal continued the New Deal in ideological rhetoric, but its actual accomplishments and tendencies laid a further basis for the politics of business-government collaboration.

Eisenhower's "New Partnership"

Eisenhower's economic policy spoke of a "new partnership" between business and government. In office Eisenhower worked compatibly with the conservative coalition in Congress to complete the dismantling of the few remaining direct wartime controls over the economy. Rent control was abolished. The Reconstruction Finance Corporation was liquidated. Government rubber plants were sold to private entrepreneurs.[14] Private power companies were favored over the TVA. Nuclear electric power was channeled for development by private industry rather than by government. Everywhere the private sector was emphasized.[15]

The "new partnership" of the conservative coalition was an economic program very different from that of Hoover and the pre–New Deal Republican party. The welfare state was accepted. Under Eisenhower, the Social Security system was even expanded somewhat. Moreover, Eisenhower accepted the New

Deal concept that the government ought to take basic responsibility for employment and the health of the economy. For example, when recession threatened in 1953, Eisenhower warned the
Cabinet that "the Republican Party must be ready to use the
full power of the government, if necessary, to prevent 'another
1929.'"[16] As recessions recurred in the 1950s, Eisenhower reluctantly came to accept Keynesian deficit spending combined
with supplemental public works programs. Thus the "new partnership" was often seen by that party's right wing as a betrayal
of pre-New Deal Republican principles.

At the same time, the conservative coalition found itself in
bipartisan agreement with many liberal Democrats on a number of other issues. Prime among these was support for massive
defense spending. After World War I, military spending had re-
verted to prewar levels. But after World War II, because of the
Cold War, Republicans and Democrats alike supported large
peacetime expenditures on the military. The defense budget
mounted to over 50 percent of the federal budget. Congress,
liberal Democrats included, showed little interest in resisting
the requests of the Department of Defense. (Recall Chapter 4.)
Moreover, the rise of what Eisenhower labeled the "military-
industrial complex" cemented institutional ties between business
and government. Military contractors became among the largest
lobbyists and providers of campaign funds.

Similarly, the conservative coalition was in bipartisan
agreement with the Democrats on the two other major spending
programs of government: urban renewal and "defense" highways. As mentioned earlier, liberal Democrats supported urban
renewal as a reform in 1948, but by the early 1950s even conservative Senate leader Robert Taft supported it. This major
spending program was supported by both parties, though liberals became increasingly critical from 1956 on. Highway spending, "the world's largest public works program," was also supported by members of both parties with little dissent. Though
a form of subsidy to business, Democrats went along for two
reasons. First, many Democrats believed that the prime objective of the postwar period was economic growth, not economic
redistribution. If subsidized transportation costs would help, so
be it. Second, highways were financed by a tax on gasoline.

Since money was not taken away from other social spending programs, it seemed a painless economic program.

How, then, was the conservative coalition different from the New Deal in matters of political economy? The main difference was on labor policy. For example, the Labor-Management Reporting and Disclosure Act of 1959 (the Landrum-Griffin Act) was passed by the conservative coalition to further restrain union activity. Though generally opposed by organized labor, union power proved inadequate to veto it.[17] In most areas, however, the difference was only one of degree. Conservatives and liberals both went along with Keynesian economics, but conservatives were more reluctant. They allowed deficits and public works when needed, but less. They gave more emphasis to the anti-inflationary side of Keynesian policy and less to the anti-unemployment side. Both went along with the welfare state, but conservatives wanted to limit its growth. They sought to limit national health care, for example, to the aged and needy rather than allow it to become a general benefit like Social Security. Or failing that, they proposed that such welfare programs be channeled as much as possible through private industry. Both conservatives and liberals favored tax favors and subsidies to business to foster economic growth, but the conservatives were more generous. Nonetheless, the conservative coalition was *less* different from the New Deal than the New Deal had been from the Hoover Republicans (or than the Republicans had been from the previous governing coalition, the Jacksonians).

Kennedy's New Frontier

Running on the issues of a "missile gap" Eisenhower had allegedly allowed to develop with Russia, and on the need to "get the country moving again" (a reference to Eisenhower's inability to prevent three major economic recessions during his term), the Democrats returned to power in 1960. Nonetheless, the conservative coalition retained control of Congress. Kennedy found himself wishing to extend New Deal welfare-state principles (Medicare, aid to education, creation of a department of urban affairs) but unable to get Congress to go along.

Kennedy was the first U.S. president to fully accept Keynesianism and try to educate public opinion about it. But this was an economic stance not very different in substance from what both parties had accepted since the war. It was a difference of degree, not kind. In tax reform, for example, Kennedy did not seek to make the income tax substantially more progressive. Instead he pushed for tax adjustments favoring business on grounds this would promote economic growth benefiting all. These included the investment tax credit, one of the largest postwar business subsidies. This tax program was opposed by organized labor, but passed anyway.

Similarly, Kennedy's labor policies did not extend New Deal principles. He did not seek repeal of the anti-union-shop clause (section 14b) of the Taft-Hartley Act, even though this was labor's number-one legislative priority. On the other hand, Congress would not have gone along even had Kennedy supported repeal. But Kennedy's Advisory Committee on Labor-Management Policy was not dependent on Congress, yet even here Kennedy's staff was one-third business representatives and one-third "public" representatives with numerous business connections. This predominantly conservative board recommended, against union protests, that the president's powers to suspend strikes be increased. The board opposed labor's corollary demand that the president be given power to change management practices during such suspensions.

More indicative were Kennedy's wage-price guidelines. Under these the unions were supposed to refrain from wage increases more than productivity gains. But smaller unions and the majority of the country's workers who were not organized at all commonly had to settle for less than productivity gains under this policy. The result was a system under which labor gains on the average would fall behind gains to business. Combined with the fact that Attorney General Robert Kennedy had made his reputation prosecuting labor officials, the Kennedy administration's policy on labor seemed quite consistent with that of the conservative coalition.[18]

Why, then, is the New Frontier remembered as a liberal extension of the New Deal? Probably for two reasons. First, Kennedy's liberal image rested on other than economic issues.

In particular, Kennedy pressed for advances in civil rights (thereby further alienating southern Democrats and strengthening the conservative coalition). He backed legislation to restrict literacy-test barriers to voting. He fought for abolition of poll tax barriers to voting. He fought successfully for legislation barring discrimination in public facilities in interstate commerce. And he increased the civil rights powers of the Justice Department.[19]

Kennedy's reputation for liberalism on economic matters rests on his confrontation with U.S. Steel in 1962. As part of his efforts to promote economic growth Kennedy had established wage-price guidelines to curb inflation. In particular he had won from the Steelworker's Union a pledge to settle for an unusually moderate increase. Only a few days later U.S. Steel announced price increases anyway. Kennedy, angered and betrayed, brought substantial political pressures against the company to force a price retraction. In a few days the smaller companies and then U.S. Steel itself backed down. But the major study of this event suggests that the price retraction was due to market conditions, not presidential power.[20] More important, the surprisingly intense wave of business criticism of Kennedy was a negative lesson. Future leaders were more reluctant than ever to directly confront large corporations. Kennedy's antibusiness image was undeserved. As one financial columnist wrote in 1963: "The Kennedy Administration is cooperating and trusting U.S. business to a degree unprecedented in modern times.... To accuse Mr. Kennedy of being anti-business is almost akin to accusing Senator Goldwater of being pro-Communist." [21]

Johnson's Great Society

In 1964 the still-powerful traditionalist wing of the Republican party nominated conservative Senator Barry Goldwater (R, Ariz.) against the wishes of a majority of Republican voters. Goldwater led the GOP to its worst defeat since the New Deal. The Democratic candidate, incumbent President Lyndon Johnson, was able to recreate a New-Deal–Hoover-Republican sort of confrontation. Johnson condemned Goldwater's "nineteenth-century" economic ideas. He spoke of the need to "save the

TVA" and protect the Social Security system. The result was a political landslide for Johnson. The 1964 elections also installed the first liberal Congress since 1948, disrupting the power of the conservative coalition.

This liberal Congress extended New Deal welfare programs. It enacted legislation providing poverty funds, aid to education, and medicare for the elderly. But the Vietnam wartime economic inflation and the return of the conservative coalition in the elections of 1966 cut short this revival of the New Deal. Concern for the health of the economy replaced concern for liberal domestic economic policy. Johnson, following Keynesian advice, brought about the tightest credit conditions in forty years in order to curb inflation. He reinstated the investment tax credit, a huge business subsidy designed to encourage economic growth. Gradually, however, it became clear that Keynesian policies were neither stopping inflation nor providing a growing economy capable of absorbing unemployment.

The Nixon Administration

In 1968 the Republican party returned to the policies of the "New Partnership." Both parties advocated acceptance of the basic institutions of the New Deal, both accepted Keynesian controls, and both favored business subsidies to promote economic growth (as opposed to a policy of economic redistribution). The inability of this program to inspire the sort of commitment evoked by the New Deal undercut the political appeal of both parties. A resurgent right wing, smarting from the defeat of 1964, continued to pull the Republican party to the right. On the left, a major antiwar movement grew to the point where a wearied Johnson decided not to run for reelection. And black rioting swept America's cities. Along with it came the rise of George Wallace and his part anti-Establishment, part racist appeal to white voters who deserted the Democratic party to support him.

The conservative coalition in Congress was further consolidated in the elections of 1968 and 1970, but the new Republican president, Richard Nixon, presided over an increasingly divided body. It was less the consensus on conservative-coalition economic policies that supported the status quo than absence of any apparent alternative.

More important, liberal economic policies continued to become more popular among traditional Republican supporters. The lack of clear contrasts between the parties favored this. For the first time in American history, a larger percentage of businessmen and professionals called themselves Democrats than Republicans.[22]

Nixon sought to shore up the political-economic program of the faltering conservative coalition. In spite of protests from the Republican right wing, Nixon used government vigorously to aid business. In a virtually unprecedented way, two giant, ailing corporations (Lockheed and Penn Central) were placed, as *Time* magazine put it, "on welfare." [23] The government took over the risk of brokerage house failures. The U.S. Merchant Marine was further subsidized. The Post Office Department was made into a corporation-like nondepartmental service. By executive order Nixon even created an import surtax (similar to a tariff), much to the pleasure of the auto, steel, and electronics industries. And Nixon proposed further business subsidies in the form of corporate investment tax credits, tax incentives for research and development, tax exemptions for profits from export sales subsidiaries, and liberalized depreciation allowances.

At the same time, the Nixon administration sought to demonstrate its compatibility with New Deal welfare-state policies. Though advocating far less than liberal Democrats, Nixon proposed not only to accept but to extend welfarism. This antagonized the Republican right wing. Nixon put forward plans for national health insurance and for family allowances.[24] And Nixon's acceptance of deficit government finance on a massive scale seemed to Republican traditionalists the final betrayal.

It was not principle but the response of now-conventional economic wisdom to a deteriorating economy that prompted Nixon. In 1971 he came reluctantly to adopt a "New Economic Policy." Wages and production had stagnated for several years. Inflation and unemployment had grown dramatically. Keynesian controls had proved too weak. Liberals like John Kenneth Galbraith were saying a more direct approach, recalling proposals of the early New Deal, was necessary.

The case for direct economic intervention was strong. Many academics had long emphasized the passing of the competitive economy in America (recall Chapter 7). Nixon's earlier efforts at voluntary price controls had proved a failure. When conventional economic thought said prices should fall because of a drop in demand, in fact oligopolies were able to increase prices anyway. As Leonard Silk wrote, "The logic of economic history was inexorably moving the Nixon Administration toward price controls." [25]

Nixon's New Economic Policy froze prices and wages. The prestigious *National Journal* suggested that Nixon's embrace of direct economic controls reflected a similar change in the thought of most top corporate and financial leaders on the Business Council (an elite body emphasized by Domhoff; see Chapter 6).[26] But these economic controls had problems of their own. Republican traditionalists felt they were socialistic. Unions were angered because the controls seemed one-sided, effectively freezing wages but allowing profits, rents, and even many prices to increase. After the election of 1972, in which the Democrats diverged from the "New Partnership" economic consensus by unsuccessfully running a candidate—George McGovern—advocating a radical extension of the New Deal (redistributionist tax and welfare policies, for example), Nixon backed away from direct economic controls. Shortly thereafter his administration was swamped in the scandals of Watergate. Nixon's domestic economic program ground to a halt.

The Ford Administration

Gerald Ford assumed office under the pall of scandal. He inherited a deteriorating economy. These factors combined in 1974 to elect the third liberal Congress of the postwar period. Ford and the liberal Congress soon came to loggerheads over economic policy. Each thwarted the programs of the other. Ford pressed for greater business subsidies to stimulate the sagging economy. The liberal Congress reluctantly agreed, reflecting its lack of a clear alternative program of political economy.

Ford proposed a $12 billion tax-rebate program, including $4 billion in business tax reductions. Congress passed a much larger tax-cut program, totaling $23 billion. The liberal Congress tried to emphasize tax cuts for lower-income individuals. Moreover, it tied tax cuts to a $2 billion increase in oil industry taxes. Stimulated in this way, the economy began a slow recovery. And bipartisan support for this sort of Keynesian intervention in the economy also slowly recovered.

The liberal Congress chose to do battle with the conservative coalition on different grounds. Liberals repeatedly pressed for and passed bills to create large New Deal-type public-works projects. The largest of these were voted by President Ford as inflationary. Similarly, the liberals in Congress pressed for national health insurance as an extension of New Deal welfare policies. Ford sought to limit the extension to coverage of catastrophic illness only. On tax reform, liberals failed to support radical redistribution. Instead a compromise tax bill was passed in 1976 providing as many new loopholes for business as genuine reforms. And neither Ford nor Carter chose to make direct economic controls an issue in the 1976 presidential campaign. The Democratic victor, Carter, seemed noticeably cool toward labor's desire to repeal part of the Taft-Hartley Act. Given no indication that Ford would seek more antilabor legislation, labor policy, too, seemed to be an area of convergence between the two parties. Except for a few lingering economic policies of the New Deal, then, the governing groups (Ford and the conservative coalition; liberal Democrats temporarily in control of Congress) found themselves in relative agreement on principles of political economy.

Summary

What do we mean when we say America is governed by an elite? Or by a plurality of competing groups? We certainly cannot mean only one thing. We cannot, for example, say that America is elitist today the same way it was in 1900. Though the general distribution of benefits in society is as unequal today as it was in 1900, America's political-economic structure is dramatically different. Similarly, the growing concentration of the American economy is simply one factor among many that disprove the myth that American politics is guided by the free competition of interests.

The question of elitism or pluralism breaks down unless one can perceive an alternative to the prevailing system. In the past, governing coalitions often provided clear contrasts with one another. The Federalists' economic policies (centralization of government and finance, for example) seemed a betrayal of congregational democracy and confederalism. The Jacksonians' dismantling the U.S. Bank seemed part of a radical program to overthrow the old established order. The Lincoln Republicans moved swiftly to construct a corporate order entirely inconsistent with the principles of Jacksonianism. And even the New Deal adopted economic policies which contrasted clearly with the Hoover Republicans (on welfarism and labor policy, for example). But in the "New Partnership" that has arisen since World War II, the New Deal has decayed. The Republican party has moved to the left; its economic programs are not those it held before the New Deal. And the right-wing Goldwater deviation of 1964 and the left-wing McGovern debacle of 1968 reinforced the moderates in both parties. While differences remain, the two potential ruling coalitions which may govern America as it enters its third century (1976–) have converged on relatively similar policies.

The moderate program of political economy calls for Keynesian rather than direct controls over the economy. It calls for moderate tax reforms which symbolically reassure the public and remove the most glaring abuses, while not changing the basic distribution of benefits in America. It envisions the slow extension of welfarism and the greater dependence of citizens on the state. It sidesteps promotion of the labor movement (yet it does not provide for its dismantling). It seeks economic growth through business subsidies and tolerates relatively high levels of inflation and unemployment. It involves businessmen heavily in the administration of this program. Despite reform efforts, antitrust remains dormant. Labor, while relatively little involved, lacks a clear alternative program. It rests content simply to demand greater welfarism than the conservative coalition would itself grant. The labor movement, in contrast to the European situation, seeks neither a labor party nor workers' control of industry. A bipartisan consensus on political economy overshadows lingering differences.

In this setting it is difficult to speak of either elitism or pluralism. It is awkward to speak of elite domination when the policies of the governors are consensual, opposed only by a minority. And it is misleading to speak of pluralism when elite policies in principle and in fact (and even in administration) favor a business class. Rather, the picture that emerges from the economic history we have described is one of a self-reinforcing political-economic system. America is not dominated by a political-economic elite. Rather America *is* an elitist political economy. The concept of political economy as a way of looking at American politics in a manner different from pluralist or elite theory is discussed in Chapter 12.

Notes

1. George E. Mowry, *The Era of Theodore Roosevelt, 1900–1910* (New York: Harper, 1958), p. 108.
2. James Weinstein, *The Corporate Ideal in the Liberal State* (Boston: Beacon Press, 1968).
3. These included the Expedition Act (hiring two assistants in the attorney general's office for antitrust action), and the Elkins Act of 1903 (forbidding railroad rebates of the sort described in Chapter 9), both progressive but relatively minor, supported even by conservatives. More controversial was the bill to establish the Department of Commerce, particularly that aspect of the act creating under it a Bureau of Corporations with power of subpoena over corporate information. With opposition led by Standard Oil, Roosevelt faced his first major confrontation with the trusts and, by exposing the secret lobbying efforts of Standard, he sabotaged their efforts and secured passage of the act. Like so many progressive reforms, however, in retrospect it is difficult to view the Department of Commerce or its Bureau of Corporations as being an example of antibusiness legislation, though some thought so at the time. See Mowry, *Era of TR*, p. 123. See also Theodore Roosevelt, *An Autobiography* (New York: Scribner's, 1920), p. 432.
4. Ibid., p. 433.
5. Arthur A. Ekirch, *The Decline of American Liberalism* (New York: Atheneum, 1967; orig., 1955), p. 174.
6. Roosevelt's labor policies started on a promising note when, in the 1902 coal strike, Roosevelt threatened to use troops to operate the mines if the recalcitrant owners (the railroads, under Morgan inter-

ests, owned the bulk of the coal fields) refused to accept arbitration or compromise. Under this pressure the railroads capitulated and accepted an arbitrated settlement. But the coal dispute was unusual. The capitalists in question were the railroads, the quintessential villains of progressive political dramaturgy. Even Hanna and McKinley had used similar pressures, in the coal strike of 1900, to obtain similar popular political effect.

7. Mowry, *Era of TR*, pp. 140–41.

8. With regard to labor, Taft's views were orthodox conservative, which is to say harshly anti-union. He declined to support the movement for labor-injunction reform and this movement remained unsuccessful during his administration. As for the railroads, though he never favored federal ownership as did leading Democrats, Taft did work for the Mann-Elkins Act of 1910, which gave the Interstate Commerce Commission further powers, though the version he supported was far weaker than that sought by the progressives (over the issue of making the new postal savings banks less competitive with private banks). And when Democrats and progressive Republicans combined to support a graduated inheritance and income tax, hitherto thought socialistic, Taft opposed it (though as a compromise alternative he supported a constitutional amendment to make such a tax possible in the indefinite future).

9. David F. Houston, as quoted in Arthur S. Link, *Wilson: The New Freedom* (Princeton: Princeton University Press, 1956), p. 194.

10. In the prosperity of the 1920s, capital at the disposal of wealthier classes increased far in excess of investment opportunity. The income and savings of the wealthiest classes continued to grow, but net capital formation as a proportion of national income was 14 percent *less* in the period 1919–1928 than it had been a decade earlier. From 1924 to 1929 the annual investment in new capital goods was actually falling. This gap resulted in investor competition for available profitable securities, inflating the securities market and consuming a large part of the nation's actual economic surplus in speculation rather than productive investment. Stock market inflation was further fueled by the Federal Reserve Board, which rapidly expanded the money supply to aid business expansion.

The decline in available investment opportunities was intimately linked to the stagnation of consumer demand. In spite of prosperity the decade of the 1920s was a period of aggressive union-busting and systematic and successful attempts by employers to increase profits relative to wages. From 1924 to 1929 there was little change in real wages and salaries, and hence little change in effective consumer demand or incentive for investment in new capital goods.

The crisis of excess economic surplus led to an inflation in the securities market in 1927–1929, a stock market "boom" that carried securities prices out of all relation to actual trends in capital formation. This trend was exaggerated by loose financial practices and encouragement of stock purchases on margin.

By the summer of 1929 many investors had become convinced of the imbalance of high stock prices in relation to stock dividends. A selling trend started and began to snowball. By October, panic days occurred on the stock market in spite of buying efforts by J. P. Morgan and others to stabilize prices. Extreme panic was reached on Black Friday, October 29, 1929. Between September and November, stock prices had lost 40 percent in value. Not only did this wipe out many individual fortunes, but the liquidity of corporations (that is, their ability to meet debts by virtue of availability of ready assets) was endangered as well. This created runs which bankrupted brokerage houses, banks, and other enterprises.

11. Barton J. Bernstein, "The New Deal: The Conservative Achievements of Liberal Reform," in Bernstein, ed., *Towards a New Past* (New York: Vintage, 1967), pp. 264–65.

12. Barton J. Bernstein, "Industrial Reconversion: The Protection of Oligopoly and Military Control of the Economy," *American Journal of Economics and Sociology*, April 1967, pp. 159–72. The WPB was led by General Electric President Charles Wilson, financier Arthur Banker of Lehman Brothers, and Lemuel Boulware of Celotex.

13. Though not as harmful to organized labor as predicted by both sides at the time, the Taft-Hartley Act provided a critical test of the strength of the new conservative coalition. As passed, the Taft-Hartley Act banned the closed shop altogether, provided that strikes could be suspended for sixty days, required that the company's last offer be voted on by the membership of a union even if opposed by union leaders, established a series of "unfair labor practices" of unions, enabled employers to sue unions for broken contracts, banned union contributions to compaigns, and placed other burdens on union leaders. Perhaps most important, the act signaled the start of an anti-union public-relations drive by employers seeking to discredit unionism. Though hardly as successful as in the 1920s—when employers were more united —without government support the growth of unions was marginal after the decline of the New Deal. But in some ways this early victory for the conservative coalition was a handicap, since it provided Truman with evidence of the fundamentally antilabor nature of even the postwar Republican party, and was a contributing factor in his reelection in 1948.

14. As John Kenneth Galbraith has noted, the RFC had been a crucial source of capital for new firms which might challenge established monopolies, such as that in aluminum. As such it was more effective than the antitrust laws; its replacement, the Small Business Administration, played no such anticorporate role. John Kenneth Galbraith, *American Capitalism* (Boston: Houghton Mifflin, 1956; orig. 1952), p. 35.

15. The Congressional Quarterly commented: "While avowing a federal responsibility for encouraging stabilization and growth, the new President and his advisers stressed the primacy of private incentive and local initiative, as in the 'partnership' approach to power development." Congressional Quarterly, Inc., *Federal Economic Policy* (Washington, D.C.: CQ, 1971), p. 40.

As historian Carl Degler wrote, "If there were any choice, the administration generally gave preference to business over government." Carl Degler, in Louis P. Wright et al., eds., *The Democratic Experience* (Glenview, Ill.: Scott, Foresman, 1963), p. 442.

16. Robert J. Donovan, *Eisenhower: The Inside Story* (New York: Harper, 1956), p. 209.

17. The Landrum-Griffin Act weighted unions down with a mass of paperwork, requiring reports of the union's business not required of their business counterparts. It barred ex-convicts from holding office for five years, thus barring from union office militants who had been convicted of Communist- and strike-related offenses. It also barred secondary boycotts, disallowing union solidarity, and it barred picketing for the purpose of union recognition. Finally, the act turned cases the NLRB declined to handle over to generally unsympathetic state courts and labor boards.

18. It is true that Kennedy's Executive Order 10988 (1962) favored unionism by opening the door for recognizing government unions, but this policy was not distinctly different from that of the conservative coalition. For example, President Nixon further liberalized policies pertaining to government unions in Executive Order 11491 (1969). It is also true that Kennedy favored the labor movement by pressing for a minimum wage increase to $1.25. But this reform was opposed primarily by representatives of marginal businesses, not by major business powers.

19. Nonetheless, an increasingly militant civil rights movement found much to criticize in Kennedy's reluctance to use direct federal force in the South or to repudiate the established Democratic organization in Mississippi and other southern states.

20. Grant McConnell, *Steel and the Presidency, 1962* (New York: Norton, 1963), ch. 8.

21. Quoted in J. F. Heath, *John F. Kennedy and the Business Community* (Chicago: University of Chicago Press, 1969), p. 125. Heath has noted in his study of Kennedy's relations with the business community: "One of the adjustments they ["establishment businessmen"] began to make during the New Frontier was to accept the new economic policies advocated by the president and his advisers. . . . Johnson basically continued the economic programs of the New Frontier. And the officials of the blue-chip corporations grew even more responsive to the new economics—and to the chief executive who used it." (Ibid., p. 128.) Increasingly, there seemed to be a convergence in economic policy between the modern Republicans and the Keynesian Democrats, however much rhetorical overlay might obscure it.

22. The Gallup Poll, cited in the *Boston Sunday Globe,* 17 October 1971, p. 37.

23. "What Congress Did for Business," *Time,* 18 January 1971, p. 68.

24. David S. Broder, "Conservatives Fear Nixon's Drift to the Left," *Boston Globe,* 22 January 1971, p. 13.

25. Leonard Silk, *Nixonomics* (New York: Praeger, 1972), p. 46.

26. See Mark Green and Peter Petkas, "Nixon's Industrial State," *New Republic,* 16 September 1972, p. 18.

12. Political Economy as an Alternative to Pluralist or Elite Theory

In the preceding chapters it has been suggested that political economy might be an alternative to pluralist and elite theories of American politics. But the political-economic approach has not yet been spelled out. What is political economy, and where did it come from?

At one time there was no such thing as political science. When John Burgess founded the first School of Political Science in 1880, he drew on scholars in history, government, law, and other disciplines. Some of these scholars had been educated in political economy. Political economy had eighteenth-century origins. It was concerned with explaining how government might increase the wealth of the nation. Later this meaning was expanded to include the study of the relationship of economic forces to political and social processes in general. Political *science*, in contrast, directed attention to the study of law and, later, all aspects of power. As political science became an established part of academic programs, political economy faded away as a distinct approach to politics.

Like other viewpoints, political economy is not homogeneous. There are political economists of the right and of the left. Some, including Marx, of course, were socialists. Others, like Anthony Downs, hold market-competition models of politics. Yet in this chapter we can observe some underlying similarities which political economists share in common. All believe, for example, that the relationship of economics to politics is the best *starting point* for unraveling questions about the distribution of power in society.

As an approach to politics, political economy is very unpretentious. It is not a grand theory of social action. Nor is it a complex method of analysis. It is not even new. Political economy is heavily historical in most cases, and the insights it suggests are often commonplace truths. No one set of political beliefs—conservative or radical—needs to be the result of a political-economic approach. But it *is* a distinct approach. It is *not* compatible with either pluralist or elite theory, for example. It *does* engender a lively debate which can fruitfully direct the student into a different way of looking at American politics. Political economy is therefore a helpful supplement to, but not a substitute for, the student's own creative insight into political affairs.

In this chapter we will first discuss the work of six authors and their colleagues. The writings of Mill, Marx, Beard, Parsons and Smelser, Downs, and Baran and Sweezy illustrate the diversity of political-economic analysis. From them we can extract some of the common themes of political economy. Second, we will recall earlier portions of this book which illustrate these political-economic themes. And we can indicate how this is different from either pluralist or elite theories of American politics.

Works That Helped Shape Political Economy as an Approach to Politics

If you have studied modern political thought, you have already come across political-economic theory. John Stuart Mill, for example, was among the foremost founders of modern liberal thought. His *Principles of Political Economy* (1848) appeared in the same year as Marx and Engels' *Communist Manifesto*. Though reflecting very different ideologies, there is some similarity between Mill and Marx in the way they looked at politics.

They both considered themselves political economists, and many of their ideas are similar. But on many other issues they differed.

The Function of Government

Mill believed government's foremost functional tendency was its role as the protector of person and property. In particular, Mill noted that governments everywhere serve to protect the "productive classes" from the masses. Marx agreed with this, but said Mill was wrong in assuming all governments were the same. Rather, Marx held, governments differ according to the stage of production in society (feudal stage, capitalist stage, for example). In each stage, production creates its own legal relations, its own form of government, and its own culture.

Capitalism, for example, generates capitalist laws, capitalist government agencies, and capitalist literature and culture. Similarly, Marx predicted that socialist production would generate socialist laws, institutions, and culture. That is, government functions to enhance the prevailing productive system. It does this by fostering a self-reinforcing set of laws, institutions, and culture.

These ideas are not new. The Federalists held similar beliefs. Madison's argument against "factions" in *Federalist,* Number 10, for example, alluded to the need to protect propertied interests from debtor factions gaining power in seven states prior to ratification of the Constitution. One need not be an economic determinist or a Marxist to acknowledge the primacy consciously given to the central production-related function of government. Similarly, Marx's idea about government being tied to stages of production is not unique to Marxists. For instance, Robert Dahl's pluralist study of New Haven (*Who Governs?* discussed in Chapter 1) contains a related analysis. Dahl discussed the evolution of city politics from rule by "patricians" (1784–1842, a preindustrial era), to rule by "entrepreneurs" (1842–1899, during the rise of industrialism), to rule by the "explebes" (since 1899, reflecting the power of workers and immigrants in later stages of industrialism). Obviously the general concepts of the prime production function of government and

the relation of productive stages to government is only a starting point. By itself, it can lead either to elite theory (Marxist,
for example) or pluralist (Dahl's) conclusions.

The ideas about the central economic functions of government are common to other political economists. One of the
most influential was Charles Beard, the only individual ever to
hold the presidency of both the American Political Science Association and the American Historical Association. His works,
including *The Economic Basis of Politics* (1922), served as a
guide for an entire generation of social scientists.

Beard cited Madison in support of the idea that government's prime function is the protection of the unequal faculties
of individuals for acquiring property. Beard also believed that
drastic changes in the economy would find reflection in changes
in politics. This, too, was similar to Marx. But it can be interpreted more broadly. It is not just changes in the basic mode of
production (such as agricultural feudalism changing to early
industrialism) that are reflected in politics. It is any drastic
change (such as the Depression marking the shift from Hoover
Republicanism to the political-economic program of the New
Deal).

Mill, Marx, and Beard were political economists with liberal or radical thrusts. But even among contemporary, more
moderate social scientists who use a political-economic approach, similar themes emerge. For example, Talcott Parsons
and Neil Smelser, writing in *Economy and Society* (1956),
emphasize the role of the polity as a provider of capital. The
government's role in increasing productivity through tax exemptions, subsidies, tariffs, and various forms of control over labor
(discussed in Chapters 10 and 11) is critical. At times businesses with a particular vested interest may resist this encouragement to productivity. In such cases government may engage
in antitrust activity, not as an "antibusiness" venture, but simply
to fulfill its role in promoting economic productivity.

Parsons and Smelser also emphasize the intricate interrela-
tionship between government's economic role and political culture. They discuss how governments evoke cultural symbols as a
crucial step in mobilizing support for the state. (This recalls Edelman's work on symbolic action, discussed in Chapter 1.) The em-

phasis on "black capitalism" during the Johnson and Nixon administrations, for instance, sought to reassure black people that they were being included in economic growth. Great publicity was given to blacks acquiring the *symbols* of capitalist success (such as ownership of small firms), even though the program had no *substantive* hope of significantly altering the structure of the economy. More generally, the state fosters a self-reinforcing cultural system. Culture-perpetuating institutions are in fact the most important elements in social control.[1]

Though the discussion above emphasizes similarity rather than the differences (which are substantial), it is still true that those who use a political-economic approach have more in common than is generally believed. These common themes may be qualified in quite opposing ways, but they are a useful starting point for nearly all political economists. Three initial points are listed here; points 4–9 appear in later sections of the chapter.

Starting Points in Political Economy

1. The normal function of government is to give primacy to the protection of property and the encouragement of economic productivity. Though other purposes are occasionally given priority, in the long run it is these functions which override the others.
2. Every system of production is self-reinforcing. Socialism elicits socialist culture, education, laws, organizations, and governmental forms, just as capitalism calls forth capitalist culture, education, laws, organizations, and forms of government which protect and nurture capitalist production.
3. To maintain system stability, the state channels resources into activities which assert commitment to common cultural values. Symbolic action to maintain the legitimacy of the state is often made concrete in "reform" legislation which reassures citizens without substantively altering the basic functions of government.

The Function of Expansion

John Stuart Mill, in *Principles of Political Economy,* emphasized the political importance of the increasing wealth of nations. It was increasing wealth which cemented the loyalty of the liberal citizen to the state. The politics of creating wealth is based on the ideology of success, not the more radical ideology of redistribution. The increased individual opportunity to succeed justifies giant business subsidies ranging from the "internal improvements" of early nineteenth-century America to the tax write-offs of the 1970s. It justifies, Mill contended, the state's avoiding a redistributionist tax policy. "Overburdening" of "skill, industry, and frugality" by taxing the wealthy would only inhibit economic expansion, dampen the opportunity for success, and undermine the liberal state.

Marx was much more pessimistic, and wrongly so, about the possibilities for continued capitalist expansion. But he recognized the truth of Mill's point, for example, in his discussion of the English working class. The English subject, Marx noted, is not revolutionary because he or she has been bought off by the industrial expansion of the nation. Later, Marx and Engels would castigate the labor movement's interest in increased wages as merely "better pay for slaves," but the political effectiveness of economic expansion was evident in their own time.

Charles Beard, in *The Economic Basis of Politics* (1922), also discussed the importance of economic growth. The dominance of economic elites depends, he said, on their providing prosperity. The effectiveness of cultural, economic, and police controls over the citizen cannot be long sustained in the absence of prosperity. Without it, the elite must yield to other governors.

Parsons and Smelser, in *Economy and Society* (1956), put forward one description of how lack of expansion is the critical component in institutional change. Institutional change, they wrote, follows a cycle:

1. Dissatisfaction arises over the productive achievements of the economy.
2. "Unjustified" negative emotional reactions and "unrealistic" aspirations are manifested by various groups.
3. Cultural pressures channel discontent into patterns not inconsistent with widely shared values.
4. Respected leaders advocate reforms, defining the alternatives.
5. Attempts are made in and out of government to implement some of the proposed reforms.

6. Innovations are accepted according to their impact on productivity and profit.
7. Accepted innovations are institutionalized.[2]

In Chapters 10 and 11, to illustrate, we noted how discontent arose with the rise of the "robber barons" in the late nineteenth century. Reforms were advocated ranging from socialism to technocracy. But extreme movements were repressed by the state, or they were unable to surmount cultural barriers which defined their goals as "un-American." Innovations were undertaken as corporate managers succeeded the older capitalist "pioneers." Family capitalistic control diminished. These changes led to higher profits in many cases (as in Standard Oil), allowing new forms of control to become legitimated and institutionalized.

Expansion still is a critical concept in contemporary Marxist explanations of American politics, as well. Paul Baran and Paul Sweezy emphasize the political role of expansion in their *Monopoly Capital* (1966). They argue that American political stability does not rest on the competition of business, labor, and other interest groups. Rather, stability rests on the common interest of big business and workers in increased government expenditures. Far from constituting a tendency toward "socialism," government's rising share of the national product has been devoted to projects socially necessary to the continued well-being of the capitalist system. Corporate growth has facilitated government expansion. Economic growth necessitates that additional government expenditures rise at an ever faster rate. The result is an economic crisis of government finance as the state tries to satisfy economic needs (for example, welfare costs of maintaining the increasingly large number of unemployed and other social casualties of the economic system) without "overburdening" entrepreneurs with taxes.[3] The solution to this crisis is elusive. Seeking it, recent governments have more and more emphasized the need for the government to intervene directly to promote economic expansion. The Republican party has shed much of its reluctance to use Keynesian and even direct economic controls and public works when necessary, and the Democratic party has come to emphasize expansion rather than re-distributionist rhetoric. This modern convergence is a corollary of the crisis of government finance and, beyond that, the threat of political instability should expansion cease.

Starting Points (*Continued from p. 331*)

4. In addition to socialization to dominant values congenial to the economic system, and in addition to the symbolic activities of government, stability has been maintained by the joint interest of capital and labor in the progressive expansion of the economy and, with it, of the government sector.

Class and Interest Conflict

The class and interest group basis of politics is laid by the primacy of the economic function of the state. Nonetheless, the liberal state is not a class dictatorship. On the contrary. John Stuart Mill long ago noted the disastrous effect on public opinion of class legislation giving different rights to the rich than to the poor. Compare, for example, America's first military draft. This class legislation allowed the wealthy to legally buy their way out, whereas the poor were conscripted involuntarily during the Civil War. The result was widespread animosity toward Lincoln, even in the North. And it led to the worst rioting America has ever experienced, necessitating diversion of large military forces from major Civil War battles so they could be used in quelling an incipient insurrection in New York. Similarly, differential legislation for blacks and whites underlay the social turmoil of the 1960s.

Mill knew that changes in overt class legislation would not alter the basic political-economic nature of government. Abolition of overt class legislation might not even affect the distribution of benefits in society. Rather, abolition of such laws serves a symbolic, moral function. It fosters belief in the justice and legitimacy of the state.

Marx felt Mill went too far in generalizing about the common belief of an entire nation in the legitimacy of the state. Marx believed it was too simple to talk, for example, about "the English people" as a whole. Most are aware that Marx preferred to discuss specific social classes rather than "peoples" at large. But most think Marx simplified society into a dichotomy: owners versus workers. Actually Marxist class analysis understands *these* categories as abstractions. That is, the broad categories based on relation to the means of production (such as wage labor and capital) must be analyzed in terms of social patterns of exchange, division of labor, the setting of prices, and so on. Thus the setting of prices determines what capital means concretely. What capital means helps determine the nature of social classes. What classes form determines what is meant by "the American people." There is a great deal of room for different interpretations of the *concrete* class structure of society, even if the *abstract* class structure of all capitalist societies (like America) can be reduced to capitalists versus workers.

Marx recognized that the division of labor gives rise to *many* roles, not just "owner" and "worker." But these roles are stratified into classes. On the one hand economic interdependence ties the classes together. For example, it is possible for the Republican party to have campaigned repeatedly on the theme that aiding business would benefit even workers. But this sort of "unity" masks an underlying potential antagonism.

Roles generate attitudes. The development of military occupations fosters militaristic viewpoints. In contrast, the development of social service work encourages liberal beliefs about reform.[4] Marx noted that the division of labor which brought about high economic interdependence also brought about classes of occupations which hold differing viewpoints. The integrative role of government continually strives to obscure differences. But reforms simply restructure (and often exacerbate) the underlying differences. For example, urban renewal (discussed in Chapter 7) at first brought various classes of interests (labor, social workers, businesses) together on a reform. But as the reform proved to be symbolic rather than redistributive in nature, the temporary unity fell apart. What was left was more bitterness, cynicism, and lack of vision than ever.

Similarly, Charles Beard understood that the diversity of economic interests is the most common and enduring source of political conflict. While ethnicity, religion, and other social forces also generate conflict, they are of lesser import in the long run. It is not an accident that the majority of Washington lobbies are of an economic character, for example. Representative democracy, Beard wrote, does not eliminate economic interests. Like other governments, it enhances the interests who benefit from the prevailing type of political economy. Nor does representative government prevent the conflict of different classes of interests. Government ideology teaches patriotism and civic participation, but underlying this is a conflict of interests never far from the surface.

But Beard differs from Marx in an important respect. He did not agree that ideas arose directly and automatically from economic conditions. Politics, the military, and the realm of ideas retained an importance independent of economics. Or to put it another way, the role sets associated with occupational classes not in direct production (such as the military, intellectuals, and the clergy) are also an important source of political conflict. These occupations are not simply "agents" of a business elite. Parsons and Smelser also emphasized the independent role of these other nonproductive classes.

More broadly, the class which benefits most from a given system of political economy (the "elite") does not "dominate" society. That is, it seeks control in its interest, but it is not a cohesive group in command of history. If that were so, history would evolve far less rapidly. Rather, unanticipated consequences of self-interested political actions are everywhere.

It is this point which is emphasized by contemporary Marxists such as Baran and Sweezy. In *Monopoly Capital* (1966) they discuss how—as capitalism in America became more concentrated, as the division of labor became specialized, and as tasks became organized and routinized—traditional values were stretched and broken. The end result is a weakened social fabric. It is characterized by alienating jobs, competitive values, and money-centered status norms.

In the area of jobs, particularly, irrationality abounds. For every responsible job (as a research scientist, for example) created by new technology, others are stripped of responsibility and creativity. For every responsible job, automation creates dozens of alienating jobs (such as keypunchers and machine-tenders). Even "responsible" jobs are stripped of their full human value by the purpose to which they are put. For example, the rise of the military-industrial complex after World War II has meant over half of all research and development moneys are military-connected. Much other research is directed toward needless consumption items.

The declining meaningfulness of jobs confronts the "overeducation" of the labor force. Cemented and stabilized by the socialization of citizens to the ideology of success, the state finds it necessary to encourage the dream that education will yield upward mobility. But in fact the great majority of upward "mobility" results from changing job structures (such as the decline of farm jobs and the rise of office jobs), not from education per se. Since World War II, education has reached a point of crisis. Millions of young Americans find themselves overeducated. That is, there are no responsible positions available to use their specialized role training. They find themselves in positions much lower than they had been expected to achieve.

Accompanying the crisis of occupational roles has been the erosion of other social values. This includes the decline of religion, the falling away from traditional morality, and even the downgrading of patriotism. Corroded by critical rationality and the reduced ability of the economic system to meet culturally induced expectations, socialization to dominant ideology no longer suffices for social control. Other, more external forms of social control become more important: economic rewards and penalties, the police and the courts. Playing a role they were never meant to assume, these institutions become overburdened. A social malaise affects the country. The integration of social relations fails to keep pace with the integration of economic relations.

Starting Points (Continued from p. 334)

5. The division of labor creates not only cooperation but also a divergence of interest between social roles. These roles and their associated interests cluster in classes of roles. This is broader than can be understood by analyzing politics in terms of individual personalities or even in terms of group politics.

6. The prime functions of government affect different classes of interests differently. Opposing class interests are mobilized when socialization to unifying ideology breaks down.

7. Stability decays when socialization is eroded. There is a limit to the effectiveness of symbolic action in sustaining the legitimacy of state political economy when system performance begins to break down.

Such breakdowns are often associated with wars and depressions. In contemporary America the main factors undermining system performance are the following:

a. The fiscal crisis of the state, based on social costs of capitalist production increasing faster than can be financed from the economy without continually higher levels of burden.

b. The erosion of traditional social controls, based on the contradiction of technology with the quality of work, and based on the diffuse effects of critical rationality of industrialism on religion, the community, the schools, and the family.

Incrementalism versus Planning

Critics of pluralist theory often hold two seemingly contradictory opinions. On the one hand they charge American politics with being highly concentrated and elitist. On the other hand they often charge that the American system so fragments power that comprehensive change is impossible.

Baran and Sweezy, in *Monopoly Capital,* are among those political economists who have addressed this question. They note that within the largest American enterprises planning is highly developed. But overall the present, highly concentrated system is as unplanned as the more competitive economy of the past. The system is unplanned in the sense that neither business nor government exerts any systematic effort that would correct the abuses of noncompetitive production or reverse the inegalitarian distribution of benefits that results from capitalism.

Concentration of the economy and of power to maintain it in its present form is consistent with incrementalism and fragmentation. As Merrill Jensen observed of the fragmented, federal system embodied in the Constitution, such a framework can be (and was) intended as a *check* upon democracy (recall Chapter 10). It can be and was an instrument of an emergent elite. Incrementalism is not the opposite of elitism. Incrementalism is a style of governing which favors preservation of the status quo, whether elitist or pluralist.

The failure to understand that concentration is consistent with absence of social planning—that elitism and pluralism are not opposites in this sense—has its origins in the early history of social science. It goes back to treating economic concentration as something independent of the pluralistic aspects of politics.

Thus Charles Beard noted that in the mid-nineteenth century, social philosophers became increasingly concerned with the justification of the expanding capitalist system. "Political economy" was dropped in favor of the narrower focus of "economics." The economy began to be analyzed independently of politics. "Of course it was absurd," Beard wrote, "for men to write of the production and distribution of wealth apart from the state which defines, upholds, taxes, and regulates property, the very basis of economic operations; but absurdity does not restrain the hand of the apologist."[5] That is, the decline of political economy went hand-in-hand with the sort of rosy justification of the American capitalist system that is represented by the present-day pluralist school.

Starting Points (Continued from p. 338)

8. A political economic system is both "elitist" with respect to ends and "pluralist" with respect to means. Elitism and pluralism may be complementary rather than contradictory. Different degrees and kinds of property and differing relations to property form the primary basis for the formation of opposing interests. The principal task of government is the regulation of these various interests in a way compatible with the preservation and growth of the economic system. The ends of this process disproportionately favor an elite, but the means utilized by a liberal state need not be conspiratorial or even require central coordination.

Parameters of Pluralism

Anthony Downs's *An Economic Theory of Democracy* (1957) is a political-economic work that discusses the pluralist means which may characterize American politics. Using a free-market competition model of politics, Downs argues that voters vote on the basis of their perceived utility or interest. To maximize votes, political parties shift to the right or left as circumstances dictate. Thus the Republican party shifted leftward during the New Deal, accepting the Social Security Act, for example. The Democratic party similarly shifted rightward after its defeat under George McGovern, a very liberal candidate. Downs's model predicts such equilibrating political shifts toward the center.

Downs also argues against the Marxist idea that the political framework of a nation (its system of courts, legislatures, executive bodies) is of no real consequence. For example, a system of single-party, majority-election districts makes voters feel that voting for a third-party candidate is "throwing one's vote away." It favors a two-party system and thwarts insurgent movements.

Downs's model emphasizes the rationality of the voter. Since obtaining political information comes at a cost of time, effort, and even expense, voters have to weigh these costs against the supposed benefits of voting. Because the expected payoff is low, most voters choose to incur little costs. They do not spend time, effort, and money to become involved or even informed. Since the costs of involvement are proportionately greater for low-income, low-status groups, they are disproportionately less involved or influential in politics. Thus Downs argues that political structure can reinforce a class effect in government.

Downs's model is limited in many respects. His emphasis on voter rationality ignores the problem of nondecisions, symbolic action, and manipulative socialization discussed in Chapter 1. It fails to draw a close connection between the economic and political realms. It gives no explanation for the elitist outcomes of the American system. But it *does* suggest how pluralist means coexist within a political-economic system which contains strong elitist traits.

Starting Points (Continued from p. 339)

9. Within the stability created by economic performance and socialization to dominant cultural values, opportunistic political parties may compete within a framework of representative democracy.

This framework is not inconsistent with either elitism or pluralism. The American political system perpetuates a two-party system which discourages insurgency.

Conclusions

The nine starting points for a political-economic approach to American politics are just that. They are points for beginning, just as this has been an introductory text. Though they are simple, they are not tautological truths. If they seem plausible to the reader, or even self-evident, many others might disagree. In particular, the political-economic approach to politics is quite different from either the elitist or pluralist.

Elite theorists contrast elitism and pluralism, whereas political economy emphasizes the systematic complementarity of the two. Elite theory emphasizes a self-conscious if not coordinated elite effort to "dominate" politics and to "manipulate" socialization. Political economy emphasizes instead the interdependence of political culture with economic systems. Elite theory emphasizes an enduring elite which renders party conflict meaningless. Political economy emphasizes instead the conflicting political-economic programs of competing parties. Elite theorists seek to show America to be elitist in both ends and means. Political economists emphasize the compatibility of pluralist means with elitist ends.

Pluralist theorists view business as one competing group among many. But political economists disagree. For them, business is a preeminent group, due to the prime economic function of the state in a capitalist society. Pluralist theorists emphasize the competition of parties, the multiplicity of lobbies, the diversity of politics, and the fragmentation of government to "show" that politics is not elitist. But political economists view these phenomena as secondary patterns within a broader system of power which favors elite interests. Pluralist theorists emphasize popular elections and the similarity of government actions with public opinion to "show" American government is democratic. Political economists, on the other hand, discount shallow readings of public opinion. They prefer to emphasize the historic evolution of given opinions and their relation to the nation's political economy. Public opinion is not treated as an independent, rational legitimator of state action.

Of course there is no one political-economic perspective. The authors cited in this chapter often strongly disagree with each other. Some would not even consider themselves political economists, at least not primarily. Nor would all accept each "starting point" listed above. But their works have shaped the political-economic approach to government. And if the synthesis of "starting points" would not gain universal consent, at least it does represent a line of analyzing American politics which is consistent with the common themes of their now-classic works.

Power and politics in America are not a conspiracy. Nor do they add up to democracy as this has traditionally been understood. If America is elitist, it is elitist in a pluralistic way. Or if pluralist, then pluralist in a way which benefits an elite. Political scientists would benefit by shedding these terms entirely. A political economy is a system of power which integrates production, culture, and power.

Power as authority (official position) is constrained by economic possibilities and political culture. Authority also functions to preserve and extend the economic system, whether in vast subsidies to business or in the recurrent repression of insurgent social movements of the left. Power as influence (resources apart from position) also reinforces the existing system since the costs of influence are greatest for those who hold the fewest resources. And even power as affinity (personality traits apart from position and resources) has inegalitarian tendencies since affinity derives from class-linked factors in no small part (examples include the self-confidence and social like-ness of attending elite schools and working in elite policy bodies, and manner of speech and social approach socialized in class-linked milieus). But more important to the perpetuation of our system of political economy than any of these overt forms of power is the implicit power reflected in the evolution of political culture in relation to political economy.

Summary

In the introductory chapter we outlined these various forms of power—overt (authority, influence, affinity) and implicit (nondecisions, symbolic action, hegemony). The failure of political science to deal adequately with the latter was emphasized. Implicit power was viewed as critical to understanding the issues which underlay the elitist–pluralist debate within political science.

Chapter 2 presented this debate in greater detail. The continuity of modern pluralist theory with earlier European elite theory was highlighted. This in itself suggested some of the false interpretations which arise from treating elitism as the opposite of pluralism. Nonetheless, elite and pluralist theory were presented as two clearly contrasting views of the nature of power and politics in America.

Chapter 3 discussed various methods of gaining evidence pertinent to the elitist–pluralist debate. These included the formalistic, decision-making, reputational, sociology-of-leadership, distributional, and historical approaches. It was pointed out how each method favors a given conclusion. For example, the decision-making approach favors pluralist theory, while the distributional approach favors elite theory.

Chapter 4 was an outline of a formalistic approach, using the military as an illustration. By looking at the constitutional and legal parameters of government, organizational structure, institutional history, and legislative records, various types of evidence were found. Some evidence suggested the pluralist view that power was fragmented among many competing groups. Other evidence suggested power operates at a relatively elite level with a minimum of significant group competition, as elite theory predicts. Yet other evidence showed the difficulty of either approach. This laid the basis for seeking an alternative theory, neither elite nor pluralist, to explain the facts uncovered. It was suggested that political economy might be such an alternative.

Chapter 5 illustrated the decision-making approach, using the escalation of the Vietnam War as an example. Here, too, some evidence favored a pluralist perspective, while other evidence favored elite theory, while yet other facts contradicted both. It was shown how the central issues of this debate shift focus from overt to implicit aspects of power.

Chapters 6 and 7 presented approaches to power which are thought to tap the net outcomes of both implicit and overt power. These included the reputational, sociology-of-leadership, and distributional approaches. While a discussion of studies of this sort showed elite theory to be far from clearly sustained, pluralist expectations were clearly not supported. If politics is "who gets what, when, and how," then in America politics favors an elite. But evidence does *not* show that an economic elite dominates government in terms of holding top positions, financing elections, or controlling policy advice. Rather, a more subtle set of processes is at work. Using urban renewal as an example, the process of business reformism was presented as one example. This process favored elite outcomes without constituting elite dominance of politics as commonly understood.

Class analysis was discussed in Chapter 8 as a way of assessing whether another, more subtle connection of economic elites to political outcomes might not be found in class-linked political beliefs and culture. It was shown that studies *do* support the idea that there is a distinctive political belief-set among business people which is not declining over time and is in contrast to general public opinion. This provides a basis for examining Marx's dictum: "In every age, the ideas of the ruling class become the ruling ideas." Given the focus of pluralist theorists on popular support for and legitimacy of the state, the question of citizenship was taken up. By examining the political-economic roots of modern citizenship (its relation to "Americanizing the immigrant"), one example was provided of the way political economy is a *system* of economics, culture, and power. This illustrated the self-reinforcing nature of political-economic systems.

Chapters 9 through 11 illustrated political-economic interpretations of American politics in greater depth, first with the oil industry as a case and then tracing American history in general. Again, evidence supported elite theory in part, pluralist theory in part, and in part neither. Again it was helpful to use an approach that emphasized system functions rather than elite will, and one that recognizes how elite interests are served in a "pluralistic" process which cannot be understood in terms of the ideology of pluralism. More broadly, American history was traced in relation to the opposing political economic programs of the Federalists–Old Republicans, the Jacksonians, the nineteenth-century Republican party, the New Deal, and the modern conservative coalition. It was found to be misleading to speak of elite domination, since governing policies were in the main consensual. Pluralist theory was misleading because governing policies in fact favor a business elite. Rather than being dominated by a political economic elite, however, America *is* an elitist political economy.

Finally, the present and last chapter has suggested some of the common starting points for political-economic analysis. These have provided the general framework for interpreting American politics in the previous chapters. While neither original nor without controversy, these political-economic starting points do provide a way of looking at American politics which goes beyond the sterile debate of the elitists and pluralists. The elitism—pluralism debate served political science well as a vehicle for discussion. But now there is a need to go beyond both. The paradigm of political economy will not be the end result of social science. The readers of this book will undoubtedly be able to think of other paradigms. But out of the discussion and debate over ideas, we will be able to better understand power and politics in America.

Notes

1. Talcott Parsons is ordinarily thought of as a functionalist sociologist. He is here included, however, because of the importance of his joint work with Neil Smelser. Parsons is often cited as believing in value- or cultural-causation explanations of society. While Parsons argues that culture is the critical controlling element discussed in the text, he does not interpret culture as the causal determinant. Rather, a sharp distinction is drawn between the terms "control" and "cause." When compared with Marx's discussion of the cultural "superstructure," Parson's views on the self-reinforcing nature of a social-cultural system are not as different as is often supposed. He does, however, ascribe a far greater degree of independence to culture.
2. Talcott Parsons and Neil Smelser, *Economy and Society* (New York: Free Press, 1956), pp. 270–71.
3. For a Marxist discussion of this problem, see James O'Connor, *The Fiscal Crisis of the State* (New York: St. Martin's, 1973).
4. For a non-Marxist discussion of the political beliefs associated with various role-sets, see R. Joseph Monsen and Mark W. Cannon, *The Makers of Public Policy* (New York: McGraw-Hill, 1965).
5. Charles A. Beard, *The Economic Basis of Politics and Related Writings* (New York: Vintage, 1957), p. 26.

Index

Abolitionism, 282, 285–286. *See also* Reconstruction
Achnacarry agreement, 242
Adams, President John, 91, 278
Addams, Jane, 217
Advocacy roles, 150–151
Alaska pipeline, 255–256
Alexander, Herbert, 187
American Assembly, 168–169
American Medical Association, 6, 8
American Petroleum Institute, 242
American Political Science Association, 41
American Protective Association, 215
Ancestral associations, 213
Anti-Federalism, 80, 277–279
Antitrust, 256–260, 298–299, 303
Armed forces, 82–84
Authority, 5–6

Bachrach, Peter, 12–14, 23
Ball, George, 139, 141, 145, 147, 149, 152
Baltzell, E. Digby, 163–165, 213
Banking, 276, 278–285, 300, 301, 305
Baran, Paul, 333, 336, 338
Baruch, George, 302
Bauer, Raymond, 8, 160
Beard, Charles, 41, 330, 332, 335, 336, 339
Bell, Terrill, 186
Berelson, Bernard, 205–206
Bernstein, Barton, 307
Bettelheim, Bruno, 10
Bolling, Richard, 63
Bott, Elizabeth, 211

Bryan, William Jennings, 288
Buchanan, President James, 283
Bundy, McGeorge, 123, 125, 127, 130, 135, 139–143, 147
Bundy, William P., 125–127, 134, 135, 137, 139, 141, 143, 169
Bureaucratic pathology, 148–151, 152
Burgess, John, 327
Business, power of, 114. *See also* Elite theory
Business Council, 50, 157, 167, 169
Business pacifism, 95
Business reformism, 189–193

Calhoun, John, 40, 42, 92, 279, 280
Calvert, Staunton, 175
Campaign finance, 186–189
Capitalism, concentration of, 181–183
Centers, Richard, 208
Central Intelligence Agency, 125, 126, 132, 135, 139, 143, 169, 223, 248
Childs, Harwood, 222
Christ, Thomas, 207–208
Citizenship, 212–224
Civic education, 220–223
Civil rights, 316
Class analysis, 32–34, 39, 71, 74, 161, 203–229. *See also* Marxist analysis; Elite theory; Positional approach
Clay, Henry, 279, 282
Cold war, 107
Collective behavior, 47
Committee for Economic Development, 167, 169

Compliance, 4–8
Conference Board, 169
Conformity, 24–25
Congregationalism, 274–275
Congress, powers of, 86–91, 93, 101, 102, 106–112, 113, 114, 115, 166, 245, 260, 261, 275, 276, 298; reform of, 63
Congressional Budget Reform Act of 1974, 90
Consensus, 24–25
Conservative coalition, 311–319
Constitution, U.S., 80–81, 91, 269, 277
Coolidge, President Calvin, 243
Council of Economic Advisers, 309, 312
Council on Foreign Relations, 167, 169
Counts, George, 221
Creel Committee, 96, 220, 302

Dahl, Robert, 14–17, 48, 65, 66
Decision-making approach, 10–17, 65–67, 70, 119–154
Defense, Department of, 84–86, 91–105, 166, 219
Democratic elitism, 31–39, 53, 55
Dexter, Lewis A., 8, 160
Distributional approach, 74–76, 174–199
Doig, Jameson, 162
Domhoff, G. William, 50, 72, 73, 166–172
Downs, Anthony, 339–340
Dye, Thomas, 162

Edelman, Murray, 20–23, 128, 203
Education, 185–186, 336–337
Edwards, Jonathan, 274
Eisenhower, President Dwight D., 100, 108, 109, 114, 130, 156, 157, 167, 168, 245, 253, 312, 313

Election Campaign Act of 1974, 188
Elite theory, 11–27, 30–57, 69, 77, 79, 106, 114, 116, 147, 148, 151, 152, 160, 163, 165, 171–173, 189, 192, 210, 261–263, 269–271, 307–308, 320, 322, 338, 339, 341, 342. See also Marxist analysis; Positional approach
Elkins, Stanley, 10
Ellis, Elmer, 222
Energy crisis of 1973, 252–255
Equilibrium theory, 47
Erikson, Erik, 19–20
Etzioni, Amitai, 4–5

Fascism, 34–37
Federalism, 273–281
Federalist Party, 80–81, 93
Food and Drug Act, 300
Ford, President Gerald R., 111, 112, 141, 206, 258–260, 319, 320
Ford Motor Company, 102
Form, William, 209–210, 211
Formalistic approach. See Structural approach
Free Soil Party, 283
Fulbright, William, 134

Galbraith, John Kenneth, 183, 318
George, Alexander, 150, 151
Goldwater, Barry, 121, 131, 133, 134, 316, 321
Gramsci, Antonio, 24
Grant, President Ulysses S., 286, 297
Great Awakening, 273–274

Halberstam, David, 121, 122, 124, 146
Halperin, Morton, 149–150
Hamilton, Alexander, 80, 277, 278
Hamilton, Richard, 209, 211

Hammond, Paul, 96
Harding, President Warren G., 243,
  302, 303
Hayes, President Arthur, 95
Health, 186
Hébert, Edward, 88, 89, 104
Henderson, David, 7
Herring, E. Pendleton, 43–45
Hickel, Walter, 256
Highway program, 313–314
Historical approach, 76–77
Hobson, J. A., 234
Honolulu Conference, 143–145,
  150
Hoopes, Townsend, 150
Hoover, Herbert, 303–304, 312
Horowitz, David, 232
Huber, Joan, 209–211
Humphrey, Hubert, 141
Hunter, Floyd, 11–12, 68–71, 76,
  156–160
Huntington, Samuel, 94

Income, 177–180
Incrementalism, 150, 338, 339. *See
  also* Pluralist theory
Interest-group theory, 39–51, 75–
  76
Interstate Commerce Commission,
  297, 300

Jacksonianism, 93–94, 96, 279–283
Janis, Irving, 148–149, 151
Jeffersonianism, 91–93, 277–279
Johnson, President Lyndon B., 103,
  110, 120–122, 127, 130–132,
  137–142, 144–147, 149, 167,
  249, 253, 316–317
Johnston, Eric, 310
Joint Chiefs of Staff, 82, 84–86,
  98–99, 101–107, 110, 114, 115,
  123–125, 135–137, 140–142, 149
Jurisprudential approach, 40. *See
  also* Structural approach

Kennedy, President John F., 109–
  110, 122–123, 125, 129, 130,
  131, 167, 314–316
Keynesianism, 306, 309, 310, 312,
  314, 317, 333
Keyserling, Leon, 179, 312
Kilpatrick, William, 221
Kirkland, Edward C., 214
Kirstein, George, 205, 206
Kissinger, Henry, 86, 105, 168
Kolko, Gabriel, 177–180
Kolodziej, Edward, 102
Korean War, 106–107

Labor movement, 95, 220, 298–
  304, 306, 309, 315, 320, 321,
  336, 337
Laird, Melvin, 103–104
Laissez-faire, 279–283
Lampman, Robert, 175
Landrum-Griffin Act, 314
Larner, Robert, 184
Laski, Harold, 42–43
Lasswell, Harold, 18–20
Legislative Reorganization Act of
  1946, 88
Lewis, John L., 306, 309
Lincoln, Abraham, 284–286, 334
Lindblom, Charles, 50
Lippmann, Walter, 43, 221
Litt, Edgar, 210
Locke, John, 40

MacArthur, Douglas, 101
Macy, Jesse, 41
Madison, James, 80, 277, 329–330
Manipulative socialization, 224, 270
Mann, Dean, 162
Mann, Michael, 24–25, 224
Mansfield, Mike, 104, 140, 141
Marcuse, Herbert, 24
Marshall, George, 99–100, 245
Marxist analysis, 20, 22–25, 32–34,
  76, 151, 210, 212–213, 224, 326–
  330, 332–336, 340. *See also*
  Class analysis; Elite theory

Matthews, Donald, 161
McCune, John, 126, 127, 135–136, 143, 144
McGovern, George, 104, 187, 319
McNamara, Robert S., 102–104, 109–110, 122, 125, 126, 127, 130, 135, 137, 139–140, 141, 144, 147
McNaughton, John, 126, 127, 135, 141, 142, 143, 147
Mellon, Andrew, 240
Mercantilism, 272–275
Mergers, 181–183
Merriam, Charles, 221
Metcalf, Lee, 182, 183
Mexican War, 283
Michels, Roberto, 35–36, 148
Milbrath, Lester, 8
Military, history of the, 89–105
Mill, John Stuart, 327–332, 334
Mills, C. Wright, 11, 12, 14, 46, 50, 51, 52, 71, 72, 113, 127, 165–168, 170–172, 262–263
Mills, Walter, 95
Mintz, Beth, 167
Missouri Compromise, 251
Monopoly, 182–183, 287–288, 310
Morton, Rogers, 256
Mosca, Gaetano, 33–35
Mueller, Willard, 183
Myths, social, 70

National Guard, 81, 95, 97
National Industrial Recovery Act, 305
National Right to Work Committee, 7
National Security Council, 86, 99, 101, 105, 137, 149
New Deal, 304–314, 320–321
New Frontier, 314–316
New Partnership, 312–313
New Republicans, 92–93, 279–282
Nixon, President Richard M., 1, 7, 104, 111, 167, 183, 188, 249–250, 253, 254–256, 257, 317–319

Non-decisions, 10–17, 23
Nye Committee, 97

Office of Management and Budget, 105
Oil industry, 231–265
Okner, Benjamin, 179–180
Old Republicans, 279
Oligarchy, iron law of, 35
OPEC, 231, 246, 249–252, 258–259
Ortega y Gasset, José, 36–37
Ostend Agreement, 242

Palmer raids, 220
Pareto, Vilfredo, 33–35
Parsons, Talcott, 330, 332, 336
Parsons, Willard, 217
Patman Committee, 184
Patriotic societies, 213
Pechman, Joseph, 179–180
Perry, Charles, 168
Pluralism, classic, 41–42
Pluralist theory, 11–17, 30–57, 70, 72, 73, 77, 79, 91, 106, 112–114, 115, 119, 146–147, 148, 151, 160, 163, 173, 189, 192, 210, 223, 261–263, 269, 271, 307–308, 320, 322, 338, 339, 341–342. See also Decision-making approach
Political economy, 77, 115–116, 263, 271–272, 277, 278, 288–289, 302, 320–322, 326–345
Political hegemony, 22–24, 270
Political stability, 49–50, 271, 331
Polsby, Nelson, 65
Pool, Ithel de Sola, 8, 160
Populism, 41, 297–298
Positional approach, 71–73, 161–173
Power, implicit, 9–27, 46, 65, 67, 68, 71, 152; overt, 1–9, 20, 67, 68, 71
Pragmatic role acceptance, 224

President, Executive Office of the, 86; powers of the, 81. *See also* individual names of Presidents.
Pressure groups, 40–41. *See* Interest-group theory
Presthus, Robert, 162–163, 171
Price, Melvin, 89
Progressivism, 41, 298–301
Prohibition, 304
Projector, Dorothy, 175
Proxmire, William, 30
Public interest, 45, 49
Public opinion, U.S., 24–25
Public policy, 49
Puritanism, 272–275

Radical Republicans, 285–287
Raskin, Marcus, 123
Rent control, 312
Reputational approach, 67–71, 155–161
Revolution, American, 91, 272–275
Riis, Jacob, 216
Rockefeller Brothers Fund, 168
Rockefeller, John D., 232–241
Roosevelt, Franklin D., 82–98, 222, 304–307, 309
Roosevelt, Theodore, 41, 240, 298–300
Rose, Arnold, 51–52
Rossiter, Clinton, 276
R.O.T.C., 97
Rousseau, Jean-Jacques, 40
Rumsfeld, Donald H., 84, 105
Rusk, Dean, 122, 125, 127, 130, 132, 135, 137, 140, 147

Scheier, Frederic, 183
Schlesinger, James R., 104–105
Schumpeter, Joseph, 37
Seniority system, 88
Shays's Rebellion, 80, 116, 276
Shepard, Walter, 227
Silk, Leonard, 319
Smelser, Neil, 330, 332, 336

Smith, Adam, 272
Smith, Al, 304
Smith, James, 175, 176
Social mobility, 204–205
Social Security Act, 306, 307, 312, 314
Sociology of leadership. *See* Positional approach
Spanish-American War of 1898, 96
Sports movement, 214–215
Stanley, David, 162
States, power of the, 80–81
Steel industry, 316
Steffens, Lincoln, 41
Steiner, Gary, 205
Stennis, John, 88, 89
Stevens, Thaddeus, 285
Structural approach, 62–65, 78–118, 119
Supreme Court, 81, 240–241, 287–306
Sutton, Francis X., 207
Sweezy, Paul, 333, 336, 338
Symbolic action, 17–23, 331

Taft, President William H., 300
Taft-Hartley Act, 311, 315
Tariffs, 287, 298–301, 303, 304, 305
Taxation, 179–180, 260–261, 301–302, 304, 309–310, 319–320
Taylor, Maxwell D., 124–125, 135–136, 137, 138, 141, 142, 143, 144, 147
Teapot Dome, 243
Thurow, Lester, 178
Tocqueville, Alexis de, 269
Tonkin Gulf Resolution, 132–134
Truman, David, 11, 39, 44–46
Truman, President Harry, 98, 101, 107, 108, 121, 130, 223, 311–312
TVA, 306, 307, 312

Urban renewal, 189–193

Van Buren, President Martin, 283
Veblen, Thorstein, 225
Vietnam War, 110, 111, 119–154

Wagner Act, 306
War of 1812, 91–92, 279, 280
Washington, George, 276, 278
Wealth, 175, 176
Weiss, Gertrude, 175
Welfare state, 304–308, 312, 314, 317
Wendell, E. J., 217
Westmoreland, William C., 124–125, 141, 143, 144, 145, 147
Wheeler, Erik G., 124, 135, 141, 143, 147, 152

Whig Party, 283
White, Leonard, 279
Wicker, Tom, 121
Wilson, Francis, 43–44, 222
Wilson, President Woodrow, 300–302
Wolfinger, Raymond, 14, 65
Wootton, Graham, 75–76
World War I, 96, 97, 302
World War II, 97–98, 106–107, 114, 115, 309–311

X, Malcolm, 9

Yarmolinsky, Adam, 100